KU-259-677

WHEN PANIC ATTACKS

THIRD EDITION

Dr Áine Tubridy

Gill Books

Gill Books
Hume Avenue
Park West
Dublin 12
www.gillbooks.ie

Gill Books is an imprint of M.H. Gill and Co.

First published 2003, second edition published 2007, this edition published 2018
© Áine Tubridy

978 07171 8049 3

Design and print origination by O'K Graphic Design, Dublin
Indexed by Cliff Murphy

Printed by ScandBook AB, Sweden
This book is typeset in 10/15 pt Formata Light., with headings in Frutiger LT Std

The paper used in this book comes from the wood pulp of managed forests. For
every tree felled, at least one tree is planted, thereby renewing natural resources.

All rights reserved.
No part of this publication may be copied, reproduced or transmitted in any form or
by any means, without written permission of the publishers.

A CIP catalogue record for this book is available from the British Library.

5 4 3 2 1

Information given in this book is not intended to be taken as a replacement for
medical advice. Any person with a condition requiring medical attention should
consult a qualified medical practitioner or therapist.

CONTENTS

The free audio downloads with relaxation, breathing
and meditation techniques are available at
gillbooks.ie/whenpanicattacks

PREFACE TO THE THIRD EDITION

Á ine was a healer and a true visionary in the crusade for mental health, sadly taken from this world far too soon. Empathy, kindness, wisdom and foresight came so naturally to our mum, so much so that it appeared entirely effortless.

Greeting her every morning, upon a small plaque in the kitchen of her country cottage home in rural Co. Wicklow, was the phrase *Happiness is an inside job.* This, for mum, was not just a frivolous saying on a souvenir or piece of art that she casually enjoyed from time to time. This was a fundamental mantra for daily living and a powerful fight response to be instilled in those in emotional peril, especially in the face of the pervasive pharmaceutical options for treatment.

In the years since her untimely passing, our family have had untold kind words and stories of hope sent to us about mum and the insights to be found in her books. The common theme of the wonderful tributes we have received, whether recounted in person though heartfelt anecdotes or indirectly via reviews online, have been of thanks for the real difference our mum made in people's lives and of the luck felt to have come across her teachings.

Colleagues are often heard to remark that, despite the title, Áine's clinical legacy here is not just helpful for dealing with panic attacks. Her closest colleague and friend of over 25 years said recently that she finds herself 'recommending the book not just to those who experience the full-blown panic attack, but to anyone who needs to understand the root cause of their difficulty in coping with this world

Leabharlanna Poibli Chathair Baile Átha Cliath
Dublin City Public Libraries

we find ourselves in'. It is certainly true to say that it's a book about anxiety, not just about panic.

Specific to the subject of panic attacks, however, the overwhelming message that can be heard loud and clear from those who have read this wonderful book is that its words uniquely make the reader feel listened to, rather than being bombarded with academic jargon and talked at. As just two of the kind reviews on Amazon so eloquently put it: 'As someone who has suffered with Panic Disorder for over 40 years, this is the first book I have read that made me feel as though the author had heard my thoughts and felt my feelings', and 'for the first time someone was able to verbalize what I couldn't'.

As Áine's kids, we feel truly blessed to have been given the gift of her having been in our lives. Our only hope for this third edition of her book is that her light can continue to shine through her words and the stories told here, and that this healing light will continue to touch those in need of help, so that they may feel the wealth of her presence as we do.

Derry, Aidan & Paula

PREFACE TO THE SECOND EDITION

Time has passed since I wrote the first edition of this book, and in that time, due largely to attracting more patients suffering from panic to my practice, and to running many seminars on the subject, my awareness of some of the dynamics driving panic have changed. Privileged to hear the variety of stories I do, I am constantly struck by its power to terrify, how common it is, its inadequate treatment, the secrecy surrounding it, and the sense of defeat and desperation of those trapped within it.

I have been increasingly aware also that many, having tried a couple of therapies, perhaps having been on different medications with no improvement, reach a point where phobic avoidance has become their only remaining tactic for controlling their panic sensations. This is an uneasy place, not at all guaranteed to provide safety, and coming with a hefty price tag, but it is the only option they can see working. I often get calls from those rendered housebound, who see their panic attacks, and the solution to them, as in a different category somehow. This is untrue: the path back is the same as for someone afraid of dogs or enclosed spaces, and it is my hope that the chapters on phobias will offer an alternative.

My training in psychotherapy – derived from the Greek *psche* meaning 'soul' and *therapeia* meaning 'attendance' – has ensured that the day is long past where I can comfortably treat this disorder as most doctors do, allopathically, which is to simply address symptoms separately from the rest of the person. Compelled to look deeper, Carl Jung's perspective resonates with mine when he said:

> We should not try to 'get rid' of a neurosis, but rather to experience what it
> means, what it has to teach us, what its purpose is ... otherwise we miss the
> opportunity of getting to know ourselves as we really are. We do not cure
> it ... *it cures us*.

So what might panic be trying to cure us of? This will obviously be completely unique for each person. Some may learn through their panic experiences to be less attached to being in control, to care less about the opinions of others, to connect with and develop more trust in their own body, to assert their rights more frequently, to become tolerant of being vulnerable and dependant sometimes, or to cease placing their entire identity in that puzzle-factory they know as their mind.

Undoubtedly some of the themes on which panic thrives reflect the societal values we osmotically absorbed while growing up. Our cultural Ostrich Approach to death and profound change, the staple diet of panic, at whatever level of our make-up, and a reluctance to provide a framework such as those that exist in Eastern cultures which might help us to fear both less. Our obsession with happiness and success, resisting any experience which drops below the culturally accepted level, side-tracking us into the socially undesirable states of fear and depression, low self-confidence and, heaven help us, non-coping. The thriving climate of secrecy and shame surrounding any difficulty having a mental component, a state of affairs which has been, in my opinion, created and fuelled by the misguided understanding and treatment of psychiatric disorders. It appears there is some way to go yet on these fronts if we want to create a less fear-driven society in which to live.

INTRODUCTION

I n my years as a doctor, first in general practice and then as a psychotherapist, I have come to appreciate that panic is fundamentally different from other disorders. Since it isn't either a purely physical disorder, making it the territory of GPs and physicians, or a purely psychological one, placing it within the brief of psychologists and psychiatrists, it tends to fall between these two stools. Although no organic cause has been found for it, it cannot be said that it is 'all in the mind', for the experience is most forcibly a highly physical one. It is, in fact, the ultimate example of a mind–body disorder, where the nebulous, non-physical, invisible world of the mind crosses over to manifest – within seconds – as chemicals in the bloodstream, which create the symptoms. Mind becoming matter.

This presents a challenge to those medical professionals who have not moved ahead towards the new paradigm – that of mind–body medicine. Without an appreciation of the primacy of thought as the engine behind panic, they will only succeed therapeutically in a sporadic fashion. Medication can dampen the reaction, but not sufficiently reliably and consistently. Meanwhile, the root cause goes unaddressed. Psychologists and counsellors, feeling the mind to be their province, may intervene by changing thinking patterns or by modifying behaviour, but unless the urgency of the survival drive is fully appreciated, it will frustrate these efforts.

Panic confounds many of our expectations as to how an illness should behave. As slippery as an eel, it can be hard to pin down. Straightforward conditions, such as pain, swellings, rashes or malfunctions of a physical nature, are all experiences you have encountered in some form before. When shown to the doctor, they are investigated, diagnosed and treated. The diagnosis is generally reasonably *synchronous* with your suspicions, and doesn't surprise you: as you feared, the swollen, painful ankle is confirmed to be either sprained or broken; or the itchy red rash is the allergic reaction you suspected it would be. Also, the symptom is reasonably *consistent*. The pain and swelling in the broken ankle isn't present only on weekdays, and the infectious rash isn't only there when you're out in public, disappearing the moment you get home.

Emotional and mental problems, while not so cut and dried, can also often be tracked to an obvious source and then be addressed. Your sense of outrage if your child is bullied at school; your fear for your safety if fire breaks out; your inability to hold back tears if you are recently bereaved: *all are logically linked to an event or thought, and there is an appropriate emotional match*. Panic, however, can occur on a day when you are relaxing, or on your holidays, when you figure you are not worrying about anything, or in the shower, or even in bed! This increases the confusion for those frantic for explanations, and it baffles the doctor who can't give them an explanation.

Some physical and emotional problems lead to certain corrective behaviours, such as lying down with a headache, cancelling a meeting when overloaded, or asking for assistance if in pain. All these are *logical behavioural responses*, and therefore nothing to be wary of or suspicious about. But where is the logic when you find yourself dashing out of banks or shops, or cancelling social engagements at the last minute, when you had planned to do the exact opposite?

Ideally, your doctor would put your mind at rest early on by clearly diagnosing panic attacks. Often, however, as months pass without improvement, confidence begins to erode, and many sufferers push for referral to a specialist. Your reaction to all the tests — ECGs, brain scans, X-rays — which come back negative, can be a mixture of relief and disquiet. As symptoms continue, you may worry that something serious is being missed.

Even when the condition is diagnosed as panic, it may merely provide a name but not a satisfactory explanation for the upsetting symptoms. How can you have such a racing heart in the absence of heart disease? Or be so breathless in the absence of lung disease? What is causing the dizziness and unsteadiness if it is not a brain abnormality? Surely paranoia indicates a psychiatric problem?

If anxiety-lowering medication is prescribed by your doctor, this can create as much concern as it eases. In our culture, the need for psychiatric medication carries a stigma that medication for high blood pressure or asthma, for example, does not, and most people don't want to take it unless absolutely necessary. Implications for the future loom large in their imagination as they begin perceiving themselves for the first time as 'someone suffering from a mental problem'.

MATCHING WITH THE RIGHT PROFESSIONAL

There are many reasons why panic is not treated as soon as it might be, or by the appropriate professional.

- Many sufferers report one or two symptoms only, usually the ones that alarm them. For example, a breathing problem will get any doctor thinking of heart irregularities long before panic. If the focus is only on breathing difficulties, asthma is a likely diagnosis, and an inhaler may be prescribed to widen the air passages. Zoning in on dizziness, unsteadiness or mental confusion may prompt neurological investigations. Nausea or bowel disturbances can lead to unnecessary probing of orifices in search of a lesion. An incomplete understanding of the full range of panic symptoms by doctors, coupled with insufficient time in busy schedules to delve any deeper, means that the relevant questions often go unasked. As Wittgenstein said, 'If all you have is a hammer, everything is a nail.'

- Even if an underlying psychological issue is identified, reliance on medication as the first line of treatment ignores the experience of many, that either it doesn't work, or its effect is only partial. The root cause remains, and lives continue to be sacrificed — sometimes literally — on the altar of panic. It has been my experience that those who find themselves in this desperate situation, where little hope of change is offered, inevitably become depressed, a diagnosis to which their entire rag-bag of symptoms is wrongly attributed.

- Counselling and/or therapy may help some people to gain insights into their fear, raise their self-esteem, learn to set boundaries, and prioritise their own needs, etc. However, there remain disturbing symptoms to be endured. Psychologists and counsellors who have no training in teaching relaxation or abdominal breathing, or who can do little to allay fears about the physical symptoms themselves, may wonder why movement is proving so difficult to achieve.

  If someone is coping with raw survival symptoms, they will find it difficult to focus on less urgent issues. Their fear of dying, or of being overwhelmed by physical sensations, will press to be addressed before they have the luxury of making more superficial personality changes. Their continued survival has to be assured first. Research has shown that information and advice on managing the symptoms of panic do not convince terrified sufferers, if offered by those who don't have any grounding in the physiology of the process. A knowledge of what is actually happening in the body — and what is not — is crucial. It seems that either psychologists need to learn more about the medical aspects, or doctors need to have more training in the psychological side, before the panic population will be adequately catered for.

- Sufferers sometimes do not consult a doctor because they dread a diagnosis of mental illness. Instead, some put up with their 'funny turns' for years, learning to manage them through a multitude of avoidance strategies, hiding them even from close family members. Others, those of the 'pull-your-socks-up' school, rebuke themselves for being weak, and soldier on alone rather than seek help.

THE NEW FRONTIER

An understanding of energy as the engine of our consciousness has had an immeasurable impact on my clinical treatment of panic. Words cannot adequately describe my excitement a number of years ago when I discovered that such a new frontier existed, one which would have such a formative influence on both my professional practice and on my personal life. As a doctor seeking to understand what causes disease and to discover effective ways to end it, and as an individual eagerly wishing to find (quick and easy) pathways to contentment, I was immensely relieved when I was introduced to healing methods using energy. Such methods are not modern. They are derived from ancient wisdom, and are at the cutting edge of many current areas of research, such as cellular biology, and the study of the very nature of the mind and consciousness.

These vibrational methods of healing extend the paradigm of mind–body medicine a stage further, opening the door into that of mind–body–spirit. Exciting as that is, some may find it too challenging for their current beliefs to cover. For this reason I have written most of this book from a perspective which does not require you to embrace the concepts set out in Chapter 8, The Chakra System, in order to follow it. However, I do most strongly encourage every reader to consider the undoubted effects that the energy exercises have on terminating the crippling condition of panic attacks. These can be done without needing to grasp fully their theoretical background; their results still apply without that.

It is my hope that this book will answer all the many questions that sufferers have, and stimulate some questions that could lead to new areas of research. If the book merely succeeds in being an interesting read, I will be disappointed. Only if it has encouraged you to make tangible and fundamental changes at every level of your life — physical, emotional, mental and spiritual — will it have achieved what I hoped it would. The deeper you go with your questioning as to the significance of your panic attacks in your psyche, the more extensive and permanent your healing will be.

PART ONE

HOW PANIC WORKS

WHAT IS A PANIC ATTACK?

KEYNOTE: RED ALERT!

H as this ever happened to you?

You're doing the weekly shopping, when suddenly everything changes. A hot, sweaty feeling creeps over you as a wave of nausea grips your stomach. *'Oh God, I think I'm going to pass out!'* Your head begins to spin, your surroundings become a blur. *'What's going on? Why has the place got so hot!'* you wonder, peeling off your jacket.

'Are you OK?' asks the assistant behind the counter, adding to your mounting suspicion that something is seriously wrong. By now your heart has begun to thump violently in your chest. *'Why can't I breathe? What's wrong with me? I've got to get out of here!'* Tightly gripping your trolley, you try to calculate whether you'd make it to the exit in time. The voice intrudes again. 'Can I do anything? Maybe you should sit down.' You notice with concern how tight and uncomfortable your chest feels and how difficult it seems to take in enough air. *'Something awful's going to happen to me!'* you suddenly think, and the next minute you find yourself bolting for the door and heading for the bathrooms.

The person staring back at you from the mirror is pale, sweaty and terrified. You splash your face with water, thinking *'I need to get to a doctor before it's too late!'* After a few attempts your trembling hands manage to punch the numbers into your mobile phone. 'John! Thank God! Something's wrong, I feel really ill, can you come and get me in the supermarket right now? Hurry, will you, I'm really not well!' Confused and disoriented, your mind races with questions, as you lean immobilised against the wall. The minutes tick by in a haze of fear, but gradually you notice that your breathing is getting slightly easier, and your heart isn't racing quite so fast. You realise that 'whatever it was' seems to have passed, leaving you utterly drained, as though a fog had descended on you.

Mythology tells us that the Greek god Pan, who was the god of nature, was an ugly, short character with goat's legs. He lived in the countryside and was known to jump out and terrify many a passer-by by uttering a blood-curdling scream that was so horrific it caused most to run for their lives and some to die of fright on the spot. This sudden, unexpected and all-consuming terror that they experienced became known as 'panic'. In contemporary times thousands experience this daily, usually in association with some sense of impending danger or threat. Experiences of such an internal attack vary:

Tony – 'It was a day I was due to give a presentation at work, not something I'd done often. As I stood up to begin, I froze. A chilly 'pins-and-needles' feeling crept over me, starting in my hands, making it difficult to feel the pages I was holding. Time seemed to stand still as I struggled to start speaking, and I felt a pressure around my throat, as though my voice was trapped and couldn't come out. My feet didn't feel connected to the ground, and a wave of nausea was building in my stomach. Gazing around at the blur of faces I realised they were all waiting for me to begin, but by now I knew I couldn't continue. In fact

I doubted I'd make it to the door without passing out. It was certainly the weirdest and most frightening thing I'd ever experienced, not to mention humiliating.'

Marie – 'It happened first at my daughter's wedding, during the service. Such a happy occasion, she looked so beautiful, and I so wanted it to be her perfect day. Suddenly I could feel my heart 'turn over' and I put it down to excitement. But it kept on thumping and I noticed a loud ringing in my ears. Feeling dizzy, I sat down and closed my eyes, telling myself that my urge to run out of the church was out of the question. The rest of the service, which seemed to last forever, passed by as though it was a dream, as though it wasn't real at all.'

Len – 'I woke up gasping for air and drenched in sweat. My heart was pounding, my chest was tight and I was terrified. I shook my wife awake and told her to get the doctor quickly, that I was having a heart attack. Throwing open the windows I leaned out and gasped for air. As I paced up and down I wondered what the hell was taking him so long. I splashed my face with water and when I saw myself in the bathroom mirror I knew this was it, the big one, I was going to die. By the time he arrived I was a gibbering, blubbering wreck, and became worse when he gave me a sedative instead of something for my heart. Did he not get it? Who was this fool? Gradually a blessed grogginess took over. Drained and exhausted, all I wanted to do was sleep.'

How is Panic Diagnosed?

If you have experienced something like this, but didn't know what it was, it will help if you answer the following questions in order to be absolutely clear that it is panic attacks you are getting. They are based on the DSM-4, the classification used by the medical profession to diagnose panic disorder. A positive answer to any four of them confirms that you are experiencing panic attacks.

Do you sometimes feel short of breath, like you can't get enough air in, making you take short panting breaths, or big deep sighs, or want to throw open the window?

Yes ❑   No ❑

Does your heart race at times, so that you are uncomfortably aware of it thumping in your chest, maybe even making you afraid you could have heart disease, or need to call a doctor?

Yes ❑   No ❑

Do you ever feel discomfort or pains in your chest, a tight or aching feeling?

Yes ❑   No ❑No

Have you occasionally felt sensations of choking or smothering, where every breath feels like it could be your last, and getting outside where you can breathe becomes a matter of survival?

Yes ❑   No ❑

Did you ever feel wobbly or unsteady on your feet, with a dizzy feeling or a pressure in your head, as though you might faint, and wonder if your 'jelly legs' will support you as far as the nearest exit?

Yes ❑   No ❑

Have you experienced sensations of tingling, numbness or 'pins-and-needles', usually in the arms or legs? Or blurring and double vision making it hard to focus normally?

Yes ❑   No ❑

Do you ever get a queasy 'knot' in your stomach, and a feeling that you might vomit, or have a sudden urge to empty your bowels?

Yes ❑   No ❑

Do you ever tremble or shake, so that it could be hard to write a cheque or hold a cup steady?

Yes ❏   No ❏

Do you feel waves of heat or cold chills pass over you, or sweat profusely at times, so that you might need to rapidly undo buttons and peel off clothes? Does it ever make you want to splash cold water on your face or plunge your hands into the freezer? Have you woken up at night with the sheets soaked in sweat?

Yes ❏   No ❏

Does your perception of your surroundings change so that you feel out of touch with your body or detached from things around you?

Yes ❏   No ❏

Have you feared that you were going to die while experiencing any of these symptoms, say from a heart attack, ceasing to breathe or some other medical emergency?

Yes ❏   No ❏

At any time did you fear losing control, or that you were going crazy?

Yes ❏   No ❏

What Exactly Is Panic?

Broadly speaking, a *panic attack is an extreme fear response which occurs when a person is convinced they are in extreme danger, although no real danger exists.*

Physiologically *panic is a sudden surge of adrenaline into the bloodstream.* Once set in motion, the surge of adrenaline molecules, known as the fight or flight response, rises to a crescendo and slowly dissipates. This primitive survival reflex is vital for dealing with danger, equipping us to fight like a gladiator or run like an Olympic sprinter. Heaving lungs, pounding heart, tense muscles, and hairs standing up on the back of the neck warn us that our life is on the line. This emergency response is essential for life in the jungle, fighting off an assailant, or reflexly responding to threats such as crashes, fires and other potential catastrophes. Whether we live or die may depend on our ability to run for it, scream for help, hide, jump aside, slam on the brakes, head for the nearest exit, or stand and fight.

Psychologically panic is a disorder of perception. *Internal sensations of the fight or flight response are being misread as life-threatening and dangerous.* This misinterpretation triggers panic in supposedly safe environments such as the supermarket, cinema, one's home or one's bed. With no obvious external threat, all the impulses to run, scream or attack are curtailed or censored, and confusion reigns. The sole task now is surviving the sensations themselves. Advancing into the depths of the supermarket can become synonymous with shark-infested waters, the distance from the door as critical as the distance from the shore. The degree of advance warning and the availability of an escape route define the level of danger.

What Course Does It Take?

The symptoms of a full-blown panic attack are similar for everyone, but vary in their combination and intensity. It is rare for anyone to experience all of the symptoms listed above. Some only get two or three of them, others more. The commonest are:

- intense fear or apprehension
- palpitations
- trembling
- breathing difficulty
- dizziness
- sweating

After a time one main symptom may begin to predominate, and the others may seem to be less to the fore. Or the panic attacks may cease as long as the person avoids certain situations, such as lifts or shops. All that seems to be left is an anxiety about going into certain situations.

The situations in which a first attack occurs are endlessly varied. It can be while doing something quite ordinary, such as watching a football game on TV, having a meal out in a restaurant, or getting on the bus home after work. On the other hand, it can be during a peak period of stress, such as going into an exam, or during a period of financial or personal insecurity, such as company downsizing or relationship breakdown. It is equally common to experience panic attacks only at night, where you're woken from sleep, gasping for breath. For most people it first occurs without warning, leaving them incredulous, shocked, shaken and utterly mystified as to what has just happened. After the attack, most people feel completely drained and exhausted.

The frequency of attacks varies. Many in the general population have one or two and no more. Others go on to have them several times a day, every other week or month, or for several years. They may disappear as mysteriously as they came, without treatment, or they may need medical intervention, as most do, before they are managed.

On average attacks tend to last between five and twenty minutes. Although you may remain 'on the verge' for days in the period before and after one, this is a state of *anxious apprehension* rather than panic itself, and will be discussed in the next chapter.

Panic attacks are exceedingly common. They occur equally in both sexes, and no particular type of personality is susceptible to them. Every age, occupation and socio-economic group experiences panic, as does every culture.

2

WAITING FOR THE NEXT ATTACK

KEYNOTE: WALKING ON EGGSHELLS

T ony – 'I don't know how I didn't eventually lose my job, because at least 70 per cent of my thoughts at work were about how to avoid that first "thump" inside my chest, when my heart would begin to race and the whole nightmare would begin. It seemed safer to out-think it and stay alive, rather than risk a possible heart attack. I reckon I deserved the Nobel Prize for ingenuity and dedication to a cause, because strategies to keep down the next one never left my mind. I would mentally scan my schedule each day looking for the "danger zones" – situations which I knew from experience might bring one on. This meant anywhere I felt trapped and unable to leave, like meetings, lifts, lunches or conference calls. I had all sorts of little side-routines in case this happened, and excuses which the boss seemed to buy most of the time. By the end of the day I would feel a pressure in my brain simply from the effort of trying to be one step ahead of things, to head off an attack. I was on tenterhooks all the time.

'I'm certain it held me back from getting on in the job. I'd always have to cry off joining my colleagues for a drink after work, or in-house training days where you'd be likely to be stuck in the one room for hours. Of course I knew that some people wrote me off as anti-social or painfully shy. I didn't care; it was the lesser of two evils. No way was I going to panic in front of people!'

Marie – 'The trouble really started when the attacks began to affect our social life. Up until then I was able to fob my husband off with excuses about feeling tired or hatching a cold or something. But then he realised that it was because I was afraid! "Afraid of what?" he'd bellow. His job involved going to a few social events each year, and it seemed so lame to be saying to him "I know it's important to you but I just can't." It caused so many rows over the years. He used to say that the person he married was a different woman, extroverted, adventurous and on for anything, that he'd somehow lost her along the way. I think it was when it began to extend to the mundane places like the kids' school, supermarkets or restaurants that he began to get angry with me for "giving in". It wasn't that I didn't love them enough to push myself – I just couldn't.

'What I could never explain was the dread I felt at the very first sign that we would have to go out socially and feeling that wave of apprehension inside me starting up. Even the phone ringing used to make me tense up, in case it meant I had to go somewhere. I felt safe at home, at least there I was more in control and could fight it off with some success. But outside my own surroundings all I could think of was *"exits, how far away are the exits!"* I dreaded that trapped feeling in queues or places where the doors were closed, anything that would prevent me leaving instantly if I had to. I always felt there wasn't enough air in places like trains or cinemas. If I could get outside, it usually eased, but it was a living hell if I couldn't! Enjoying things would have been a luxury; it was enduring and surviving them that I found hard. For years, events like family weddings or christenings became a blur of watching for exits! And then of course there was the clock: *"How long more till it's over and I can go home and feel human again?"* It was all about "keeping the feeling down", whatever that took. If anyone could have read my thoughts I'd have been taken away by the white coats for sure.'

CONSTANT VIGILANCE

That first panic attack is a terrifying event, a life-and-death experience, and as such it leaves a deep imprint. Like an earthquake, it is not easily forgotten. It is difficult to write it off and go on as if it hadn't happened. After the first few you can feel as if a ferocious beast has taken up residence inside you, who always has the potential to rise up and run amok, and each subsequent attack is like waking it up again. Once aroused it rips and roars through you, unstoppable and outside of your control. When it's over you feel shocked, exhausted, disillusioned and beaten up. In between attacks the monster sleeps, and you tiptoe around it. Your only hope of avoiding attacks from then on is to keep it from waking. Since it seems that prevention is your best policy, you're on guard all the time, never really taking your eye off it.

Like any efficient bodyguard, your radar system quickly becomes an expert on the subtle nuances of the beast's behaviour, those early tip-offs that it's beginning to stir. Although you are quite unaware of it, your nervous system is becoming intimately familiar with the activities and situations that rouse it. Cautious of whatever normal healthy pursuits cause a rise in your heart rate, make you break a sweat, or breathe a little faster, you become subconsciously wary of heated discussions, watching thrillers or exciting sports, sex, running up stairs, and warm, sweaty environments. So you begin avoiding these triggers, without knowing why, making lame excuses to yourself and others. This mental policy of being constantly on guard pays off, the rationale being that if your scanner picks up any slight change occurring in your internal environment (like a house alarm scanning windows and doors), this can give you vital minutes in which to escape, and abort an attack.

Imagine your response if your home was broken into, not once, not twice, but three or four times in the same week. After such serial breaches of security, you'd be thinking of little else. Suspending your normal routines, battening down the hatches, you'd turn your house into a bunker. This is what your life becomes when you are always vigilant of the next panic attack, all the worse if the potential assault is going to be an 'inside job'. There's no place left to hide, and fear eclipses normal life.

All your thoughts, feelings and behaviours are now focused on preventing another attack. While for some the fear is of the actual experience of panicking – that wave of nausea or dizziness, terrifying racing heartbeat or wobbly knees – for others it's the out-of-control feeling of not being able to get your body to 'behave itself' or to stop your mind spinning. Or the worst dread can be worrying what people will think if they notice you look sweaty or nervous, whether they'll ridicule you or shun you. Besides the constant anticipation of an imminent attack in the present, at another level your mind is concerned for your long-term future if the attacks continue – what it means for your sanity, your job, and your prospects – assuming you survive the next one.

A BODYGUARD IS BORN

With your energy sapped, and a shorter fuse, you snap easily at others. Simple tasks become too much, and social events are an ordeal. Your concentration and capacity to make decisions isn't good, and even deciding what to wear or what to cook for dinner becomes a trial. This state of 'living on your nerves' means that you may find your sleep disrupted, your eating pattern changed, and alcohol, cigarettes or other substances functioning more and more as a sedative or anaesthetic.

Physically this state of constant vigilance is draining. Becoming your own bodyguard means you're never off duty. Many lose motivation for exercise, sex or creative outlets. Others describe themselves as looking at life 'through a pane of glass', at a distance, one step removed, as though they were a spectator witnessing themselves going through the motions of living. There's a sense of disconnection with projects, people and plans.

Many don't pick up the fact that this is subtly different from what they've known as stress in the past. So they soldier on, trying to manage it alone, hoping that when the stressful period is over, all will return to normal. Others, desperately searching for relief and urgently needing a 'jump-start' to boost their flagging energy, describe their state to their doctor, who diagnoses them as clinically depressed, and starts them on anti-depressant medication. Unfortunately, this often makes matters worse, since these are 'uppers', substances whose purpose is to add a buzz to the system, which in this case is already over-stimulated. Medication prescribed to reduce anxiety can take the edge off the vigilance, but many find this disconcerting, because now their security system feels dopey and unreliable, and they can feel more vulnerable than ever to another attack while their defences are relaxed.

Understanding this state of constant watchfulness and ever-readiness is central to the treatment programme in Part Two of this book, because it explains many of the seemingly 'out-of-the-blue' attacks which occur confusingly at times when you didn't feel particularly on edge and therefore weren't expecting one. While you may not have been anticipating one, your bodyguard was!

AVOIDANCE – LIVES ON HOLD

Because that first attack can be so disturbing, most people will go to great lengths to avoid another. So when a trip to the supermarket, town centre, cinema or bank looms, and you've had an attack in a public place before, your radar begins to check internally to see how you're feeling about that. Your intellect may be saying 'Don't be such an idiot! The shopping simply has to get done, no copping out, get a grip on yourself,' but at the level of our primitive life-and-death protective mechanisms, you're hearing 'Are you crazy? No way am I going in there again!' This instinctual part of you makes you hold back and find other ways around it, finding excuses and strategies that would get you off the hook – and keep you safe.

The term given to those who find the intensity of the panicky feelings unsustainable while out in public, and who have developed a phobia about leaving home, is agoraphobia (from the Latin phobia – avoidance, and agora – the market-place). This is a psychiatric label that is both unhelpful and stigmatising, besides failing to capture the essence of the behaviour. A high percentage of agoraphobics are experiencing panic attacks, so strictly speaking it is not a separate illness. If you got a nasty shock every time you touched a certain light switch, it would be considered the action of an intelligent person to avoid touching the switch repeatedly. Yet if a person listens to their 'bodyguard' and tries not to put themselves in the way of another terrifying panic attack, they are unfairly stigmatised.

Many can only continue a normal social life by relying on various 'safety measures' being in place before they'll go out – adaptive strategies like having a few drinks on board before arriving at a social event, sitting near exits, altering their work schedule to avoid heavy traffic, and of course never being without their mobile phone. Bringing someone along, even if it's a young child, can act as a distraction and somehow create an illusion of safety, because they could alert someone and arrange your dispatch to the hospital if necessary. Superstitiously, certain talismans or objects are carried around, such as the phone number of a therapist, a (sometimes empty) bottle of pills, a bottle of water, or antacids. Although buffers such as these can help, the danger is that when they're unavailable, all hell breaks loose and you can feel more unsafe than ever.

Situations from which escape is not easy become a problem. The urge to run is so strong that it becomes agony to have to attend meetings, go to church or the cinema, remain at dinner tables, stand in long queues, engage in conversations that are not easily interrupted, sit in hairdressers', barbers' or dentists' chairs, or take taxi rides. Inveterate travellers may begin to find flying or taking trains a nightmare for the first time in their lives.

Many decide not to 'give in' to the urge to avoid things, and push themselves to continue in their normal routines. In doing so they live with permanently high stress levels, since such events are a part of daily life. Others, unable to tolerate such stress, opt for a 'smaller life' which, being less interactive, holds less potential for attacks to occur. Both stances are understandable, and have a certain logic to them, but a high price is being paid. *Life is being endured rather than lived to the full.*

PARALLEL UNIVERSES – INSIDE VERSUS OUTSIDE

With your focus permanently in emergency mode, it is difficult to be present to, and involved in many of the ordinary details of life around you. You find yourself living in two parallel universes – your external life and your secret internal panic universe, one competing with the other. Since your attention can't always be in two places at once, the panic world usually wins out. You may find that at meetings at work your mind is preoccupied with whether or not you can get a seat near the door, or what excuse you'd give if you needed to leave, rather than on what's being said. Or your son's graduation passes by in a blur because all you can think of is your churning stomach. These lapses in concentration create extra worries. You wonder if others notice, and you have to keep checking whether your work standard is suffering. Balancing the two worlds consumes enormous amounts of energy, leaving you chronically irritable, frustrated and drained.

The thought of having a panic attack in front of others can be a fate worse than death. You fear being misunderstood and judged harshly. *'They might think I was drunk, drugged, weird, strange or mad! I'd die of embarrassment!'* Your thoughts run riot. *'What if I vomited in a restaurant, shouted out some obscenity in church, or had to positively demand that they open the emergency exit door on a plane?'*

Next to the fear of making an absolute fool of yourself in public is the fear of being exposed as a panicker. Most would prefer to keep it a secret at all costs, and many don't confide in even their closest relatives and friends. Your preoccupation with the judgement and criticism of others, *the public gaze*, is fed by the stigma associated with all mental distress. This paranoia leads to loneliness and alienation, and obviously over time diminishes confidence and erodes self-esteem. Friends and relatives become frustrated and angry at your 'stubbornness', and you can feel misunderstood and isolated. Self-loathing and shame are therefore inevitable travelling companions of panic. *'I feel it's so stupid to be reacting like this, I'm weak and useless, I'd be better off dead.'* These are depressing thoughts and many are diagnosed with clinical depression without the panic element ever being discovered. Others begin to rely on alcohol to get them relaxed enough to cope, even carrying around a hidden bottle for medicinal reasons.

This is what life is like for many who panic. However, this is only a surface description of the phenomenon. The key to eliminating it is through a thorough understanding of how it works at the deeper levels. By peeling back these layers you can see why and how your mind creates this state of fear, what hormones it uses in the bloodstream to do so, and what thoughts take over. Only then can you participate in dismantling it. In much the same way as those with diabetes need to understand the central role glucose plays in their disease, and the part they themselves play in making it go up or down, and how this influences their symptoms, so you need to understand the underlying causes of panic attacks. This makes you an active agent in your own healing, taking responsibility for the role of these attacks in your life, and as you take more control, you end the climate of disempowerment and vulnerability you may have been living with.

3

WHY THIS, WHY ME, WHY NOW?

KEYNOTE: THREATS TO IDENTITY

W hy this? Why me? Why now? These are questions that preoccupy people as they're trying to make sense of their panic attacks. It is important that they get accurate answers, otherwise there is a chance they may incorrectly assume that it's part of a serious psychiatric illness. This then leads to escalating levels of fear for the future, untold damage to their self-esteem, and often depression.

Mark – 'I always knew that as part of my job as a policeman there were going to be times when I'd be involved in life-threatening incidents. Over the years there were countless serious run-ins with thugs of all sorts. Weapons of every kind were involved. Of course you'd come in for your share of injuries but this never put me off being one of the first in there. I even had a bit of a reputation as being one of the toughest in our station, and certainly someone you could rely on in a tight spot.

'However, nothing could have prepared me for the effect that last incident had on me. My partner was badly stabbed in the back of the neck as she bent down to handcuff a guy on the ground. I thought I had it covered but he seemed to come from nowhere. As he turned on me, we eyeballed each other, and I thought for the first time in all the years in the service, "This is it." He swung at me but by some miracle I escaped the blade by inches. The image that still stays with me was that look. He meant to kill me, not just injure me, and I felt every bit of the closeness to my last breath in that moment. I got a kind of preview of what "meeting your maker" meant, and the enormity of death hit me.

'In the weeks that followed I hardly recognised myself. Although I was back on the job, I was waking at night soaked in sweat and gasping for air. Sometimes as I went upstairs to get dressed for work, I'd get shaky and dizzy. And whenever a call came in to the station to answer a call, I'd have to work hard at hiding the fact that I could hardly breathe, and make excuses about the heat to explain the sweating.

'But the thing that I asked myself all the time was why now? Why after all the years of dealing with violence was I having this reaction now? And why me? The girl who got stabbed was handling it better than I was! And what did that mean? Could I not be counted on any more? Or would I have to be put on "soft duties"? I thought that maybe this was what people meant when they said someone was cracking up. I genuinely didn't feel I was half the man I used to be, and I felt ashamed for letting myself down like that.'

Pauline's story also shows how confusing the experience of panic can be, and how central the need to make sense of it is.

Pauline – 'My hysterectomy was planned months in advance, and I was looking forward to finally getting some relief in that department after years of trouble with fibroids. I told them at work that I'd need a few months off, thinking I'd be back to normal in no time. However, three months after the operation I was still having to take the odd nap in the afternoon, since my energy hadn't really come back to normal.

Having been fit and energetic all my life this really threw me, as I always used to pride myself on being able to cope with anything and reliably bounce back. I found myself oddly annoyed when my sister took over my role of cooking Christmas dinner. When my elderly mother told me that she had got her neighbour to take her for a fitting for a hearing aid, because she didn't want to burden me, I felt like an old car thrown on the scrap heap.

'What upset me most was finding out that during this time the company I did clerical work for decided that I was "superfluous to their needs", and I found myself prematurely retired. One day when I felt particularly drained, I remember lying in bed thinking *"this is what it's like to be old"*, and from then on every time I felt tired I'd tense up at the thought, and give myself a pep talk. I noticed too that my sleep wasn't good and I always felt particularly "iffy" first thing in the morning. Then I had my first panic attack. It happened on the way out to play golf. I knew it was a bit soon after the operation, but I was so frustrated by then. As I changed in the dressing room I could feel it engulf me like a wave – my heart began to pound, and my chest tightened up till I could barely breathe. The room began to spin and I had to sit down. There was no alternative, I just had to say I felt unwell, and I fled the place.

'From there things just went downhill – the harder I tried to get on top of it the worse it seemed to get. I thought it was due to "hormones", but my doctor informed me that as my ovaries hadn't been taken out that wasn't the reason. The last straw was his suggestion that I possibly hadn't adjusted to the fact that my childbearing years were now over! I felt that more than anything I needed to understand why this had happened. I was always the sort of person to cope well if I knew what to adjust to, but this time I was stumped. What was I doing wrong? Surely it was better to be trying to get back to normal rather than wallowing at home playing the sick role? And how come this hadn't happened five years ago, when we were under far greater stress when my husband's business had been in trouble?'

WHY IDENTITY MATTERS

Mark and Pauline's stories both share one of the essential ingredients of panic: a threat to their identity. The fact is that humans need consistency to be able to function. Continuity and reliability are necessary ingredients to face any challenge. The general of an army needs to know he can rely on numbers, fitness, commitment, etc., to engage in battle. A competitive runner needs to know she can count on her physical fitness, and her racing speeds confirm to her that she can. Similarly, we all crave a sense of 'sameness' about life in order to cope with the challenges it throws our way.

In order to feel safe, it is important to be able to take for granted that you'll be the same person tomorrow as you are today, that your personality and your physical body will 'be there' for you. Unconsciously you presume that tomorrow you'll have two arms and legs, the full use of your eyes, and a brain capable of recognising your children, remembering your mother's birthday and navigating your way to the office. Your personality traits define you, as much as your height, build or hair colour. You know yourself to be 'the sort of person who is … honest, competent, safe from harm, punctual, reliable, knowledgeable, strong, able for anything, financially secure, respected by others, healthy, loved, attractive, successful…' The list is endless. Now you're caught in a catch-22 situation. You need the consistency to feel somewhat secure. Yet if you invest too much in the status quo continuing, you may not be flexibile enough to allow for an unscheduled change in your make-up. As you struggle to integrate the implications of such change on your identity, the reverberation can be felt as a panic attack.

Flu may render you temporarily 'weak' physically, or an argument may render you temporarily 'hated' by your partner. Neither sits easily if you know yourself to be 'the strong one' or 'dearly loved', but the shift in terms of your identity is still minor. What a different story, however, if the flu turns into encephalitis or chronic fatigue syndrome, or the argument leads to your partner permanently leaving you. Now a *psychological earthquake* has occurred, as it radically alters the future 'you' – in a way you may not like at all, a way that may instil a lot of fear within you. It's like living inside a stranger.

THE IMPRINT LEFT BY DEATH

Mark's panic was a response to a change in his existential experience, in the sense that he grasped for the first time *what it may mean to physically die*. We all have a certain degree of denial about the fact that one day we will cease to exist, that physically we are not immortal. In most Western countries, attention to the next leg of the journey is minimal, and even considered by some to be downright morbid. So it can be quite a jolt to suddenly become aware with absolute certainty, as Mark did in the moment when he saw the intent to kill in his assailant's eyes, that our last breath could be imminent. As this realisation sinks in, there are often no words to adequately describe how you feel, since death is such an abstract concept. Usually what is registered, however, is intense fear, and the adrenaline rise that goes with it may be enough to generate a panic attack.

This is why panic attacks are so common after a bereavement, an operation, an assault, a car crash, or sometimes even if we experience any of these second hand, as a witness. They are exceedingly common in post-traumatic stress disorder and also following drug-induced 'boundless' experiences, where there are dramatic shifts in consciousness, which, until they are made sense of and integrated, can be very frightening. Near-death or out-of-body experiences, and spiritual openings where other dimensions of consciousness are accessed, can seem like imminent annihilation, and can elicit panic. Birth can be a similar existential challenge, most especially if it was a traumatic one, where the life of either mother or child is in doubt, or perceived to be.

Some traumatic experiences are far-reaching and very deep, going to the very core of our existence, and confronting us with versions of reality we never thought possible. For example, it is a gigantic shift in a child's consciousness to take on board that the father they trusted to love and keep them safe has either abandoned them, abused them, or has suddenly died. Or for a wife to discover that her husband, who she thought loved her, has been having another relationship for several years. Or that your nest egg has been mishandled by your accountant, leaving you penniless, or that your teenager has a malignant cancer.

Such shifts in your view of yourself, the world and the future can be too enormous to comprehend all at once. Instantly your identity changes from 'feeling safe and trusting of the world' to 'insecure and vulnerable'. Your old framework effectively 'dies', and what is terrifying is the fact that there is a time-lag before another can be hastily constructed to replace it. In the interim your mind frantically buzzes with all kinds of questions for your future, like whether you'll survive, or if you do, whether it's wise ever to trust again, to relax, and take your eye off things. *'After all,'* says your bodyguard, *'such a stance left you open and vulnerable before, so why trust it any more?'* There is a doubt present now as to how the 'future you' should ensure your safety.

OTHER DEATHS – SOCIAL, FINANCIAL, RELATIONSHIP

The harsh judgement of others, such as may follow a demotion, a jail term or a business failure, can mean *social death* – the end of your social role as you knew it. On a more ordinary level, the very thought of 'what people would think' if you failed an exam, made an obvious mistake or failed to meet an important deadline and let others down, can make you cringe at the thought of *being annihilated by the public gaze*. Having a panic attack in front of others can fall into this category, and for some this would be a fate far worse than physical death!

In Pauline's case, her discomfort was about a change in her social experience of herself – from a competent, healthy, reliable, youthful woman, to one who had limited energy, whom others could no longer rely on for help, and who was now fearfully aware of old age because of its similar characteristics. It was her own abhorrence of such a possibility that rattled her. With her old identity temporarily undermined, and no other one yet formulated to take its place, there was essentially no 'Pauline' there to count on.

Similar losses of role identity follow the breakdown of relationships, where one's identity as part of a couple shifts back to that of being single, with all the new social challenges that presents. Even some new mothers are overawed by the responsibility of their new role, albeit welcome, as their own conditioning regarding 'good mother' standards leading them to feel inadequate for the job. Yet others baulk at the inescapable proximity of the baby, forever encroaching on their own independence in a psychologically needy way, and panic at the thought of their individuality being swallowed up in the merging process.

The factor that determines whether an imminent identity threat will trigger panic or not boils down to the degree to which we feel equipped to deal with it. It's an internal power balance. This explains the range of individual differences in sensitivity to bereavement, to losing control of our mind or body, to being judged by others. If the skills are there in your personality to deal with these situations they won't faze you. If they are not, such a state of vulnerability may cause you to panic.

THE JUMP FROM STRESS TO PANIC – FEAR OF THE FEAR

Many would say, months or years later, that although they can understand how the original stress could have caused panic attacks, they remain mystified as to why, now that the stress has passed, the panic remains. They'll say that their greatest worry now is simply that they'll be condemned to having panic attacks forever. There's a feeling that however bad the original difficulty was, it didn't constrict their life so much, it seemed more understandable, the stresses they were dealing with seemed more normal, and they knew it would eventually end, unlike their feeling about the panic attacks.

The reason for the persistence of the attacks is that although the original fear may have been about dying as a result of an assault, or not being able to survive financially, or of being socially alienated, *their fear now is the panic experience itself*. While the external threat has left, an internal one has replaced it. The good news if you are in this category is that while no one can guarantee you safety from harm from outside stresses, you can learn how to feel safe from what comes from inside of you.

4

BEHIND THE SCENES OF A PANIC ATTACK

KEYNOTE: THE FIGHT OR FLIGHT RESPONSE

A s astronomical events go, a full eclipse is a dramatic, exciting experience that fills us with wonder and awe. Certainly the most unlikely feeling we have as we watch it unfold is fear. Why is that? It's because we know what's happening, and that what's going on behind the scenes is not harmful. So we're relaxed and interested as we observe it unfold.

Contrast this with, for example, an indigenous tribe in darkest Africa, watching a full eclipse for the first time. Suddenly and without warning, their sun is obscured and their world is plunged into complete darkness in the middle of the day. Terrified, they presume this is the end of the world and anxiously anticipate worse to happen – the ground to open up, the village to be set on fire by lightning or some such freak act of annihilation. Living as they do very close to nature, depending on it for their livelihood and respectful of its wisdom, a reason for this freak of nature is urgently sought. The elders meet and confer and, steeped in a tradition based on forces of good and evil being expressed symbolically through such very events, an interpretation is made: 'The gods have vented their anger by taking away the sun to punish us for not paying enough homage, and it will not be returned until the situation is atoned for.' So a ritual is hastily done, beasts are sacrificed, prayers are chanted and forgiveness is sought. Within hours, before their very eyes, their sun is returned, the elders are praised for their wisdom, and a tribe now much more attentive to the gods' wishes breathe a group sigh of relief. The 'emergency' is over.

Thinking of this scenario, we can see plainly what is fact, and what appears to add up, but is actually fiction. These days, we have the astrological information that explains why the sun disappears and why it later returns. Although it may be our first time witnessing a full eclipse, our educational system and the media have seen to it that we are intellectually familiar with the concept. So the climate in which we observe an eclipse is one of eager anticipation, curiosity or even indifference, but certainly never fear or terror. *Knowing the facts behind the scenes* can decide whether we feel safe or threatened by an experience.

Since panic is a terrifying experience, with the added horrifying dimension that it is happening inside your body, it means the same as the misinterpreted eclipse would to the unsuspecting natives – imminent harm of an unknown kind. Just as astrological information would change their perspective, *medical information will change your perspective*, so it is essential that you really know what is happening when you panic, and what isn't. This can help you to begin to understand it as *a highly unpleasant, inconvenient physiological experience, but not one that will harm you*. The same kind of information is presented to expectant mothers in ante-natal classes, and has been crucial in reducing their anxiety and influencing the entire birthing experience in a positive way.

As we begin to unpack the experience of panic, you'll see that it affects three main aspects of your make-up. You have specific fearful *thoughts*, you feel certain fearful *sensations* in your body, and you begin *behaving* in fearful ways. This chapter is about how panic is expressed through these three aspects, and what sequence of internal chemical events occurs. Later on you'll be able to see how certain interventions can affect different parts of the sequence, interrupting the attack.

THE ADRENALINE CASCADE – FIGHTING OR FLEEING FOR SURVIVAL

There is no evidence for any biochemical abnormality that causes panic specifically, but what has been found is a general *hyper-arousal of the adrenal system*, which occurs in all of us whenever a challenge is presented. It is the part of your nervous system that gears you up to handle incoming threats.

Panic always starts in a climate of stress, pressure, fear or anxiety. Although this will ring true for most, it may puzzle some people because they might not have thought of the time around their first attack as particularly stressful. On closer inspection, however, they'll usually agree that it was at least a time of challenge or struggle, when there were extra demands to deal with. It rarely begins at a time when life is at its most peaceful, when everything is stable and free of worries.

These challenges are usually traumas and distresses of an obvious kind, such as a bereavement, car crash or assault, or a difficult time in a relationship. Life thrusts all kinds of challenges on you unpredictably and your level of stress is a reflection of your effort to overcome them while still maintaining the old status quo, and as much of your essential identity as you can salvage. Sometimes, however, the extra demands may be the kind that one would ordinarily think of as positive, even sought after, such as a new baby, a promotion, a house move, or life-enhancing surgery such as a hip replacement or a by-pass operation. Alternatively, a first attack may occur at a time when life in general is OK, but a bad trip with a recreational drug introduces you to an experience that others may find innocuous but you personally find to be highly anxiety-provoking.

The specific nature of the threatening ingredient in such experiences will be covered later. Our initial task is to take a look at what they all have in common, what fuels them – *the adrenaline molecule*. An understanding of the chemical pathways that mediate fear is basic to eliminating panic, because it can allow you to reframe symptoms that you may have been misinterpreting as potentially harmful, and see them instead as unpleasant but harmless.

FEAR KEEPS YOU SAFE

All our emotions have a function, and fear is designed to alert us to the presence of any dangers which could be potential threats to the continuity of our status quo. Threats can be small, such as the fear of being late for an appointment, or large, such as the fear of death. Each day we all oscillate back and forth along a spectrum ranging from fear to safety, making the necessary adjustments needed to return to the safety end of that continuum, even if we've only left it for a short time.

Fear	——————————————	Safety

Fear cautions you to 'pay attention and get ready' for change. It is your alarm system. Just as the presence of pain at the physical level prompts you to be observant and if necessary to take action, fear urges you to mount an instant response if all is not well. In this sense it acts like a messenger. You can choose to act on it or ignore it but you are always warned!

So once a perception of threat is on board, how is that translated into action? What's the route by which a mere thought in your mind, an abstract concept, a non-material item of information, becomes translated into action? How does that impulse end up as a physical response that is now measurable, in terms of speed or power or blood chemistry – in other words, a physical response that 'exists'? Medicine is moving into a new paradigm that views the mind–body as one unit rather than as separate, unrelated compartments. An undeniable link has now been traced between thoughts and feelings and their effects on our physical existence. Scientifically the pathways are clearly documented as to how, for instance, goose-bumps 'know' when to appear on your arms, or hairs to stand up at the back of your neck in response to watching a horror movie. Your physical experiences of sexual arousal or a vivid nightmare are recognised to be the end result of images being presented to your brain, which stimulates the creation of chemical molecules in your bloodstream, making your body react accordingly.

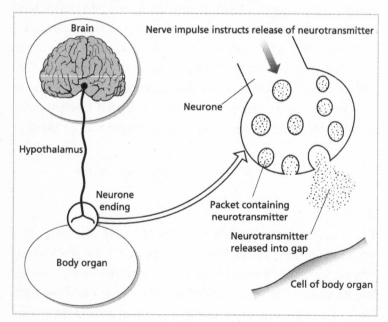

FIGURE 4.1 THE ADRENALINE CASCADE

The fear cascade happens through the manufacture of the neurotransmitter hormone adrenaline and its cousins, which the brain delivers into the bloodstream following your initial perception of danger. As you cross over from feeling confident that you'll be on time for your plane, to knowing you'll miss it, your blood adrenaline will rise as it prepares you to with cope with the consequences. In the moments after receiving the news that your child has been hit by a car, your adrenaline climbs to help you deal with the implications. Walking into an interview, you experience a mini-surge to spur you on to best advertise your attributes. A chemical boost is needed with all these challenges in order to energise your system, hone your senses and increase alertness, and hopefully, with the task achieved, to place you back in the safety zone.

FROM CAVE TO URBAN JUNGLE – THE FIGHT OR FLIGHT RESPONSE

Our cave-dwelling ancestors faced many fears, most of them about their physical safety. It was vital that an automatic response could be relied upon to take over if they were presented with some overwhelming danger. They had to be able to rely on themselves to take immediate decisive action, to attack or run, without thinking, in a reflex way, like when your arm shoots out to break your fall if you trip.

Even in today's hectic 'urban jungle', such reflex mechanisms are still necessary. If you saw a car speeding towards you as you were crossing the street, you'd need to act quickly to save your life by jumping out of the way. No time for deliberation. Your rational mind is hijacked into emergency mode and your primitive brain does the deciding for you. Minutes later on the footpath, you may become aware that your heart is thumping, you're shaking and breathless, and for some time later you may be tense and jumpy.

The process that has just taken you over, and saved your life, is called *the fight or flight response*. It is so named because it is aimed towards preparing you to fight the 'enemy' or flee the danger. Without it you might have been killed. So its purpose is to protect you, never to harm. If the danger you face is clearly external, then the response works well by helping you to defend yourself. It causes an explosion into action.

However, if the danger is perceived as coming from inside you, your first instinct may be to resist it, rather than express it. This happens because there is a mismatch between the seemingly neutral setting you are in, and the urgency of the feeling that you are in danger. Your brain is puzzled and confused as it looks round the supermarket and sees everyone else strolling calmly around, while on the inside you couldn't feel more terrified if your trolley had burst into flames. As a result you censor the outward expression of your fear, judging it inappropriate. Now instead of an explosion into action, an implosion occurs and the full force of it is felt all over your body. This experience is terrifying and leads to the state of excessive vigilance about such a thing ever happening again.

Many who are living through a stage of life where there are many daily challenges experience high levels of adrenaline all the time, or in isolated peaks. *Anxiety is the term used to describe the clinical picture caused by a slow constant drip of daily adrenaline, while an intense rush of it suddenly entering the bloodstream is referred to as panic.*

Several factors distinguish these first cousins from each other. Firstly, the smaller number of molecules released into the bloodstream distinguishes anxiety, something familiar to us all, from panic. Secondly, the symptoms of anxiety, although unpleasant and annoying, rarely frighten us, while most people find the symptoms of panic terrifying, some more than others. This is a very important factor, because feeling afraid (of the way the fight-flight response makes you feel) will prompt the release of more adrenaline, and that alone will shift anxiety up a gear and tip it over into panic. A vicious cycle of *fear of the fear evolves*, in which your attention zones in on monitoring any potentially dangerous bodily sensations. Later we'll come back to this essential point since much of the treatment approach in this book rests on understanding it.

HOW AND WHERE ADRENALINE ACTS

Once in your bloodstream, adrenaline targets those parts of your body that will be instrumental in getting you to safety. You experience this increase in adrenaline as symptoms such as:

* shortness of breath
* palpitations/fast heart rate
* discomfort or pains in the chest
* feeling smothered or choking sensations
* feeling faint, unsteady, or dizzy
* numbness or tingling in the extremities
* hot and/or cold flushes
* sweating
* trembling or shaking
* nausea, knot in the stomach or diarrhoea
* perceptual changes, feelings of unreality
* fear of dying
* fear of losing your mind or going crazy
* fear of losing control and doing something bizarre
* an overwhelming feeling of terror, or ominous sense of something bad about to happen

When danger is perceived or anticipated, your brain sends messages to the 'emergency wing' of your autonomic (or involuntary) nervous system, also called the sympathetic nervous system, to release neurotransmitters and fuel and get your body prepared for action, as described below. At the same time it alerts the 'restoration wing', called the parasympathetic nervous system, to return equilibrium and 'mop up' once the crisis is over. This ensures that the emergency response has a ceiling, and once this is reached the dampening down process is initiated. So your nervous system can't get stuck in 'panic mode' indefinitely. (This shut-off mechanism is an important reassurance for those who fear their panic attack will never end, and it can be purposely activated by using the techniques in Part Two of this book.)

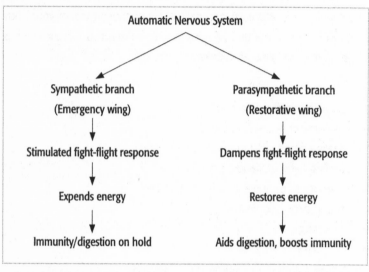

FIGURE 4.2 THE AUTONOMIC NERVOUS SYSTEM

- ***Muscular effects.*** In order for your caveman ancestor to fight with a predator, or for you to jump clear of an oncoming car, your muscles need to become instantly active and strong. If this is happening on an ongoing daily basis, you may feel tense, restless and fidgety, your muscles may ache and you may tremble and shake. Tension headaches, back strain or jaw pain from clenching or grinding your teeth at night are all signs that you're running a high muscle tension. Tasks that require a steady hand, such as writing cheques or pouring coffee, can become a problem. If the muscles in your throat tighten up it can feel like you have a lump there, or it may be difficult to swallow, or you may develop a stammer.

Since the purpose of the increase in tension is to propel you out of the situation through action, anything that blocks your exit can seem intolerable. You begin to dread going to places where easy escape is blocked, such as the cinema or church, because they frustrate this urge to flee.

- **Cardiovascular effects.** Extra demands are placed on the heart whenever your muscles become more active. The quantity of blood it pumps around the body must increase quickly to provide these working muscles with the necessary nutrients – hence the term 'pumping iron'. Adrenaline ensures that the heart rate speeds up and pumps more forcefully.

The distribution of blood flow also changes. It is redirected away from limbs at the periphery, towards the centre where it is needed for the vital organs. Adrenaline makes this happen by narrowing the diameter of the smaller vessels and widening the larger ones that supply the muscles. This has a survival value in that if your caveman ancestor got bitten or wounded on his hand or foot, he would be less likely to bleed to death, since there would be less blood there than usual. (In first aid terms, something tight acting as a tourniquet wrapped around a bleeding limb is seeking the same effect.) On a daily basis, it means that your hands and feet may feel colder when your adrenaline is high, and you could feel pins and needles or numbness in them, a reflection of the reduction in blood supply to the nerves in the skin.

The flow also reduces to areas not essential to the emergency effort, such as the skin. This is why people often look pale after having had a fright, or bad news. The blood has drained from the tiny arteries in their face towards the centre, where it's more useful. The same dynamic causes fainting under extreme stress, as the blood drains from the head area, resulting in a temporary loss of consciousness. (For those afraid of fainting it is important that they learn to see this manoeuvre as restorative rather than harmful – see Chapter 5.)

- **Respiratory effects.** To prepare for action you need to take in more oxygen than usual. Adrenaline increases the number of breaths per minute, a phenomenon known as *hyper-ventilation*. To you this feels like breathlessness, choking, smothering sensations, sighing or simply an inability to get a satisfying 'deep enough' breath. The effort may cause your chest to feel tight or even painful. A side effect of faster breathing is that the blood supply to your head is reduced. Although in no way dangerous, this can cause dizziness, blurred vision, loss of concentration and confusion, all unpleasant and frightening symptoms. It is estimated that hyperventilating, either acutely during an attack, or chronically in between them, is a factor in 60 to 70 per cent of panic attacks.

- **Sweat gland effects.** With such vigorous activity going on in the muscles your body temperature rises, so in order to cool down you produce more sweat. This adaptive response also has survival value since it makes the skin slippery, so that an assailant will find it harder to grab hold. For you it may mean waking at night soaked in sweat, having to change shirts more often, or finding your hands becoming damp.

- **Other physical effects**. Many other internal variables change to prepare you for a struggle.

Fuel is made available through the release of glucose from the liver, and cholesterol, normally broken down and cleared out of the blood, instead hangs around in case it's called for. While neither of these states are of concern in the short term, they can lead to diabetes and arteriosclerosis (coating of the arterial walls with cholesterol plaques, leading to their blockage) if the fight-flight response goes on uninterrupted for years.

In an attempt to prevent bleeding to death in the event of a gash or a bite from a predator, our forebears needed to increase their *blood-clotting factors*. This ensured that a scab would quickly form at the site. These days our predators are unlikely to cause such physical damage, so this part of the response only serves nowadays to increase the danger of an artery blocking up, since our blood is now travelling through them more slowly, like orange juice as compared to water. Add to this the narrowing of the artery's diameter, also caused by adrenaline, and it's easy to see how stress is associated with a much higher incidence of hypertension and heart attacks if it is long-term.

Digestion is suspended while adrenaline levels are high. After all, digestion of your breakfast or lunch is not a high priority when you're looking into the jaws of a lion, and can always be attended to when the emergency is over. This go-slow in the digestive system is felt as a decrease in saliva production (giving you a dry mouth) nausea, a heavy feeling in the stomach, and diarrhoea and/or constipation.

Extreme fatigue is the end result of a chronically aroused nervous system. This is due to a combination of interrupted sleep, metabolic overdrive and the consumption of vast amounts of energy by the personality in the attempt to integrate and process the latest challenge.

EXAGGERATED INTERNAL FOCUS OF ATTENTION

Mentally, adrenaline brings about changes in how you think and how you pay attention, which helps you to foresee emergencies and challenges.

A state of hyperalertness develops. This enables your hearing to become sharper, and your pupils to dilate to allow in more light, all with the goal of bringing in more information and increasing your awareness of danger. Your brainwaves become predominantly of the faster type, known as beta, to speed up the processing of danger signals. Many who panic feel a constant buzzing or bursting feeling in their head, and worry about a brain tumour. This state of mental 'ever-readiness' can mean that you are plagued by racing thoughts at night, which can disrupt your sleep, or distract you from your study or work during the day. It also makes it hard to switch off and relax during weekends or on holidays. This 'adrenaline high' is unfortunately the staple diet of many who do battle on a daily basis with the clock, the money markets, or the cultural 'scales of perfection' against which too many of us have been trained to measure ourselves.

Back in the days of the caveman, it was essential that adrenaline provided him with a hefty dose of fear. Enough of this would motivate him to defend himself or run from danger. Curiosity or bravery would be misplaced and counterproductive in facing a charging lion. The greater the number of adrenaline molecules in his bloodstream, the more insecure he would feel, and the more he would (wisely) overrule any information presented to his intellect that 'all is well'. He could not afford to believe rational thoughts seducing him into feeling safe, because too much was at stake. So *a high level of mistrust, suspicion and even paranoia make up the emotional territory that go with this chemical profile.* These feelings are relatively short-lived in a caveman-predator situation, where the adrenaline is burned off in the course of the struggle. However, in our modern urban jungle scenario, where one challenge follows hot on the heels of another, consistently high levels can be the norm, which means constantly viewing the world through spectacles tinted by insecurity, lack of trust and constant vigilance.

Feelings of unreality or depersonalisation are common, and some individuals have an out-of-body experience when they panic. These are a side-effect of some of the energy-field changes that occur during panic, which are explained in more detail in Chapter 8.

Feelings of dissociation, bringing with them a sense of unreality and disconnection with yourself and your environment, are common. This is termed depersonalisation when it refers to a change in your self-awareness during which you feel detached or removed from your own experience, your body and mind seeming unfamiliar to you in some way. It's been described as 'robot-like, acting a part, made of cotton-wool, lifeless or dead, being a spectator, not doing your own thinking, observing the flow of ideas in your mind as independent of you or happening to someone in a film'. You may even feel as though you are standing alongside, above or behind your body, or as though it has shrunk or expanded in size.

Derealisation, on the other hand, refers to a change in your experience of the environment around you, as though there's a space between you and it. Descriptions include 'looking through a veil or pane of glass, being in a goldfish bowl, daydream-like, objects appearing smaller than they should be, shimmering, lacking solidity'.

The phenomenon of dissociation has as yet been poorly researched, but would seem to represent a shift in consciousness which is accompanied by changes in your energy field (see Chapter 8 for more detail). In the same way that you would reflexively withdraw your hand rapidly from a naked flame, or run away from smoke to avoid hurt, some people unconsciously dissociate at the slightest whiff that the sensations are about to begin, so great is their fear of what will happen next. It's essentially an out-of-body experience much like that which occurs to a person during a rape, or who is caught in a car that has been in an accident, or in the post-operative phase. Its goal is to render the trauma sensations less intense, because they're being experienced from a 'safe' distance. While this may be so, once your bodyguard gets wind of it, and your mind tries to interpret this shift, it becomes a source of worry and concern, so the important thing to know is that these symptoms are completely harmless, just another expression of panic, and do not in any way herald the beginning of a mental disorder or psychiatric problem, although this is most people's immediate fear.

Many who panic report that their dissociation feelings can precede or trigger their attacks, rather than follow them as an effect. Some speak of having had a tendency to 'trance-out' since childhood, and of this tendency being activated again in adulthood as a result of major stress, or not eating and sleeping properly, both well known to trigger feelings of not being 'grounded'. Such trance states can be induced within seconds, when a person is relaxed and/or staring: out of a window, while driving, watching TV or fluorescent lighting, using a computer or when absorbed during a conversation. Some nocturnal panic attacks may be explained by such shifts in consciousness, on the interface between deep and dreaming sleep.

In the face of a serious challenge it pays to be focused and not to get distracted from the task at hand. During periods of adrenal overdrive we may lose interest in our home, our children, our beloved garden, or sex with our partner, focusing instead on nothing else but the emergency. In survival terms this is completely appropriate in short bursts, but you can easily see how it can erode and change your personality over the long term, leaving you too joyless, cynical and blunted to derive pleasure from life. Instead, the main 'feel-good' factor has been replaced by the secure knowledge that you have triumphed over the adversary, 'won the day', become the victor, and secured your fortress. How many such daily battles are technically won in the world of work, our predominant war-zone, without the realisation that we are losing the entire war by letting inner peace slip out of our grasp.

THE FILTER OF PERCEPTION – HOW THE INITIAL ATTACK IS MISINTERPRETED

If you see a car travelling along the road you know one thing for sure – it has petrol in it, otherwise it couldn't be moving. Likewise, for the symptoms of the fight or flight response to be present, this means that a high level of adrenaline must be present to fuel it. Adrenaline manufactures the symptoms of panic as surely as the flu virus causes the symptoms of flu, or the petrol allows a car to run. Like the old song says, 'love and marriage, horse and carriage – you can't have one without the other'.

At times of stress or challenge, when the adrenaline level is running high, some people will experience a panic attack, others tension headaches, others irritable bowel or insomnia. Many (up to 10 per cent of the population) who experience one or two occasional attacks, even if they didn't realise they were particularly stressed, never have another. This is referred to as 'non-clinical' panic. The feature which seems to distinguish this group from those who go on to have more of them, is that *they do not interpret the symptoms themselves as harmful.* In this way one person may find their first panic attack thoroughly uncomfortable and disturbing, but they are not terrified by it. Their belief system, the filter through which they perceive the experience, seems to be able to incorporate such an unpredictable and incomprehensible event without attaching an ominous meaning to it. To them it just happened, it doesn't have to mean something, or be a sign of anything in particular.

The group who go on to develop regular panic attacks do, however, worry over its significance. They misinterpret the racing heartbeat to mean an impending heart attack, the dizziness a brain abnormality for sure, or the 'jelly legs' to mean early multiple sclerosis. They seem to have a heightened awareness of and sensitivity to the symptoms of adrenaline, and become concerned about its effects, while the former group do not. Their inability to control and terminate an attack troubles them in terms of trusting themselves to handle it in the future. It may have been their first truly out-of-control experience in their lives. These factors make that initial 'out-of-the-blue' attack a more frightening experience for this group of people. It is this difference that is thought to prime them to turn their focus inwards, looking for the next attack, creating the state of 'ever-readiness' or vigilance. Why does this excessive sensory sensitivity develop in this group?

If an assailant threatened you and you experienced your 'alarm system' going off, and the adrenaline cascade began, you'd understand that the assault had been the trigger, and your attention would be devoted outwards to discern whether your attacker had gone or would come back, or to calling the police to catch him. Your brain doesn't like having no explanation for something as serious as a survival threat, so if your alarm has gone off and you feel terror, and *if no obvious source of threat can be found in the environment, then the search turns inward.* As you internally scan your body looking for a likely reason for your feeling of danger, listening for 'noises', *you notice, question and misinterpret some of its normal functions as dangerous.*

TWO PLUS TWO MAKES FIVE – WRONG!

Every event that impacts on you is analysed and recorded by your brain. Based on how they feel, experiences are broadly assessed as nice or nasty, good or bad, comfortable or unpleasant. This information is stored in your brain's filing system for future reference and is referred to instantly if any similar situation arises. It's as though a folder is opened in which the images, the bodily sensations and the verdict, 'good' or 'bad', are recorded. Also recorded there is a recommendation, from a survival perspective, of what to do should they recur – 'go towards' if it was comfortable, and 'pull away' if it was noxious.

If you noticed your skin felt numb and tingly, and you couldn't figure out why, your brain would begin to search its files to see if this 'puzzling incoming input' has ever happened to you before. If nothing comes up, it will cross-reference to all the reasons it has ever read about, seen on TV, heard others discuss, etc. Unfortunately the brain is oftentimes more desperate than it is efficient, and it can isolate a piece of information out of context, and seize it as gospel truth. And of course who's to challenge it; so you begin relating to an item of misinformation as something to be afraid of, when in fact it's merely puzzling but innocuous. You think 'I must have a brain tumour. Wouldn't that make you dizzy?' Although incorrect, the misinterpretations are accepted as if they were true. They also carry more threat than the truth would, so instead of being afraid of a mildly unpleasant sensation like dizziness, you are now afraid you may have a really serious, potentially fatal medical illness. This really gets your adrenaline flowing, and the end result is that *you learn to fear the sensation itself*, because that's the initial trigger. It becomes the 'cue' to a panic attack.

Panic attacks can therefore be seen as a phobic-like reaction that develops as a result of repeated associations between certain bodily 'cues' (palpitations, dizziness, breathlessness) and the high adrenaline surge that the fear of it triggers.

The problem is that a person learns to initiate the alarm in response to these cues, and lives in a constant state of anxiety over the possibility of future alarms going off. For example, if mental ill-health was related to in your family as a 'fate worse than death', with a shudder of fear and abhorrence, and during a period of intense stress you feel like you're now losing control of your sanity, you'll be a lot more disturbed by a 'mental' symptom than someone whose family had an attitude of compassion and tolerance. You may therefore fear that you're going mad if you have an irrational urge to run out of the room or (mis)interpret moments of confusion, or lapses in memory (like forgetting your way home or where you parked the car). *Understandable as these thoughts are, they are incorrect and damaging as they increase your adrenaline further.* An important step in gaining freedom from panic is the re-education of your belief system, rooting out misinformation and replacing it with the truth.

Without you even being conscious of the search, your brain might find matches for your current state in unpleasant experiences you had forgotten happening to you in the past. For example, you could have been separated from your parents as a small child and felt insecure and abandoned. Perhaps your heart was racing at the time, and you felt nauseous and terrified. Or when you had an anaesthetic in hospital for a tonsillectomy, missing your parents and feeling sick, you may have had similar symptoms. Or when you heard the news that your granny had died. Or perhaps it was even before you could talk, like when your brother locked you in the wardrobe as a toddler, or during the perilous journey down the birth canal.

It is possible to have stored memories (as images) of these events but not be able to remember how your body felt at the time, especially if the memory was recorded in the pre-verbal years, before your thoughts occurred in the form of words, but merely as perceptions. Even if that information has slipped out of your conscious awareness, your unconscious always makes a record of it (just like your computer 'saves' material in case you forget to). Without your knowing, a pairing has occurred, and the unconscious elements, the bits you've forgotten, such as the fear and sense of threat, can still influence you in the present day. You have 'learned' to fear that experience. This explains how you can find yourself caught in the throes of an attack seemingly 'unawares'. Rather than having clear thoughts of danger, you experience shorthand vague 'impressions' of danger. Your internal scanning mechanism, your bodyguard, will have picked up, below the radar of your consciousness, what it has come to recognise as signals of 'danger' – a faster heartbeat, a series of shallow breaths, a tightening of the muscles. It might even have been during your death in a past life that you made the association that these symptoms always precede trauma. How this works is explained later on, but while it is academically interesting to follow the trail back to the original threat, *it is not necessary to retrieve these old memories in order to overcome panic.*

For now, the first step is to increase your awareness that a sequence of events is occurring when you have a panic attack. Although it may seem like attacks happen 'all of a sudden', there is actually a beginning, a middle and an end to them. You need to learn to slow down the process by becoming aware of the individual components. Only be doing so can you gain some control of the way it unfolds.

INTERRUPTING THE CYCLE OF FEAR

This concept of triggers or cues is important for treatment. If all panic attacks are triggered (although they may have slipped in below the level of your awareness), this implies that they are in fact not entirely unpredictable, or 'out of the blue'. One of the most terrifying aspects of panic attacks is this quality of having no control over when they come. You may feel less at their mercy if you realise, for instance, that the reason for some of them might be that when you feel an argument brewing or if you're hurrying, your heart rate rises without you realising it, and acts as an internal trigger, starting off an attack, rather than some mysterious process such as mental illness or a brain tumour. This allows you the opportunity to decide in the future to examine the level of conflict in your life, or to be less hurried, and thus introduce an element of control over the frequency of attacks.

Likewise, if you realise that it is the learned fear of the symptoms themselves that keeps you constantly apprehensive, and if you become less afraid of having a fast heart rate or being breathless, then this is another area you can learn to control. Furthermore, if you know that once you break the association between certain thoughts and the ensuing sensations, you will no longer trigger the fight-flight response in the first place, then controlling those catastrophic thoughts makes sense as an important part of treatment. These steps are clearly laid out in Part Two.

If you live in a state of continual hyperarousal, this means that you will be experiencing triggers or cues, such as a racing heart or fast breathing, on a continual basis. Therefore it will help your panic attacks to reduce your overall level of adrenaline (this is covered in more detail in Chapter 17).

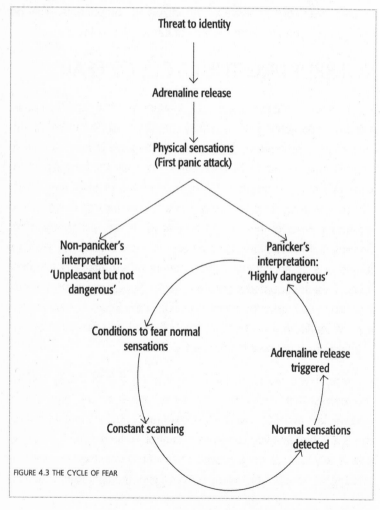

FIGURE 4.3 THE CYCLE OF FEAR

5

MYTHS
ABOUT PANIC

The cycle of fear is triggered and then fuelled by the *inaccurate meanings* attributed to the experience of certain sensations. These beliefs distinguish those who panic from those who don't. This chapter is about identifying some of the specific fears shared by many who panic. Later on you will learn how to challenge these fears, and replace them with facts.

In this chapter try to push yourself to eliminate vague global terms for how you felt, such as 'terrified' or 'awful' or 'like something bad could happen any minute'. If you try to tease out and identify specifically what you are afraid of, then a more medically accurate explanation can be given which can address that fear, and lower your adrenaline. It may even head off its rise in the first place. So you need to ask – 'terrified of what?' And what specifically was so awful about it? And what exactly did you fear could happen next? Precisely how did you see it affecting the future?

COMMON FEARS

① *Am I Going Mad?*

Because of the unusual mental changes that occur during panic, many believe that their sanity is in question. After all, it seems pretty strange to be at an office meeting or in the supermarket one moment, and convinced that you're going to die if you don't get outside the next. The undeniable sense of losing touch with the normal world as your inner universe takes over can cause you to feel 'unreal', floating and disconnected, as though you were perceiving life through a pane of glass. Many who experience the demons of paranoia, self-doubt and utter naked vulnerability for the first time, can only interpret them as madness. Never realising that intense emotion could cause such psychological earthquakes, they assume they have a serious psychiatric condition.

A constant buzzing sensation in the head is sometimes misinterpreted as mental illness. In fact it is an expression of excessive beta brainwave activity, which occurs with increased adrenaline, and it is harmless. This symptom goes with the territory when your brain is in overdrive, looking for answers. When you are worried, and focusing all your attention on what's happening inside you, you can tend to zone in on it like you never have before, presuming that it is ominous.

Many of the mental faculties that you are used to relying on become compromised when adrenaline rises. Like an overloaded food processor, your brain can feel like it is seizing up. You can find it impossible to make decisions, to remember where you left things, or to muster up enough concentration to read. This fugue state can give you the alarming feeling that the command post has been left unattended! Unable to totally trust yourself, you increasingly need to double check things, which adds extra strain. In some cases, people may forget names, or get lost on their way home, or in a distracted state be unable to remember how to start the car.

A doctor's visit following a panic attack may accelerate rather than alleviate concerns about your mental health, if he or she advises you to take a few days off, and gives you a prescription for Valium. Where has the person gone, you may ask, who left the house that day with not a thing to indicate anything was wrong with their mind? As the weeks go by, if you find yourself avoiding certain places, sitting near exits, taking the odd drink 'to calm you' before going out, and, most disturbing of all, finding that you are now relying more on the medication, you may incorrectly conclude that you do indeed have a psychiatric disorder.

The commonest fear is of a mental state known as schizophrenia. The schizophrenic inhabits a different reality than everyone else (this is called psychosis). They have their own unusual beliefs, called delusions, an example of which would be to think that the TV was communicating directly with them, or that alien life was issuing them instructions. They frequently hear voices, or see people who the rest of us can't, and who may be instructing them to do certain actions. Their thoughts and speech are frequently disjointed and disorganised, often to the point of not being able to hold the thread of a conversation, and its content often seems nonsensical.

This disorder typically begins very gradually, not suddenly as panic does. It rarely first appears in people over 25. Those who become schizophrenic have usually shown some mild symptoms of anxiety or eccentricity for much of their lives. Many are loners who were often 'odd' children spending most of their time on their own, avoiding their peers, and finding socialising difficult. Unlike the Nobel Prize-winning mathematician John Nash, portrayed in the movie *A Beautiful Mind*, many never manage to successfully complete school, leave home, become independent, develop intimate relationships or hold down a job.

Panic never progresses on to become schizophrenia, and it is not one of the initial signs of schizophrenia.

The other psychiatric disorder that people worry about developing is manic depression, also referred to as bipolar disorder, because it manifests as a 'high' or elated and 'low' or depressed state of mind. Again, during the psychotic state of elation the manic is not sharing the same reality as others, and may imagine themselves to be someone grandiose, such as Jesus, or a famous rock star or an astounding success, much sought-after in their own occupation or field of interest, ignoring all evidence to the contrary. They cannot conduct a normal life while psychotic, their flights of fancy generating loud and fast speech and non-stop action, such as spending sprees or all-night partying. The manic phase, which is constant and does not come and go in waves as panic does, can last for weeks or months before finally burning out, or has to be terminated through the use of sedative medication, and depression follows. Mania is a state characterised by over-confidence, and there should be no confusing it with panic, where the opposite is the case. Also, although there can be a tremendous degree of activity in the mind in panic which is difficult to turn off:

Manics experience none of the physical symptoms of panic at all, particularly the fear.

Manic is covered in more detail in my book *Depression – An Emotion not a Disease*. Panic and depression can be linked, but not in any genetic sense. Many of those who have not been fortunate enough to receive a prompt, correct diagnosis and effective treatment can become depressed as time drags on. There can be few experiences worse than having to face fear on a daily basis, feeling totally at the mercy of such disturbing symptoms, which are holding your life to ransom. It is depressing stuff to see your chances of a promotion or relationship fall outside your reach, or to find your life gradually constricting and your urge to continue living slowly diminish. Many become suicidal. Much of the depressed feeling is the effect of having no control, feeling utterly helpless and disillusioned with various interventions, including medical ones, because they haven't worked. So once a good treatment programme begins which instils a sense of personal control, the depression lifts as a consequence.

Depression will only accompany panic if the panic attacks have been inadequately treated.

Admission to a psychiatric hospital should never be necessary for panic. Many fear that they will start down some slippery slope where life as they know it will cease, where long-term medication will render them stupefied and slow, in and out of hospital for years, and unable to relate to, or support, themselves or their family. This is an inaccuracy, since most who panic couldn't even be identified by those they work with, or socialise with, even though it may be disrupting their lives quite considerably, so it could never be confused with any major psychotic disorder requiring hospitalisation.

The importance of eliminating such misinformation as this from your thinking cannot be emphasised enough. If, when you experience the first symptoms of panic, you automatically go on to have fears that you will become psychotic (go mad) as a result, then a cycle of anxious apprehension is set up where you are continuously frightening yourself and raising your own adrenaline just by thinking about it. A psychological 'own goal' if ever there was one! These distinctions are covered in more depth in my book, *Going Mad? – Understanding Mental Illness*, co-written with Dr Michael Corry.

② *Could a Panic Attack Cause a Heart Attack?*

This is one of the commonest inaccurate beliefs about panic. Some of the symptoms of panic are similar to those of angina and heart attack, such as palpitations, breathlessness and chest pain. Since everyone knows that you can die of a heart attack, people begin incorrectly diagnosing an imminent heart attack, and of course assume they are about to die. So, fear of the next episode of panic translates into fear of dying of a heart attack! Little wonder that they remain in a state of 'ever-readiness', internally scanning every heartbeat for any irregularity.

In angina, chest pain is the main symptom. This means pain, not the vague chest achiness or tightness from breathing fast during a panic attack. It is generally directly related to effort, in that the more you exercise the worse it gets, and it usually subsides with rest. *Palpitations are not a feature of angina*, nor are trembling, feelings of unsteadiness, or having an urge to escape.

If you had palpitations to begin with and developed slight chest discomfort or pain later on, then this is panic, not heart disease.

Angina is therefore different from panic, which more commonly happens when you're doing nothing energetic. For example, panic could occur when you're watching TV or sitting at your desk at school or at work. Although there is some overlap, in that heart symptoms can occur when you're stressed, and panic symptoms can occur when you're exercising, panic occurs more often at rest, which is a major difference from heart disease.

Ventricular fibrillation, the cardiac irregularity that is the cause of most sudden cardiac deaths, is the one featured most often in the movies and on programmes such as ER because of its drama value. Since it requires the emergency use of the defibrillator, it succeeds in injecting a 'fear of death' tone into the scene, which heightens the emotional tension by making us anxious about the character's survival. While this may work for the movie-makers, it creates a false sense of fear in the viewing public at large as, like all stereotypes, it is built on a shred of truth and large dollops of inaccuracy.

Ventricular fibrillation has a completely different presentation to a panic attack. It generally occurs in *those who have well-established heart disease already under treatment*, so if you have been checked by your doctor for any other reason (such as for an insurance policy) and heart disease was not picked up, you need not fear that your palpitations are of this category. The essential disturbance is a disorganisation of the heartbeat that results in the heart muscle being unable to work, the pulse ceasing, and death ensuing within approximately three minutes. The patient is gripped by an excruciating, crushing chest pain, they collapse on the ground, cannot speak or move and have no pulse.

> If you can freely move around, talk and can feel a pulse, even if you have the sensation of your heart 'jumping out of your chest', or mild pain or tightness, you are having a panic attack rather than a heart attack.

Most importantly, heart disease will produce electrical changes, which are picked up easily on an ECG, whereas in panic the only change will be a more rapid heart rate.

> If your ECG is clear, you are experiencing panic attacks, not heart disease.

In the 1980s some researchers suggested that there was a relationship between mitral valve prolapse, a common completely benign cardiac condition which shares some of the symptoms of panic but which is distinguished by the presence of a heart murmur. I recently had a patient terrified by her pharmacist who told her to go have her heart examined, as MVP was a likely cause – totally untrue. Current more up-to-date studies using echocardiograms have found no significant link between the two, so it is important to remember when you are catastrophising, panic attacks do not cause valve prolapse.

③ Could I Lose Control?

You may fear that you will 'lose the run of yourself' when you panic and, not knowing what you're doing, will then go berserk, shout something out, push people or make a fool of yourself by acting irrationally. Or you might feel capable of taking a knife and stabbing someone, or holding a child's head under the water in the bath for no reason. Although these things *never* happen, they are very common fears, but are based on an inaccuracy.

The point of the emergency survival response is to get you to safety. It does not give you the urge to hurt other people who have done nothing to threaten you. How would that help your survival? Although some of the behaviours you might have when you are afraid, confused and distracted, such as turning your car around and driving straight home, or hastily leaving a meeting, may seem to you like losing control, in fact they are entirely controlled and focused in the direction of getting you to safety and avoiding what you fear. The only control lost is that the rational voice of conditioning that says 'play it safe, don't upset the apple cart' is drowned out as you plan your exit. This can be a disturbing feeling for people who usually restrain their emotions and find spontaneity uncomfortable. For people who always need to do things 'the right way', letting go can imply chaos. They find it disturbing to think that one aspect of their mind, the primitive, threatened part, can over-ride the will of their logical, rational mind wanting to keep the lid on things. The thought of doing so in full view of others, and the judgement they imagine that would bring, adds to their fear.

Equally primitive is the fear of your bowels deciding to relieve themselves of their own accord without your consent. Medically, the only conditions in which such incontinence can happen involve deterioration of the nerves which supply your anal sphincter, as happens in old age or paraplegia, the paralysis following severe physical trauma like car accidents or other such injury. If you have neither of these, then you, like the rest of us, can say 'no, not yet' to that muscle if you are not near a toilet, and 'yes, now' if you are sitting on one. It cannot open involuntarily, but confusion can arise because often in the throes of severe bowel cramps and gurgles, a person, on reaching the toilet, produces quite a lot of diarrhoea, and makes the medically incorrect assumption that if they hadn't got there an accident would have occurred. It wouldn't, and it doesn't, but a phobia of being far from a toilet can develop from that point on.

④ *What If I Collapsed or Blacked Out?*

You may fear that you will black out or become paralysed, only to come to some time later in hospital, or worse, the police station! Many people see nerves as being like electrical wires, which can short-circuit when they become overloaded, leaving you unable to function.

Panic attacks are associated with arousal of the sympathetic branch of the nervous system. Fainting as a result of panic is *extremely rare*, because it requires parasympathetic nervous system activation, a physiological pathway working in the opposite direction. The moment you faint the nervous system begins to compensate for that. *Within seconds* it corrects the imbalance by widening the arteries again and restoring consciousness. This mechanism automatically restores normality quickly, without you having to do anything. Also, fainting is a familial trait, so if you haven't fainted ever in your life until now, it is unlikely that you will begin to. It usually affects people who become nervous when exposed to blood and injections, and this is because of overly strong parasympathetic activation.

Many people are afraid to be alone during or after a panic attack in case they might be unconscious for long periods of time, and could even die before anyone finds them.

> It makes no difference medically whether someone is with you or not during an attack because there is nothing harmful that can happen to you.

Although you may feel better having someone there, and feel it may help your attack to finish sooner, this is only true because it helps you to feel less afraid.

⑤ *Maybe I Have a Brain Tumour or Other Serious Disease?*

Some of the panic symptoms such as dizziness or light-headedness, unsteadiness or lack of balance, numbness or tingling, weakness or double vision, lead people to believe they have a brain tumour, brain haemorrhage, cancer or multiple sclerosis. As with heart disease, the pattern of occurrence of the symptoms is radically different, a fact not appreciated by the 'amateur doctor' which so many become as they frantically search for reasons for the mysterious symptoms.

A brain tumour or haemorrhage is accompanied by signs that a space-occupying lesion is growing in the brain. Such symptoms might include a constant violent headache, complete loss of power in a limb, blindness in an eye, or slurring of speech. This severe disease will never come and go like panic, here one day, then gone the next. Once the symptoms begin they are constant, and will stop you functioning normally within hours. *If your panic has been going on for several months or years, you do not have any of these serious diseases*, because they progress more rapidly than that.

Dizziness and numbness of the fingers, or sometimes lips, is very common in hyperventilation, and is often misinterpreted as multiple sclerosis. Do the exercise in Chapter 11 to see if hyperventilation is a feature for you – this may bring on the symptoms, showing you that nothing but fast breathing is to blame.

⑥ *What If the Attack Didn't Stop?*

You can't get stuck in a panic attack.

Although during an attack it can seem as though it will never end, panic attacks are time-limited and can only go on for a certain length of time, after which they stop by themselves.

This is not possible because as soon as one part of the nervous system, the sympathetic branch, is aroused to the fight-flight response, another branch of it, the parasympathetic branch, sets about restoring balance and dampening it down. It's like a trip-switch which ensures it only goes on for a designated time and then burns out. So, your own nervous system sets about bringing it to an end, even though your intellect may not feel able to. It's as if adrenaline only has a certain amount of time to pull off its rescue mission and get you to safety before other chemicals in the blood begin to digest and destroy it. If you stop creating these chemicals, by reassuring yourself that you are not in danger, but instead 'wait it out', *the panic attack will always end by itself*, whether you fight hard to control it or try to escape the situation.

⑦ *Could the Next One Be Worse?*

It is important to realise that *there is a ceiling to the intensity a panic attack can reach*. Once you're experiencing the symptoms listed on page 31 it can get no worse than that; there are no other surprise symptoms. Many who have been having panic attacks at full volume for years still feel each time the attack is over that they were 'lucky it didn't get any worse'. Although the attacks may have always remained basically unchanged in character, each time one occurs, many fear it is 'the big one'. In their minds there is still a possibility of appallingly harmful and terrifying symptoms, which have never happened, but which they suspect could one day occur.

Although it is true to say that panic attacks can range from 'not so bad ones' to 'awful ones', *the worst ones you've experienced to date are probably as bad as it is going to get*. Panic goes to its limit quickly, so if you've had more than three or four of them, you've already reached it. In fact often the first one is as bad as it gets. So try to stop frightening yourself by visualising 'the attack to beat all other attacks'. Focusing on it only has the effect of raising your adrenaline level and increasing your chances of having one.

⑧ *What Will People Think?*

The preoccupation with social humiliation if you're seen to be sweating profusely, if you faint, vomit, tremble, blush, stammer or do something that makes you look inadequate, stupid or foolish is understandable and one of the commonest dreads. This fear is not based on any medical misinformation. Occasionally panickers are in truth thought less of, or assessed as 'weak' by others if they display some signs of 'not coping'. What is rarely true, however, is the fact that such judgemental people would be in the majority, or that the result – being exposed as vulnerable – would have the devastating effect you anticipate it would. This hypersensitive black-and-white thinking only serves to raise your fear levels.

FACTS

❶ *Panic Attacks Can Run in Families*

There is research to suggest that panic runs in families, but this does not mean that it is genetically passed on. In the same way that good manners, dress codes and social responses are taught, we quite possibly also imitate our parents' physiology in certain situations. A child, in utero or as a babe-in-arms, may notice that a subtle speeding up of breathing rate is common when the adults are distressed, that muscles tighten up when they're under pressure, or that restlessness or avoidance accompanies worry. Although these learned tendencies may be there in your case, you can still learn to respond in ways different from your parents, since the response is not laid down in your genes, but is merely a reaction.

❷ *Panic Attacks Can Begin During Sleep*

Many panic attacks occur during the night, the majority within one to four hours of sleep onset, the time during which slow-wave sleep is most prevalent. During this phase, eye movements are reduced, blood pressure is lower, and heart rate and respiration slow down. However, such relaxation can be interpreted by someone whose nervous system has been in overdrive as 'your bodyguard has dozed off! Wake up!'

Peaks and valleys in heart rate also occur during the day. Those who are more anxious during the day experience more peaks during sleep. If you are one of those people who are particularly sensitive to, and have unconsciously learned to fear such peaks of sensation, then this may have a different impact on you than it would on someone who is less sensitive.

Our internal scanner doesn't pick up on what is not relevant to it in terms of survival, but remains personally 'attuned' to what it considers significant. A mother may sleep through a fairly loud sound such as a truck going past the window, but if her baby sniffles or cries she'll hear it, even if the sound is faint. Cues portraying danger are meaningful and, once registered by your primitive brain, may wake you.

Someone worrying over money or their relationship may have as many peaks in arousal of their nervous system during sleep as those who panic, both tossing and turning restlessly. However, since the worriers have not associated the normal symptoms of arousal with danger (heart rate increase among them), they don't react to all the heart rate peaks. Since it doesn't act as a 'fear cue' for them, a panic attack is not triggered. So those who are merely worriers but not panickers can experience identical peaks of heart rate and other variables (like sweat or breathing rate), but don't relate to them as cues to start producing adrenaline. Even when the conscious mind is asleep, the unconscious is on the job, scanning for danger. Because of this, many with post-traumatic stress disorder wake frequently in the throes of a panic attack as their sleeping brain picks up images of danger on their inner screen.

❸ *Some Panic Attacks Begin When You're Relaxing*

It can be mystifying how a panic attack can occur at a time when your mind is not worrying, like when you're doing something seemingly neutral, like watching TV, or preparing dinner, and this lack of a time connection can add to the air of unpredictability and irrationality panic instils. These are times when the trigger for the attack is unconscious and most likely physiological in nature, rather than linked to any specific stressful thought or challenge.

Possible reasons include the minute shift in consciousness which goes with the tendency to dissociate while staring, and as part of the body's effort to compensate for chronic hyperventilation. In this case any change in CO_2 level is registered and reacted to, as occurs whenever muscles are resting or standing still, and may explain why so many report feeling agitated in queues.

For those who have been in fight or flight mode for a considerable time, even years, a relaxation exercise may cause them to feel most vulnerable and exposed when they drop their guard, and the reduction in heart rate or the relaxing of muscles may paradoxically signal a possible breach in security, and frighten them. It feels to them like their bodyguard has gone off duty, and they react with a surge of adrenaline just when others would be reducing theirs.

It seems that the fear of losing control and fear of the sensory side-effects of both relaxation and meditation can, in susceptible individuals, cause panic attacks. The very fact that their internal physiology changes *at all* (even though its objective is to move them in the direction of feeling better) is perceived as a threat. In the same way, some women panic more during the pre-menstrual period, again simply in response to normal fluctuations in physiology picked up by an over-conscientious radar.

If you recognise that you have in fact been harbouring any of these common fears, keep them in mind for unpacking in more depth in Chapter 13 where you will learn how to permanently dismantle them.

6

TRIGGERS FROM THE PAST

KEYNOTE: CONDITIONED TO PANIC

One of the most challenging aspects of panic is unearthing the source thought or image, the one that begins the cycle, the initial cue for the entire adrenaline cascade to begin. What threat has your mind reacted to that you may not even be aware you were thinking about?

In terms of timing, it can be baffling to find yourself having panic attacks or avoiding situations now, when life is fairly routine and settled, as opposed to times in the past when there was much more turbulence and you could at least see clearly why you were stressed. People often lament that if it weren't for the attacks, there would be nothing holding them back in their present life. They find it really disappointing to have a good relationship spoiled, or to have to pass up a promotion or a trip, just because of a hangover from the past.

The reason panic attacks can continue after the initial stress is because of a phenomenon called *the conditioned response* (see page 42). We have all had the experience of picking up a smell, perhaps 'baked bread', and suddenly finding that our grandmother pops into our mind. It is as though 'baked bread' and 'granny' go together for the great computer inside our head. When 'baked bread' is presented to it, the search programme comes up with some of the contexts in the past where that occurred, and on average 'granny' has the highest correlation with it. You can see her kitchen, feel the heat from the Aga cooker, see her flour-covered apron, smell the aroma, and almost taste the hot-buttered crispy fresh bread in your mouth. Overall you remember the 'safe and loved' feeling whenever you visited her house.

Likewise, a particular old song might conjure up memories of your first love, and nostalgia for being in love for the first time, and Christmas trees might remind you of your innocent excitement about Santa's arrival.

Here's how conditioning occurs. The aspect of you that keeps an 'eye' on the level of danger and monitors how great is the chance of another panic attack is your memory. Encoded in the archives of your primitive brain, in a folder entitled 'threats to survival', is a full description of the initial attack, and even before that, any similar threatening experiences in your past. Like the black box of an aircraft that has crashed, it contains all the information in the 'snapshot' your mind took of the experience – your heart rate, respiratory rate, sweat, muscular tension, thoughts, emotions, and what each of your senses was perceiving. Sights, sounds, touch, are all imprinted there exactly as they occurred at the time. Also encoded is the bottom-line appraisal of how the experience affected you – terrifying, to be avoided at all costs.

That memory comes as a whole package, all-or-none style, with the result that if you tap into one aspect of that old experience, its travelling companions appear too. So some perceptions are thrust into the foreground of our awareness by default, simply because they are packaged with another one, just like baking smells automatically bring with them memories of granny, whether you wanted them to or not.

In the case of panic, *a feeling of being threatened is piggybacked onto certain normal internal physical sensations.* Every day your physiology is constantly adjusting itself in order to meet the demands placed on it. If you decide to take exercise, your physiology has the job of seeing that enough blood is delivered to your working muscles. If a virus has entered your system, your immune system has to mount an aggressive response if you are to throw it off. A heavy dinner requires different digestive processes than your morning toast. So physiological rearrangements are a constant, never-ending, normal occurrence.

Imagine, however, if one of these adjustments became twinned with fear in your memory. If one particular time when your fight or flight response was gearing you up for a challenge, and part of that involved a rise in your heart rate, and you simultaneously felt very afraid, *a memory trace would be laid down* which included all these elements. Just as 'baking and granny' are linked like Siamese twins, from now on so would 'racing heart and terror'. You stimulate one and you call up the other.

This explains how you can find yourself caught in the throes of an attack seemingly 'unawares'. (You are truly unaware, because this process is an unconscious one.) It can occur while you are sitting quietly in front of your TV, or while watching a football game, or during love-making, or while you are asleep.

Rather than having clear thoughts of danger, you experience shorthand vague 'impressions' that something is wrong. (A mother will likewise pick up her baby's subtle movements or whimpers even behind a backdrop of traffic noise outside, because they are important to her. She need not necessarily remember thinking 'the baby's awake'. Her sister sleeping down the hall may not hear anything because it doesn't have the same importance for her, nor may her husband!)

This process happens because your internal scanning system is always looking for signals of danger without you being aware of it. It isn't football or sex that you fear, it is the physical accompaniment that goes with them (the twin), such as the racing pulse, the panting breaths, the active muscles. These may have all occurred once before, during some initial fearful experience, and many times before during panic attacks themselves, and now you're conditioned to fear them. Uncoupling these is an important step in treatment, where you need to learn to feel the sensations that the archives of your mind has classified as 'unsafe', and re-classify them as 'unpleasant but not dangerous'.

MISSING PIECES OF THE PUZZLE

This phenomenon was first demonstrated by a Russian psychologist called Pavlov, who would ring a bell every time his dogs were about to get their food. Over time the dogs associated the bell with the imminent arrival of food. Whenever the dogs heard the bell, saliva was automatically produced, as it normally is, in readiness for digestion. This response is a reflex, and happens without consultation with the brain. (We all know the phenomenon of drooling after having a delicious meal described to us!)

What Pavlov noticed was that after a while, if the bell was rung and no food appeared, the saliva was produced anyway. The instruction to begin salivating was paired now to the bell sound as strongly as it was to the food. Anyone observing the dogs who only caught the end of the experiment, and did not know that food had ever been part of the sequence, would have a hard time explaining why the dogs were salivating after hearing a bell ring! The logic behind it is hidden to them, and the resulting behaviour, salivation, looks like a decidedly odd response to a ringing bell.

Sometimes you remember why you hate a thing, a feeling or a person. You remember clearly what you were thinking at the time as you re-run the mental video of the experience. In other words, *you are well aware of and can easily recall the memory and the reason for your reaction of dislike now.* An example would be someone who abhors alcohol because it reminds them of their drunken father, or someone who is terrified of hospitals because they remind them of their mother's slow painful death from cancer. In these examples you are making an appraisal of something that, based on your known past experience, recreates the emotion of dislike and encourages the 'pull away' reaction whenever it recurs. *It is logical to you why you react in the way you do.* In order to react differently to alcohol and hospitals, this association that your mind has made would have to be modified and new interpretations inserted. So the belief that 'drinkers are to be avoided' or 'hospitals are where people die' may have to be examined as to whether they are serving you in your present life or restricting you, an important step in treatment which psychotherapy can encourage you to make.

For others, the 'pull away' reaction may automatically happen without the memory to go with it, as a conditioned response whose origin is unclear, as in the example of the dogs. Just as the 'food/bell/salivation' sequence changed to 'bell/salivation', *one piece of your initial experience may have dropped out of your awareness.* This can happen if those details were too traumatic to be integrated by the psyche at that time.

DELETED MEMORIES

For example, a young girl may have lost any awareness of the details of her father abusing her, but may find herself inexplicably reluctant in adulthood to leave her children alone with him. The sequence 'sexual abuse/fear/avoidance of father' has lost the initiating component and now plays itself out as 'fear/avoidance of father'. The abuse memory is lost to her awareness or recall, but her primitive brain's interpretation still firmly stands – its advice is to 'pull away'. So, unaware of that traumatic memory, she doesn't know why she reacts as she does with fear and an adrenaline rise, just as the last-minute observers of the dogs wouldn't know why they were salivating. *Her reaction may seem illogical both to her and to others* in this case, because the 'logic', the first element in the sequence, is hidden within the conditioned response. What may seem like an inappropriate reaction – that of denying a grandfather access to his grandchildren – has a sound survival basis and is in fact highly appropriate.

In other cases, an interpretation may have been made based not on direct experience but on something that a person has read about or heard second-hand. An example of this would be if your mother always cautioned you to be wary of certain things, such as thunderstorms, or certain ethnic groups, without explaining why. In these cases, like the other example, you might find yourself inexplicably fearful *with no logical present-day reason for the fear*. What is different here is that nothing negative ever actually happened to you in connection with thunderstorms. The logic for the initial reaction was apparent only to your mother, and the conditioned response, the advice that thunderstorms can be dangerous, was the piece registered by your brain.

Panic symptoms can become the terror-filled end-point response to events that happened in the past, just like the dogs' salivation. It is often not at all clear why a certain sensation, such as difficulty breathing, can instil a feeling that survival is threatened rather than merely annoying you because it is unpleasant. What is safe to assume, though, is that the lost component that originally accompanied it was interpreted as a life-or-death issue, if it triggered the fight–flight response.

Psychotherapy is useful here to try to track back and, if possible, fill in the blank in the sequence:

$$(???) + (\text{physical sensation}) + (\text{fear})$$

While retrieval of the details is not essential in order to uncouple the physical sensations and the ensuing panic, it can help make the entire experience more logical and allow the sufferer and others to stop blaming themselves. This can in some cases be enough to allow a person to reframe the sensations from an adult perspective, one in which they have more manoeuvrability and power.

For example, the journey through the birth canal might have the components of 'trapped and constricted', 'respiratory difficulty', and 'high adrenaline'. In adult life it is conceivable that in certain situations such as lifts, or if life circumstances dictate that there is no room for manoeuvre (trapped and constricted), a person may be unconsciously reminded of that perilous journey, and simultaneously feel afraid and unable to breathe.

Peggy's story illustrates how present-day panic attacks can have their origins in the past. At the age of eight she was taken from the playground by a local man, brought to a derelict building and brutally raped in the toilets there. Since he used a broken bottle she sustained severe vaginal injuries and spent several months in hospital. With the passing years, Peggy became a nervous, timid child who never went out much except occasionally in the company of her sisters. She had many nervous habits, among them always needing the front door to be open at night, wanting to sleep downstairs, spending much of the day standing outside in the front garden of the house, and sometimes inexplicably rushing outside in the middle of meals. She would go to the local pub only if she could get a lift or a taxi, but would never go on foot.

Her husband was her first and only boyfriend ('I could trust him') and she had four children. During sex she said she would 'space out' until it was over, and she gave it up once they had completed their family. All the family thought Peggy was odd and somewhat stupid, with all her strange habits that she refused to discuss. The relationship with her husband was not tranquil, as he would frequently lose his patience with her and shout at her. After these episodes she would be nervous for days and had been prescribed anti-depressants over the years.

At the age of fifty-two, following a minor car accident in which the other driver got out of his car and began shouting loudly at her, she became hysterical and had a severe panic attack, which resulted in her being brought to the local casualty department. Although the accident had shaken her, it was fairly minor, and it was obvious even to Peggy that her terror was an over-reaction. When she subsequently developed disturbing nightmares, she was refered to me for psychotherapy. She had in fact been having panic attacks for years, and confided that she feared that the other driver, who was drunk and abusive, was actually about to kill her.

It was during deep relaxation exercise that Peggy got her first insight into the source of her problem. Although she hadn't forgotten the fact that she had been raped, she could not remember many of the details of the experience, and had not made any connection between that and her subsequent nervous nature. She thought that all her 'odd' behaviours were due to the fact that she was stupid. Her mother had blamed her for going off with the man and not having 'more sense'. It was swept under the carpet and never mentioned by the family. When she turned into such a nervous child they reasoned that this dullness was the cause, which was reinforced by the illogical nature of her behaviours.

On one occasion, while practising her relaxation exercise, she could clearly hear (for the first time) her rapist's voice saying to her: 'Your father sent me to bring you home.' This meant that he must not have been a stranger to her. Other memories that re-emerged included noting that he had worn spats on his shoes, that when he had taken off his shirt she had seen a tattoo on his arm, and that he had smelled strongly of sweat. She remembered that he shouted loudly all the time he was with her, and threatened to kill her if she ever told. She recalled again the terror she felt as he blocked the door to the toilets so that he would not be disturbed. She recalled thinking 'if that door is closed I'm dead'. Retrieving the images helped piece together many loose ends for Peggy.

The driver of the car that had crashed into her at the age of fifty-two had unwittingly brought back several of the elements that had been present during the rape but lost to her memory. Just like 'baked bread and granny', she gradually began to recall the others. Like her original assailant, the driver was drunk and abusive, and she was once again shaken, hurt and feeling she could have died. Although unable to process an experience of such traumatic magnitude as a child, the ball was rolling now, and integration of these parts of her history was the goal.

Her terror of being in a room with a closed door now made sense, as did her need to sleep downstairs – for a quick get-away. Her certainty that her breathing would stop whenever she got frightened was a result of being held by the throat. Since the derelict building in which she'd been raped was on the way to the local pub, she now knew why she refused to pass it on foot, and why she was terrified of any aggression whatsoever on the part of her husband. Most startling for her was the moment she recognised who her attacker was, by the shoes he wore. She knew a man locally who wore spats. He was married to a friend of her mother's. All the family knew she feared him, because she would run to her room if he had occasion to come to their house. When his wife died, fifteen-year-old Peggy had adamantly refused to go to the funeral, causing a row at home. Nobody, even Peggy, knew why before now.

Peggy's opinion of herself changed dramatically. She went from being obese to a healthy weight, became interested in clothes for the first time, and began to venture out to the shops alone. She could stay inside the house now with the doors shut, and would sometimes sleep upstairs in the bedroom. Knowing where her fears came from allowed her to see that she was no longer in any danger as her attacker was now an old man. Most importantly, she knew now that none of her reactions were 'stupid' but highly intelligent, advising her to keep away from certain situations and from him.

Now that she was able to see that what had once been a useful survival response had now turned into a life-restricting habit, she had more motivation to uncouple the two. She learned to feel the unpleasant sensations and know that, unlike during the rape, they wouldn't kill her, and that this time she could do something about them.

I call these un-integrated experiences, where the details are effectively 'frozen' because they could not be processed by an immature psyche at the time they were experienced. Sometimes the reason why they cannot be accepted by and integrated into the person's psyche is that the implications are too contradictory and disturbing to take in. A child's mind may shatter under the realisation that a trusted parent could abuse her. She thinks 'if the adults who are there to protect me are untrustworthy, then maybe that means I can never be safe in a world run by adults?' At some deep level her psyche decides that it is wiser to 'airbrush out' those details and keep the illusion of safety intact.

However, while your mind may find it expedient to remove one piece of the sequence, it rarely removes all of it, and the untidy loose ends that remain are often the primitive brain's survival wisdom (which, if you remember, is outside the reach of logic for just that reason, so it won't be overlooked during an emergency!).

HOW FAR BACK DOES THE PAST GO?

Dr Brian Weiss, a Miami psychiatrist, in his brilliant book, *Many Lives Many Masters*, looks at past lives and their relationship to our present experiences. In it he recalls Catherine's story. She came to him with panic attacks and after over a year of psychotherapy they were no closer to a resolution of her crippling condition. He decided to use hypnosis to see if there was anything that her unconscious mind might reveal while in a trance state, which her conscious mind was reluctant to acknowledge.

As he was regressing her to before the age of two, she suddenly began to relate to him the details of what she was experiencing while in the trance state. The fact which astonished him was that she was describing herself as a child, not in the US in contemporary times, but in Egypt many centuries before! Catherine had recalled a past life. She proceeded to recount many events that happened to her there, with historical details of what her life was like, and even described to him how she experienced dying. Her father then was her current boyfriend and the dynamic between them was repeating itself. She recalled over sixty more past lives in the following months. In the course of that time her panic attacks ceased, even though they never discussed what she told him during the regressions. The therapeutic effect seemed to come from re-experiencing the traumatic times, and passing through her death again. Certain elements which were filed within her memory bank under the label 'threatening', fell away as they were recalled to her memory. The beliefs that said 'you won't survive this' were challenged by her realisation that this couldn't be true if she always went on to live another life. She learned that there really was no reason to fear death, that her mortality applied only to her physical body, but not to her soul, which went on existing as a continuous thread through the identities of many lifetimes. As she let go of that survival fear, her panic attacks faded.

The concept of karma is fundamental to many Eastern traditions of belief. It is best seen as *your beliefs as to what you deserve in this lifetime, or what you expect to happen to you*. Someone who experienced many lifetimes of powerlessness, never able to make anything happen for themselves, might bring into this lifetime the expectation that this one will be no different. 'What's the point, nothing ever works' will be their script. In this sense, karma is really a conditioned response, except the cause-and-effect trigger is from a previous lifetime.

It is conceivable that our fearful associations stem from our experience in the womb or within the birth canal, a time that, since it preceded sight and the use of language, was dominated by sensation. Surely a babe in utero, sharing its mother's blood chemistry, must register subtle changes within her system in response to stress? It isn't stretching the imagination too much to propose that the baby makes a connection between loud, shouting voices, a defensive tightening of its mother's muscles, and the surge of adrenaline as she feels afraid of someone's anger. If that child ever finds itself exposed to verbal aggression in its life, then a rise in adrenaline, and possibly a panic attack, could be the legacy of that in-utero experience. Many memories are very effectively accessed and integrated through the use of re-birthing or holotropic therapies, using hyperventilation (since it is almost universally an element in traumatic experiences) purposefully to trigger memories of past experiences and unite them as an integrated whole. The end result can be a reduction in the arousal of the nervous system, as fear-filled sensory memories, inaccessible to language, literally 'come to mind' and can be processed.

It is by no means essential to retrieve lost memories in order to eliminate panic. Regardless of the trigger, in all cases the adrenaline surge that is conditioned to follow it still needs to be dampened down.

POST-TRAUMATIC STRESS DISORDER – WHEN THE ALARM WON'T STOP

If a person witnesses or experiences a traumatic event involving actual or threatened death or bodily harm, to which they respond with intense fear, helplessness or horror, it is known medically as post-traumatic stress disorder (PTSD). A few months after such an event (technically more than six, within medical diagnostic criteria), the nervous system of someone with PTSD is still caught in a cycle of excessive reactivity, and is not settling down.

Road traffic accidents, plane crashes, violent rapes and assaults, natural disasters and war are all common sources of this disorder, because as life-threatening events they leave a death imprint. Anything heralding an imminent change in your identity elicits the activation of your primitive survival response. Its aim is not only to prompt you to find safety, but it will remain in place until it is certain that the danger is over and that you will not be exposed to a similar experience before you have fully recovered.

Once you're out of danger, the focus shifts to the risk of a future recurrence. Your internal bodyguard means to see that you don't become complacent or relaxed for some time yet, to ensure that you stay 'on alert' should the danger return unexpectedly. A logical tactic. Anyone who has had their heart broken will relate to the lingering mistrust in love that follows being betrayed. Or the uneasiness following a car accident, when traffic moving at ten miles per hour seems to be speeding.

This is carried to an extreme in post-traumatic stress disorder, as your surveillance system can keep you trapped for months or years in hyper-alert, never off duty. It does this by repeatedly re-running the traumatic event in your mind, day and night. Like a security firm going over every minute detail, it is looking for any slip-ups in your attention while the event was happening, which might have contributed to the breach in security that led to you being exposed to the trauma. As the video in your mind rolls, you don't just see the images again, you experience many of the fearful feelings vividly. These emotionally charged flashbacks and nightmares can stimulate panic attacks, because the material being presented to you on the screen of your mind is as fresh and realistic as the day it occurred. It can feel to you as though you're in danger of dying all over again.

The alarm will only cease when your primitive brain is completely satisfied that you are not in danger any longer, and that adequate safety measures have been put in place for the future. That day arrives in different ways for different people. Sometimes with every day that goes by, the simple passage of time tells them that they're safe and are in fact surviving. With their continuing identity no longer in doubt, the fight or flight response can finally settle. Or when they know for sure that they will never interface with those dangers again because they've left the hazardous job they had (such as the police or fire service), or a relationship that was abusive and in which they never felt secure.

Others come to the existential realisation that we must accept death as an inevitable part of life, because it is going to happen to us all one day. This acceptance defuses the sense of death being a danger. Making their peace with it brings a sense of serenity. As long as they know their soul is immortal they can give up any resistance they had to the death of their physical body.

PORTRAIT OF PTSD

Panic attacks frequently affect sufferers of PTSD. Psychotherapy is crucial to provide an explanation for the many unusual mental and physical symptoms that accompany this condition, as a reassurance that madness is not imminent. Unfortunately, symptoms such as insomnia, anxiety or depression are often treated medically in isolation, and the experience as a whole is never processed. My book *Going Mad? – Understanding Mental Illness*, co-written with Dr Michael Corry, documents in more detail the very common fear of insanity that accompanies many of the symptoms of PTSD. So much worry and damage to self-esteem could be avoided by a clear understanding of these phenomena.

- *Hypervigilant*, your adrenaline running high, you're on guard and wary all the time. Suspicious and paranoid, you blow things out of proportion. Panic is never far away. You often feel your heart racing and your breathing laboured, and you sweat profusely. Your muscles can go into tension spasms. Tremors are common.

- *You startle easily*, jumping in alarm at a sudden sound such as a door banging or the phone ringing.

- One of the first casualties is *sleep*, which is also one of the last things to return to normal. This causes extreme fatigue and allows no let-up from the constant barrage of mental imagery. Your mind is in 'on mode' all the time.

- Intrusive vivid *images of the event haunt you*, replaying the trauma over and over without mercy. Such is their intensity that you feel as if you've been catapulted back into the initial trauma as if experiencing it for the first time. These flashbacks can occur when least expected. John, who had been brutally bullied by a teacher at school, found himself shouting 'get away from me, leave me alone!' and running from the office as his boss came towards his desk. His mind was literally reliving the beatings meted out by that teacher, so much so that he actually saw the man's face, not his boss's.

  This persistent re-running of traumatic events on your screen of perception is comparable to a Vietnam veteran, newly returned from the front, being repeatedly compelled to watch the horrific opening scenes of the war movie *Saving Private Ryan*. Every re-run re-opens the original trauma, and what is so frightening and dispiriting about these re-runs is that they can't be voluntarily stopped. You get frustrated trying to explain to others how something in the past could still be so 'real' in the present. Months later, smells, sounds and tactile sensations may remain vivid and disturbing. Three years after his ordeal, Steve, a policeman serving with a rapid response unit, could still smell the gunpowder from a Kalashnikov assault rifle that was discharged at him from close range.

- *Nightmares* destroy your sleep and can be so terrifying that you eventually dread the moment when you close your eyes.

You regularly wake up soaked in sweat, in the middle of a panic attack. Bizarre sleep patterns become the norm, and sleep deprivation is common.

- *Avoidance strategies.* In a desperate effort to control your escalating anxiety levels you avoid everything associated with the event. You try not to talk about it, and you avoid the scene of the trauma or any reminders of it, such as TV programmes. If you've survived a car crash, you'll postpone driving. If you've been raped, having sex can trigger a flashback.

- *Emotionally you're on a roller-coaster.* You experience the full spectrum – panic, anger and rage, episodes of crying and sadness. Feelings of hopelessness and despair become the norm. As a result, being in the company of others becomes an extra stress because of the unpredictable and hair-trigger nature of your emotional outbursts. Ordinary life is merely a memory. Suicide passes through your mind – 'I don't want to be here.'

- *Paranormal experiences* that occurred at the time of the traumatic event are difficult to make sense of, and therefore your mind is drawn to them. Such experiences include time standing still (where the traumatic events happen in slow motion), apparitions and visions of dead loved ones, 'out of body' and 'near death' experiences. From a viewpoint outside your body you may have felt that you were looking down on yourself while trapped in a car, on the operating table, or in the process of being attacked. It is as though you were watching a drama unfolding in which you were the main player.

The 'near death' experience has the added distinction of the sensation of moving up a tunnel, at the end of which is a white light, perceived as being the next life. There, you may have met dead relatives or heard a voice from the earthly plane calling you back. While being wheeled into an operating theatre with multiple injuries, David felt that he was dying. He experienced himself travelling up a tunnel and emerging into a light-filled area where his dead relatives were standing at the entrance. One told him 'Go back, your time hasn't come.'

- *Shutdown and shock.* It can seem as though you're looking at life from behind a glass pane. A state of emergency reigns. You may feel totally dislodged or fractured from your usual ways of thinking, feeling and behaving. 'Normality' has disappeared. You feel alienated, split off, de-skilled, dazed and anxious. You wonder if you're mad. Your work, leisure and family life is turned upside down.

- You live in *parallel universes* – your ordinary life and your extra-ordinary inner world. Because you're in emergency mode, you can focus on nothing else but the trauma and what will become of you. As a result of not being fully present, you have trouble with your short-term memory, your attention span is limited and poor concentration is the norm. Inevitably you make mistakes and lose confidence in your ability to carry out simple tasks. You start to feel 'stupid' as names are forgotten, car keys are lost, conversations become difficult to follow, and the execution of routine tasks requires more focus than you're capable of. Your inner movie constantly distracts you.

- *Emotional numbing.* You may find that after six months or more, in an effort to dampen down your emotional distress, you unconsciously anaesthetise your feelings. You 'numb out'. Feeling as if you're in limbo, much like the 'walking dead', you merely go through the motions of living. You neither express emotion nor register the feelings of others. This state of suspended animation can be extremely distressing for those around you, making them angry and concerned as you become ever more unreachable. 'He's in his own world and has tuned out what's going on around him. A train could pass through the house and he wouldn't notice!'

- *Collateral damage.* Another way of numbing your pain and inducing sleep is to use alcohol and other substances. As you increasingly withdraw into your own world, your relationships suffer, deadlines cease to exist and problems at work arise. Now chronically awash with adrenaline, suspicion and paranoia increasingly alienate you from others. In order to distract yourself, to the annoyance of others, you keep frantically busy and 'on the run' from the feelings and images that flood in as soon as you stop. Out of character behaviours such as gambling and promiscuity can begin. Feeling you've nothing to lose, you might engage in reckless behaviours and expose yourself to unnecessary risks. The character played by Jeff Bridges who survived an air disaster in the film *Fearless* is a good example of a PTSD sufferer. He balanced on the ledge of a tall building, jay-walked through fast-flowing traffic, drove his car into a wall and ate food he was known to be dangerously allergic to.

- You feel *misunderstood by others*. Much to your surprise, sympathy and support for your difficulties is time-limited and starts to wane. A recognised ritual exists in traumas such as bereavement, whereby support is given immediately and recognition of the impact acknowledged. Flowers, cards, phone calls and practical help follow. There are no similar rituals in place for the post-traumatised individual, who can feel ignored and rejected. After a number of weeks questions may be asked of you, like 'When will things settle back to normal?' and 'Shouldn't you be back in the saddle by now?' Subtle innuendoes are made which have a judgemental air about them. 'He looks fine and he's able to mow the lawn, why isn't he back at work?' It may be inferred that you're 'playing it up', 'malingering', or 'milking the system'.

- *Socially you withdraw*, fearing the judgement of others. Now it is easier to avoid situations where you might have to explain yourself. Doors aren't answered, phone calls aren't taken, and you start living like a recluse. Bitterness and cynicism may set in. If you had your way you would hide away in some isolated sanctuary. There you would be free to eat and sleep when you wanted, act out your distress without concerning others, and have no responsibilities.

- *Past the heal-by date.* As the months and years roll by, you're shocked that normality hasn't returned yet. 'How can it take so long!' You become increasingly frustrated and impatient with the healing timeframe. A beautiful insight into this was unfolded in the book and film *The Horse Whisperer*, the story of a post-traumatically stressed horse named Pilgrim, who was brought to a horse whisperer for healing. The owners of the horse, on pressing the horse whisperer for a definitive heal-by date, were always greeted with his knowing reply: 'That depends on Pilgrim.' He acknowledged the unique nature of the horse and its healing timeframe, which could only be assisted but not hurried. Impatience had no place here.

- *Grief eclipsed.* Your anxiety can be so much in the foreground, and your mind in such turmoil, that there's often no room for grieving for what has been lost. This could be the loss of a physical function through disability, loved ones who died in the same trauma, or your career and financial earning power. You may sense a dam-burst of grief awaiting when the mental spin-cycle stops.

- The problem of the *'extra piece'*. Before long you know you'll never be the same again. You're like Humpty Dumpty falling off the wall, breaking into hundreds of pieces. On attempting to rebuild yourself you find extra pieces, which means that your life can't be rebuilt in exactly the same way again. The pieces of the traumatic experience are just too different to be incorporated. Where before you may have fitted hand in glove into a couple relationship or a working life, now you may feel at odds, sensing that there's a mismatch.

- *Fear of stigma.* You may be the kind of person who has always been wary of psychoactive medication, and the last place you ever imagined ending up in was a psychiatric hospital. Suggestions that you need one or the other can be terrifying, confirming your worst fears that you're going mad.

7

PSYCHOTHERAPY

Symptoms of ill-health can be related to in two ways. If you experience them merely as an inconvenience, an unpleasant nuisance that limits you in terms of choice and the control you have over your life, then your primary task is to remove them speedily and efficiently so that the status quo returns. This is the prevailing medical view.

The other view you could take is to wonder if they could have a function. What if, aside from being distressing and annoying, there was some logic explaining their presence? The holistic viewpoint would hold that what affects one part of an organism influences the health of the entire structure, whether that refers to bodies, plants or the environment. Our natural tendency is to move towards health and wholeness, much as plants seek the light. Could it be that symptoms may be helping you do this, by alerting you when balance and harmony have been lost?

The pain of a rotten tooth acts like a red flag marking the spot, alerting you to the real problem – the decay underneath. As it increases in intensity, you plan an urgent visit to the dentist. So the pain itself, the symptom, is not the primary issue; meeting the conditions for dental health is. And few would continue giving painkillers for a severe abdominal pain, or that rotten tooth, knowing that this will only mask what is lurking underneath. In this sense *symptoms act as messengers*, bulletins to jolt your awareness, announcing 'Look here, look here!'

Unless they're very intense, most of us tend to ignore many of these SOS calls. We continue working too hard, despite the joyless striving that characterises life on the treadmill. In spite of daily headaches or insomnia, we may relentlessly push ourselves towards unattainable goals, or turn a blind eye to obvious family dysfunction in the interest of short-term peace. As long as the symptom isn't too bad and doesn't bring us to a halt, we try to ignore it.

When the physical body begins to go out of balance, it sends signals that are not as easy to ignore as the psychological ones. You may become aware of aching muscles and parts that stop working properly. You notice rashes or swellings, and you wonder what they mean. In this sense they function much like the indicators on the dashboard of your car, *making you aware of a need* that the car has, to be filled up with petrol or to have the brake fluid checked. Once that's done they leave you alone again. Their only role is to interrupt your stream of consciousness for long enough to get the job done.

How can your psychological needs make themselves known to you if you keep ignoring them or anaesthetising them? It would be considered unwise and irresponsible to paste over the dashboard so that you were no longer bothered by that flashing light. Yet this is what is routinely done with psychological 'messages'. The awareness and appreciation of distress is not given much airtime in our culture, and a so-called 'strong' character has as its hallmark a stoic attitude, the ability always to cope, to control emotions, and not to allow setbacks to change your plans.

At a societal level, the denial of psychological symptoms is actively encouraged and validated. Anaesthesia comes in many forms. Alcohol takes the edge off distress, recreational substances help us zone out of it altogether, and prescription drugs mask it in a more socially validated way.

Whatever about emotions such as anger or sadness, fear (medicalised as anxiety) is one of those which, as soon as it raises its head, is 'shot on sight', medicated out of existence with hardly a question being asked as to its significance. Many emotional experiences, such as low self-confidence, shyness, indecision, guilt, shame, even compulsive giving, are really all variations of how we express fear. Valuable opportunities are lost, due to medicalisation or anaesthetising, which could be used to discover whether *encoded in the symptom, your fear is a message about what you need in order to regain balance.*

ENCODED MESSAGES – ATTENDING TO THE NEEDS OF THE SOUL

Like a fish in water, we often can't see the impact on us of the milieu we're immersed in, that cultural and familial 'soup' that, unbeknownst to us, is the driving force behind many of our desires, fears and opinions. We have been so conditioned to think, feel and act in ways endorsed and validated by our society that, like the fish, we don't see these viewpoints as separate from us, but experience them as part of the very fabric we're made from. This symbiotic relationship is not all bad, because while we're young and dependent on those very support structures for our survival needs, it pays to know what the rules are so that if we obey them we are cared for and supplied with the necessary basic ingredients to grow to physical maturity. Society benefits from this trade-off by having a method by which it can create order and control, avoiding chaos through tempering the expression of individuality, too much of which could lead to anarchy.

It is often at times of distress, or when life doesn't seem to be running as smoothly as usual, that we can catch a glimpse of how our surrounding milieu influences and shapes us. Like a fish who has just landed on the deck, gasping for life, who suddenly realises, by its absence, that a thing called water even existed before!

> *In the middle of the road of my life*
> *I awoke in a dark wood*
> *To find that the true way*
> *Was wholly lost.*

These opening lines from Dante's *Commedia* remind us that we are all on a journey, treading a path, although the destination is not always clearly apparent. At times we feel 'in sync' with the direction it is taking, happy to be carried along by its momentum, healthy and carefree. At other times we feel rudderless, lost, thrown off balance, when nothing seems to flow and we're even unhappy in our own skin. It is on these occasions that people find themselves asking the 'big questions'. Why am I on the planet? In what direction does my life purpose lie? Am I getting the most out of my life?

It seems that the deepest part of us is asking fundamental questions about the very substance underpinning our existence, the fabric we're made from. It is times such as these, these 'dark nights of the soul', that present us with questions we often haven't ever contemplated before, and may not be able to answer alone.

PSYCHOTHERAPY – INSIGHT, CLARITY AND WISDOM

The word 'psychotherapy' is derived from the Greek word 'psyche', meaning soul, and 'therapeia', meaning attendance. In its truest sense this is what its function is, to give a voice to, support for and validation of the needs of your soul. Psychotherapy attempts to clarify how the deepest aspects of your psyche speak through your distress, announcing itself through your desires, emotions and behaviours. Frustrating situations, obstacles, and individuals who appear to be holding you back, all take on a significance when held under its microscope and observed from another perspective.

This is often not possible to do alone. Enmeshed as you are in your conditioning, programmed to see things only in certain ways, and reacting in knee-jerk fashion to events, your perspective is contaminated. Laden with hidden meanings, it lacks that more balanced gaze of a scientist looking at the subject of study with more objective eyes. A psychotherapist can encourage you to focus on the 'big picture', on the long-term trends evident in your life, prompting you to assess whether your choices are as informed as they could be, or are born out of the urgency of raw survival. You can begin to explore the direction your life journey is taking and decide whether or not it resonates with what you sense your purpose or destiny to be. In this way you can bring more conscious awareness into all aspects of your experience, and *become accustomed to making your psyche or soul journey a constant point of reference.* This acts as a mast to which you can hold, a compass with which to navigate, and a map onto which you can plot your thoughts, emotions and behaviours, asking if they concur with the direction you feel your soul, as opposed to your personality, wishes you to move. An awareness of your spiritual dimension brings new significance to the other aspects of your being, giving it depth and substance. We then make the transition from human beings having the occasional spiritual experience, to spiritual beings having human experiences.

In days gone by, this perspective would have been provided by the medicine man, the shaman, or the priest. In recent times this task is falling more and more to the doctor or psychiatrist. Unfortunately, since their training is not in the realm of the soul, in order for the message to be recognisable to them it has to be encoded in their language, in medical-speak. In this way your soul's 'mayday' signal has had to be translated into a medical symptom.

Teresa's daughter Anna was getting married, and while this should have been a happy event, she had begun to feel increasingly nervous about 'the big day'. First her sleep became disrupted, and she found herself lying awake for hours going over what she'd wear and say. Then she noticed herself unable to make decisions or even read the paper, her mind was so cluttered with worry. Finally she began having panic attacks in the supermarket and, after having to call her friend several times to bring her home, she had to accept that her stress level was unmanageable. Having tried sedatives a few years before when her mother died, she knew that something different was called for, as she couldn't afford to be spaced out on the day of the wedding. A series of psychotherapy sessions threw some unexpected light on the problem.

She and her husband had divorced eighteen months previously after thirty-two years of marriage. In shock, she had retreated inside the family home, engaging little with anyone except a few close female friends, who she suspected were now tired of hearing about her plight. Too ashamed to discuss it, she had told her own family that they were working on a reconciliation. It wasn't that they were ever that close, in fact they had the classic 'cold marriage' where she did her thing and he his. So she raised their two children, Anna and Clare, provided the traditional homely comforts, entertained when necessary, and complacently turned a blind eye to the fact that she and her husband had nothing but a business relationship. The family were well provided for, and the years rolled by painlessly enough, each absorbed in their roles.

Anna's personality was like her father's, and she never really got on with Teresa, although neither had ever addressed the issue. Both girls had a confidence Teresa knew she lacked, and they never sought anyone's approval, often to the point of bullying her into doing what they wanted. They also didn't have her 'sense of the family', as she put it, and they found it irritating to have to endure family gatherings of any kind. Her own father was a domineering kind of man who could never understand why she couldn't command more respect from her husband and children. He liked things to be 'a certain way', and often criticised her efforts. His approval was important to her and she wanted the wedding to go off without a hitch.

This didn't look likely, however. Anna was insisting on the smallest possible number attending, excluding many of Teresa's family. She was also insisting that she did not want any presents, as she was going to live abroad after the wedding. And also that she wished her father's new partner to attend. This presented Teresa with several unbearable dilemmas. Firstly, what should she do with all the presents already sent to the house? She just could not bring herself to send them back as Anna suggested and risk being thought discourteous, and she felt guilty and dishonest about sending thank-you letters for them when in truth Anna hadn't even opened them.

Secondly, her family were all going to know there was no hope of her husband returning when he appeared with a lady on his arm, and worse, that her own daughter's loyalty seemed to lie with them rather than her! How would she survive her father's ridicule? And the seating arrangements? Would this 'new woman' of his be at the bridal table where Teresa would have to tolerate her all day?

Lastly, how would her family members who hadn't been invited ever forgive her? It was always the custom in her family to invite everyone. There seemed no workable solution, and she increasingly felt like an animal going to the slaughter.

During our sessions, many of the family 'codes' were made more explicit, as well as some of the origins of Teresa's behaviours. Her upbringing had been very traditional, and the group rules always took precedence over those of the individual. Everything had to look right for the public gaze, no matter how unhappy that made you. It had never before occurred to her to question that way of living. Besides, women in her family didn't question things, their role was always to take direction from the men. Her mother had commanded respect, but rarely went against her father. He regarded Teresa as a mouse because she hadn't been able to 'hold onto her husband'.

When she thought back over the years, she realised she had ignored the fact that she had allowed herself to be taken advantage of, thinking she was being a good wife. Her husband would demand dinners to be given for large numbers of colleagues at the drop of a hat, and often had the house full of visitors, which she found exhausting but whom she tirelessly catered for without objection. Although she often suspected he had other women, she turned a blind eye, afraid to believe that her 'cold' husband could in fact be capable of warmth and affection, which she finally knew was true when she saw him in the company of his new partner. She realised she had been foolish, too afraid to rock the boat, and intimidated by his powerful personality, which so resembled that of her father.

Meanwhile, the panic attacks worsened, occurring almost every day. Her friends offered advice, to stop playing the 'poor me', to empower herself, to enrol in an assertiveness course, to challenge her daughter, to stand her ground with her family. But as the day approached she couldn't see any feasible solutions to her dilemma, and remained frozen in fear. Her daughter spoke to her less and less, telling Teresa to pull herself together and not spoil her 'big day'.

Although psychotherapy had helped her to see the problem more clearly, Teresa felt that the required changes were too much for her just then. All she could see was social scorn, and she felt powerless to stop it. On the morning of the wedding she felt more fear than ever before in her life, and could only attend the wedding with the assistance of several sedatives. Her memory of the day remains a blur. She regretted that the high point of it was leaving after the speeches, after which she sat at home alone crying.

In the following weeks the attacks began subsiding as she thought about the day less and less. We continued working together and she learned new ways of relating to her family. Gradually she began to value her own wishes and acquired the skills needed to have them met. Now she felt more able to cope with people's disapproval and ceased trying to please everyone.

Her symptoms had led her to a situation where she could no longer ignore her need to mature into her own woman, to stop behaving like a dependant child with no power of her own, especially with men. Only when her old identity was under imminent threat of annihilation did she make the transition from anxiety to panic attacks, when the prospect of being at the mercy of the public gaze was more than she felt she could survive, given her existing personality. Through psychotherapy she began shaping a different identity and developing the necessary new skills for life as a woman in charge of her own life, which would allow her to be less vulnerable in the face of future change. She could understand better why her daughters felt such impatience with her devotion to convention and obligation. Anna could see it for what it was, fear, and had little respect for that stance, having such a strong character herself. In time, Teresa was able to take more responsibility for the breakdown of her marriage, realising that her husband must have lost respect for her inability to be an individual as she took refuge more and more inside the role of mother and homemaker.

Only an emergency, such as the panic attacks presented, would have jolted Teresa out of her old identity and encouraged her to forge a healthier new one. Healing was achieved at a deeper level than would have occurred if her symptoms had merely been eradicated by medication alone. In her case her soul journey expressed itself in ways our culture rarely expects, not through religious attendance, prayer or charitable works, but through everyday difficulties.

Paddy had been a grocer all his life. Now, at forty-eight, he was head of the fruit and vegetable department in a large supermarket, a post he had efficiently held for twenty-five years. In the last few months he had become increasingly tense and irritable, finding it harder each day to feel motivation for the job, and wanting only to flop in front of the TV in the evenings. Just back from a holiday, ordinarily Paddy would be feeling refreshed, but the trip abroad had been stressful, since on the fourth day he had had a severe panic attack, followed by a few more in the next week.

He had found the holiday crowds difficult to cope with, distracted by the buzzing in his head and the constant feeling of being unable to breathe, and he found sitting in the sun made him feel worse. Spending most of his time in the apartment, he only joined the family in the evenings, which he found long and exhausting. The plane journey home was terrifying for him, because he was so convinced by then that there was something seriously wrong with his mind. Never having been ill in his life, he began to worry about the family's future if anything happened to him. After seeing his doctor on his return, he was referred to me for relaxation training using biofeedback.

It emerged that the previous year his wife Kay had returned to work on a part-time basis as a publisher's assistant. Paddy had been happy to see her getting out again after all the years at home with the children, and a little bit of extra money was always handy. What he hadn't bargained for was her rapid advancement to assistant editor on a full-time basis some months previously. The change in people's attitude towards her both pleased and disturbed him. When asked why, he couldn't explain, except to say that he probably would have preferred it if things had remained the way they'd been throughout their marriage. Something was different now, and it unsettled him.

Paddy had lost his father at the age of twelve, and he, his three sisters and his mother had gone to live with a relative. Apprenticing himself to an uncle who owned a grocer shop, he learned the ropes there, eventually landing his present job, a very lucrative position for a 23-year-old man with a young family. But twenty-five years later the pressure to provide a higher and higher standard of product was increasing, with the public becoming ever more particular and demanding. Kay had subtly begun to suggest to him that at their age they should be enjoying life to the full, and with her salary now at quite a substantial level, maybe he should consider taking a less stressful job with fewer hours elsewhere. While of course this made intellectual sense to him, he found himself oddly resistant to the notion.

After some weeks of therapy he could see a pattern. Whenever he thought 'work' he tensed up. His biofeedback readings confirmed this, and he found it difficult to relax his muscles once his mind turned to the job. He had always worked to full capacity, feeling that all success depends on sheer hard work. For as far back as he could remember he had 'given his all' to his job, as if his life depended on it. In a sense it did. His had been the only wage coming into the house after his father died. His experience had taught him that 'if the breadwinner stops working the family's survival is on the line'. His mother had depended on him to fill the role of 'man of the house'. It had been his identity for all the intervening years since childhood, and he felt it was threatened now with Kay's promotion. He wasn't sure what the meaning of work was if it wasn't to keep the wolf from the door. He had never had the luxury of thinking about it in terms of satisfaction or fulfilment; all he knew was that it paid the bills and that made him feel secure and confident in who he was.

Discussions with Kay in therapy enabled him to reframe some of these identity issues and open up to the notion of trusting her to take over the role of primary breadwinner. In time he could see this as liberating rather than threatening, and his panic attacks subsided. His psyche had reached a fork in the road, and a new identity was required for the next leg. He could insist on staying the same in the face of changing times, or he could adapt to this different stage of life and let go of the old Paddy, the identity that had helped him survive his childhood. Like a foot whose toes are being pinched by a shoe it has outgrown, he was feeling the constriction. Without the insights he got from psychotherapy he wouldn't have known that the distressing symptoms were really an indication of the need for expansion and maturing, rather than trying at all costs to reinstate the old status quo. His body communicated to him through the panic attacks, the biofeedback machine telling him that his fear had its genesis in the work role, and allowing the conversation about change to develop.

8

THE CHAKRA SYSTEM

There is an aspect of us that, like the gauges on a car, that constantly monitors how balanced our system is. If we lean too far in one direction, like the petrol gauge tipping toward 'empty', it picks up the need for readjustment. Like a silent witness, this concerned presence acts like a compass, and when we stray from the point of balance that is right for us, it gives us a nudge, which we experience as a symptom. The owner's manual for a car, or the care instructions that come with an indoor plant, announce the individual requirements that will keep it healthy. As human beings we don't have these to refer to, only the obscure clues we get when distress or disease tell us to do a maintenance check in order to regain optimal functioning. *Cracking the code of how your own 'vehicle' communicates to you* is essential work if you want to stay within the healthy zone, and symptom-free.

What exactly is this aspect of us that 'steers' us in certain directions and not others, that seems to have a 'vested interest' in *our* progress? Is it the same thing as the force that animates all living things, the life-force that programmes the daffodils to come up in spring rather than autumn, that sees to it that night follows day without ever getting muddled up and missing the odd one?

If you cut your hand, once you have been to the doctor and had a few stitches, who or what now completes the healing? Not your brain, for it could be asleep or concentrating on other things. Where do the instructions come from to deliver enough immune cells to the site to fight off infection, or the requisite number of clotting factors to form a scab and prevent excessive bleeding? How do these processes 'know' when they are needed? *There would appear to be an innate intelligence always acting in our favour that is outside the awareness of the conscious mind.* It takes care of everything from regulating your heartbeat, sustaining a pregnancy, and navigating you to your workplace, while at the same time healing your wound, and all without consulting you for instructions. It appears to be trustworthy too, because if you leave it to 'do its thing', take your eye off it and check back in a few weeks' time, you'll find the wound perfectly healed.

This creative intelligence has certain requirements, however, to do its job well. *It works optimally if its basic demands are respected.* So you don't dirty the wound by digging in the flowerbeds, or cause it to sting by immersing it in washing-up liquid. And you certainly don't keep picking the scab off just to check that all is going well underneath! It is also asking you to allow the hand to be 'off duty' until it heals, and to pay attention to symptoms such as pain. Most of all, it needs you *to hand over to and trust in its wisdom.*

We achieve optimal results if we learn to observe the ways this creative intelligence works and try to move with it rather than against it. Just as the farmer notices that seeds planted in spring yield crops, while those planted in winter don't, and the sailor sees that he gets to his destination faster if he avails of the wind in certain ways, so we can harness the life-force running through us in our best interest. *The same vital force that animates every living thing is localised within each of us in a personalised version.* Just as a drop of seawater is made of the same 'stuff' as the rest of the ocean, at a quantum physics level the human body is made from the very same raw material as all other living matter – energy. It breathes life into us at birth, and its withdrawal marks our death.

Many know it as Spirit, which comes from the Latin noun *spiritus*, meaning *the breath of life*, or animating force. As the drop is to the ocean, many know the Soul to be the aspect of Spirit that locates itself within us individually. Soul is generally understood to relate to that part of a human being which has the capacity to oversee and direct its progress, and which survives after the death of the physical body, to rejoin the 'ocean' of Being to which we all ultimately return.

The Indian poet Tagore captures its essence:

> *Thou hast made me endless,*
> *Such is thy pleasure.*
> *This little flute of reed*
> *Thou carried over the hills and dales*
> *And breathed into it*
> *Melodies eternally new.*
> *This frail vessel*
> *Thou emptiest again and again*
> *And fillest again and again*
> *Ever with fresh life.*

How does the life-force exert its influence on living things? How do the cycles of the moon affect our body fluids, so that more epileptic seizures and other mental and physiological phenomena occur during a full moon? And how does a hibernating animal 'know' when to wake up in the spring, or birds spread the word to each other that there are nuts available in the bird tray in your garden? This information is transmitted electromagnetically through the vibratory frequencies accessible to each particular species. Like a personalised language specific to them, each 'hears' the life-force whispering to them as *impulses of energy carrying the information they need* to make life run according to plan, like a radio wavelength broadcasting only to them.

MORE THAN MEETS THE EYE

While we may think of ourselves as solid matter, as much as we do the chair we sit on, one look down a microscope shows that at a quantum physics level we are made up of a collection of constantly moving protons, electrons and neutrons. The 'dance' they engage in, the particular arrangement in the surrounding electromagnetic field that they assume, dictates whether they are recognisable as 'human', 'horse', or 'tree'. And even though we feel that we begin and end at our skin, in fact we are surrounded by an energy field that extends outside our body. It vibrates outside the range of frequency of our senses, and is therefore invisible to us.

Although this field is non-material, its presence is scientifically proven. Can you see the waves passing from one mobile phone to another, or from the TV station into your set, or from a computer on the other side of the world to your email address? Then how do you know they're there at all? You realise that they are beyond your perception, but since the end result is beyond doubt (you hear the voice or see the picture), grasping the mechanics of how it happens is not vital in order to utilise it.

Every living thing is surrounded by this egg-shaped energy field. It functions much like a lung, not only transmitting but also receiving, processing and integrating any energy impacting on it. It doesn't end at the body surface but penetrates right through our physical matter to infuse every cell. Just as every movement is picked up by the beams of your burglar alarm, every cell in your body is bathed in and influenced by your energy field. Your field is, in turn, under the influence of all that impacts on it from the wider world, such as temperature changes, noise levels, TV, phone and radio waves: even the movements of the planets have already affected your field before they reach your body surface.

All the bodily functions are orchestrated through the movement of positive and negative ions across the cell walls. Oxygenation, food absorption, detoxification, and generation of nerve impulses are carried out, and like a huge metropolis that never sleeps, your body keeps receiving the electromagnetically transmitted instructions that prompt it to grow, replicate, defend and repair itself. It does this whether you are in a coma, sleeping, dreaming or awake, so its watchful intelligence is not mediated by your conscious awareness.

Your mobile phone only receives calls made to your SIM card, and your bank account only gives out money at the ATM machine in response to your PIN number. Likewise, your energy field can screen out 'messages' from the life-force that are not intended for you, but for your horse or your bonsai tree. It does this through *the chakra system*.

YOUR MULTI-DIMENSIONAL ANATOMY

In the same way that the conductor of an orchestra provides an organising force that coordinates all the individual musicians participating in playing a symphony, so your energy field provides a map according to which operations unfold. This is called *the energetic template*, and it holds the script that your body follows as it evolves into a mature human being. It was present even before you began to grow into a fertilised egg. These incoming vibrations are of too high a frequency to be processed by your five senses. They need to be converted into a waveform that your cells can recognise, rather like phone waves translate into something we know as the human voice. A series of step-down transformers called *the chakras* become the sense organ for these higher frequencies.

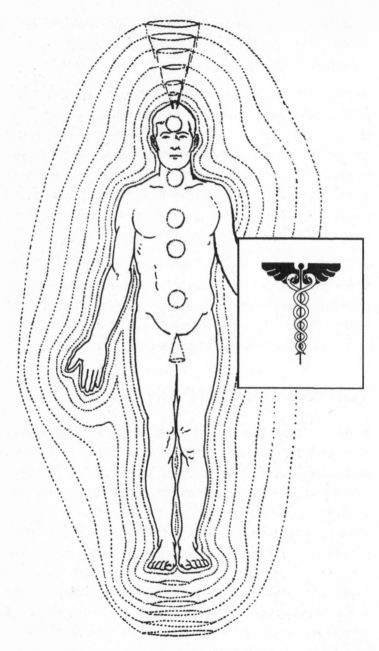

FIGURE 8.1 THE CHAKRAS AND THE ENERGY FIELDS

The chakras are vortices of energy, rather like small satellite dishes, which are found at clearly definable anatomical positions. Each is associated with a major nerve plexus and endocrine gland, and together they create a regulatory system that drives your physiology. When imbalance occurs it may activate your genes to produce illness, or even generate the hormonal climate within the central nervous system to produce symptoms of madness. On an everyday basis it is responsible for the creation of your thoughts, moods and emotions, through the endocrine glands which govern the workings of your brain.

The seven major chakras run along the central axis of the body, from the base of the spine to the crown of the head. Each can be seen as a floppy disk that not only contains old programmed sub-routines, but takes in new information, filters it and cross-references it to see if it is 'compatible' with its programme. Like a circuit board, all seven are interconnected, and are as individually 'wired' as the electricity board in your house, quite distinct from that of your next-door neighbour. In it are lodged all the elements that make up your personality, from the things that anger you, inspire you, bore you, frustrate you, to what food you prefer, to the weather you feel most comfortable in.

The question that naturally follows is – for what purpose does this energetic 'computer bank' lodge all this information? One reason is so that you stay being identifiable at a personality level as 'you', in the same way that your physical features allow me to recognise you.

The other reason requires us to ask a more profound question: Why are we here? What is this journey about anyway? Your entire spiritual agenda is encoded in your chakra system: what your soul is trying to achieve as far as your life path goes, what psychological skills your personality requires for that purpose, and what obstacles must be transcended for it to happen. It is that part of your energy system that has all the wisdom and karmic imprints you have acquired in other lifetimes, all the suffering and joy and the beliefs resulting from those

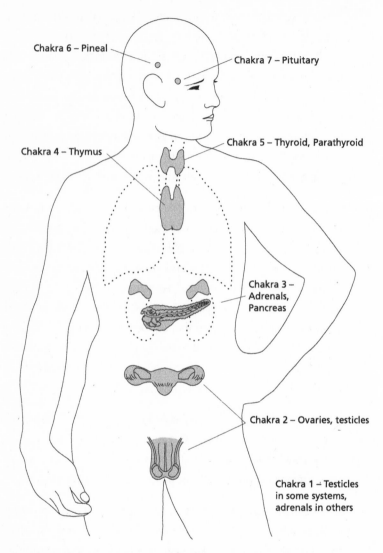

Chakra 6 – Pineal

Chakra 7 – Pituitary

Chakra 5 – Thyroid, Parathyroid

Chakra 4 – Thymus

Chakra 3 – Adrenals, Pancreas

Chakra 2 – Ovaries, testicles

Chakra 1 – Testicles in some systems, adrenals in others

FIGURE 8.2 COMMON ASSOCIATIONS BETWEEN THE CHAKRAS AND THE GLANDS OF THE ENDOCRINE SYSTEM

experiences, all the prejudices and fears. Your chakra system facilitates these in being activated and expressed in this current lifetime. It is that part of you which will go on after your physical body dies. To know if it functions well, *you must begin looking for the signs that tell you if it is in harmony or not.*

This means *listening to symptoms and becoming conscious of what they're trying to tell you*. For example, if whenever your boss or boyfriend criticises you, you become anxious and your self-esteem plummets, these feelings may be suggesting that your yardstick of self-worth is too often located outside of yourself, making it necessary for you always to please people and seek their approval before you can feel worthwhile. Since this makes you feel vulnerable and out of control, perhaps you would feel less so if you became more self-referred and learned to rely on your own judgement.

If you always feel pressured within your family to 'fall in', to succeed in the way they approve of, and dread visiting them, couldn't that feeling of dread alert you to the possibility that you need to become your own person even if they alienate you as a result? Or if you are someone who finds it hard to 'let go' and really enjoy yourself, or who can't relax recreationally or sexually, shouldn't that reticence encourage you to explore why?

All these difficulties, and their symptoms, are reflected in an imbalance in the chakras. You can learn to use this information to learn about yourself and bring harmony back. Panic attacks hold quite specific information about your identity and can be an indication of how great your attachment is to a particular identity, sending ripples of fear through the system if any substantial change is detected. Over-attachment can be restrictive if growth requires that we let go and move into a new phase. This battle between the soul's intention for us to move to a new experience, and the personality's terror at the necessary change, are played out in the energy field and the chakra system.

THE CHAKRA SYSTEM

The degree of harmony between the seven chakras influences the level of performance of every physical, emotional, mental and spiritual function of our mind–body–spirit organism. Such balance can depend on the degree of openness or closure at any given moment of an individual chakra, or all of them.

Chakra imbalance usually begins within a context of fear. This can happen following a range of life difficulties such as childhood traumas, physical pain, social conditioning, deprived and oppressive environments, mental and emotional shocks, and prolonged stress – anything that constricts our unique personal consciousness and its full expression.

The first chakra (see Figure 8.3) is located at the base of the spine. The verb that best describes it is 'I have' or 'I exist'. Its primary role is to *secure the survival of your physical identity.* Your first chakra will urge you to get enough sleep, to eat, to find a place to live, a means of independent income, and what measures to take in the face of danger. It can be compromised in the face of survival issues and threats to existence, and activates the adrenal plexus to initiate the adrenaline cascade during panic.

The appropriate response to a radical change in identity, particularly of a survival nature, is encoded in your first chakra. This is based on lifetimes of experience. So for a workaholic, it is this chakra that may issue the warning 'you stop work and you die!' It vibrates at the *red* end of the colour spectrum.

The second chakra is located below the navel and its verb is 'I feel'. As the centre of your *emotional intelligence* it influences your ability to experience pleasure and to avoid pain. It mediates how you respond to change, experience your sexuality and deal with the issues of intimacy, parenting, relationships and community. Many of the irritable bowel sensations so common to anxiety and panic are due to excessive activity in this chakra as it attempts to process change and the emotions it brings. Its vibration is *orange*.

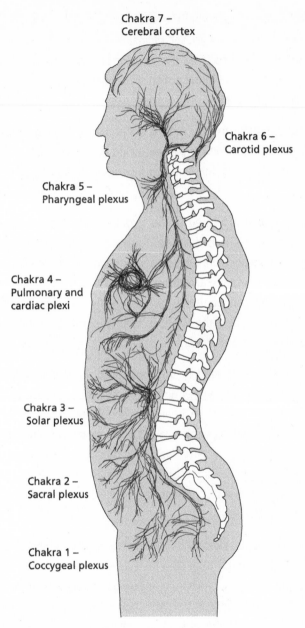

Chakra 7 –
Cerebral cortex

Chakra 6 –
Carotid plexus

Chakra 5 –
Pharyngeal plexus

Chakra 4 –
Pulmonary and
cardiac plexi

Chakra 3 –
Solar plexus

Chakra 2 –
Sacral plexus

Chakra 1 –
Coccygeal plexus

FIGURE 8.3 CHAKRAS AND NERVE GANGLIA

The third chakra is located in the solar plexus and its verb is 'I can'. It deals with *individual identity*, self-definition, ego strength and willpower – the ability to influence your life. Its issue is personal autonomy, 'fire in the belly', and is vital to the notion of standing on your own two feet, and defending yourself.

The 'butterflies in the tummy' feeling, or the nausea that can accompany panic is actually the feeling you get when your third chakra wisdom doesn't cover the situation, and you feel out of control. Its vibration is *yellow*.

The fourth chakra is located in the middle of the chest, behind the breastbone, and its verb is 'I love, I accept'. It is through this chakra that you feel *unconditional acceptance* of yourself, others, and reality as it is rather than as you'd like it to be. Much chest tightness and hyperventilation can be from the unforgiving 'heartless striving' of perfectionism, pushing the limits of what is comfortably possible to achieve. Its vibration is *green*.

The fifth chakra is located in the throat and its verb is 'I speak'. It helps you to *express yourself* and explore your special talents, to be authentic to your true nature, hear other people empathically, put form on your ideas, and think symbolically. It is associated with creativity and your 'public face'. Some can't swallow or they feel a tightening of the throat when they panic, and misinterpret this as a literal closing of their windpipe, when it is in fact expressing an imbalance in communication. Its vibration is *sky blue*.

The sixth chakra is located in the centre of the forehead and is metaphorically referred to as 'the third eye'. Its verb is 'I see'. It deals with *insight*, reflection, intuition, visualisation, thoughts, and the realm of abstraction. Imbalance in the sixth chakra is reflected in the inability to see clearly, losing the plot, fragmentation, inflexibility, rigid belief systems, delusions, poor concentration, hallucinations and nightmares.

During times of stress this chakra is often overloaded, looking for a solution, and there is a heavy, 'full' or buzzing sensation in the head, which is a reflection of the chakra attempting to understand the situation. Its vibration is *midnight blue* or *purple*.

The seventh chakra is located at the crown of the head and is associated with beliefs about how the universe works, spiritual understanding, your connection to other dimensions of consciousness, and your place in the grand design. The verb is 'I know' and the vibration is *purple* or *white*.

THE ENERGY FIELD AND PANIC ATTACKS

The following information and the specific exercises that are particularly helpful during panic attacks were recommended by clairvoyant and spiritual teacher Walter Makichen, director of the Center for Self-Teaching in Sacramento, California.

What is happening in the energy field before and during a panic attack? The trigger is a (conscious or unconscious) perceived imminent change in identity. This can occur during times of extreme stress or radical change, such as following a bereavement or relationship breakdown. Or during intense fear such as accompanies bullying, accidents or attacks. Or it can be a period of financial uncertainty, or when you are feeling overwhelmed in your job – when you're out of your depth and you aren't sure if you'll manage the situation. Next, one of two pictures results – either all the chakras 'pop open' and the field is flooded, leading to a terrifying inflow of energy, or they all close down, leading to a cutting off from the life-force. The net effect is the same, *a great sense of helplessness and impending doom, and a fear of being utterly defenceless.*

CHAKRA FLOODING

Since the chakra system usually functions in a state of varying degrees of closure, screening off any excessive incoming input, the experience of *chakra flooding*, in which the individual is bombarded by information from the environment, is a new and unfamiliar one. Now everything becomes real, including all the non-physical dimensions not normally available to your consciousness. Suddenly thoughts seem real. The thought forms 'You're going to have a heart attack!' or 'Quick, get out or you'll stop breathing!' become compellingly true. What exist normally as whispers in your consciousness become amplified when your chakra system is wide open, and seem to be screaming insistently at you to respond. If you're in a crowd, it appears as if people are literally pressing onto you, so the feeling of not being able to breathe properly feels quite real at the energetic level. As you become aware of the surrounding energy fields intermingling with yours, you can lose your breath, and it seems as if there's nowhere to hide. There is no sense of the individual identity present to make a balanced assessment of the situation, no one who can stand up and announce reassuringly 'My chakras are all open, that's all this is, nothing to worry about.' With no centred calm voice, the fight or flight response is triggered.

The experience of an open chakra system is one which few people are already prepared for, or have the skills to handle, so most find it startling and terrifying. If you are the kind of person whose sense of survival depends on the 'inner you' remaining untouched by the world, and intact at all times, this kind of sudden opening is horrifying. This especially applies to those individuals who are the observing type, who prefer to watch rather than participate in the world, and the greater part of whose reality occurs in their head, where they can regulate the amount of energy coming towards them. With their chakras wide open, they have switched out of a reality they can comfortably handle, into one in which they are helpless.

On occasion, it is one particular chakra that opens to its fullest, usually the third, which manages most of the fight or flight issues we face. Bombarded with new information, which the other chakras, because they are not so open, can't help it to handle, it becomes overloaded and confused as to what the solution is. These are the sort of panic attacks in which a person has a tremendous urge to act, restlessly moving around, and unable to settle, nervously fidgeting or talking compulsively. There is a basic underlying fear at their third chakra, and whenever it is triggered, the urge is to 'do something, act!'

If they are not aware at all of the presence of such a trigger, they will give a story such as 'I don't know why, but I just had to leave the restaurant.' This is the kind of trigger to a specific chakra that could be unveiled in psychotherapy, and a solution discussed as to how to deal with that particular challenge if it recurred. For example, they may have an insecurity about whether they can make interesting conversation or relate well to people, and when they find themselves seated beside an important or intimidating person, they may find themselves unaccountably panicky. *All types of panic are underpinned by the individual's belief that they are helpless.* There is a common feeling of being lost and rudderless, lacking the skills to cover the situation. The solution obviously involves helping them find a way to 'ground' into the new reality they find themselves in, to find a way of feeling intact within it.

PARANOIA AND PROJECTION

If only one chakra opens fully, an individual then finds themselves at the mercy of whatever skills are in that chakra, or are lacking there. Each chakra has the ability to make things real to us, and what we perceive through it becomes the truth. The excessively open chakra acts like a magnifying glass, blowing small things out of proportion.

For many panickers it is the opinion or judgement of others that causes the greatest fear and can be the trigger to their attacks. If *paranoia* is a major factor in the anxiety symptoms, which is often the case if the sixth chakra is the main one that has suddenly opened, the individual may feel like their head is exploding. The energetic dynamic is that their sixth chakra, acting like an antenna, and being in a more open state than usual, is taking in more information but doesn't know how to interpret it. They are picking up energy from others, such as thought-forms, and trying to understand them (the job of the sixth chakra) at an intensity that is new for them, and they find it frightening.

Since their chakra system is not usually in such an open state, they would not be accustomed to having access to the private thoughts of others, including self-critical ones. In our culture anything not immediately understandable is the enemy, and instils a sense of threat. Tuning in on, but not being able to make sense of, these critical thoughts of others is an intolerably confusing situation. As a solution, *they project onto the situation the notion that the other person is having those critical thoughts about them*! Now they're back in familiar territory which they have expertise in. They can now go on to run through familiar grooves in their mind. They have felt hurt and rejected before, experienced judgement and ridicule, and feel no stranger to embarrassment and shame. The 'truth' that their projection provided, in the form of a paranoia that 'they think I'm stupid', has returned them to familiar ground, even though it is inaccurate.

EXPANDED UNIVERSES

Some panic attacks are a response to a larger universe that we know is there but which we find difficult to accept. The trigger may be a fear of life in general. For example, a hesitant type of person who leads a 'little life', lacking in risk or unpredictability, may find the cut and thrust of normal existence constantly challenging. In such a person, whose chakra system is protectively closed most of the time, a rapid succession of events, which others might handle with ease, would swamp their chakra system. In other instances it may be an experience of limitlessness, such as being up above the clouds in a plane, or out on the ocean, that emphasises the vastness of the universe, a concept that they usually manage to keep in their unconscious.

Those who have experienced a psychotic episode or post-traumatic stress disorder have encountered a version of the universe that they never knew existed and cannot easily interpret. Other dimensions of being, such as the non-physical, have become known to them. Out-of-body or near-death experiences, where people find themselves looking down on their own body from above, or travelling up a tunnel toward a white light, can occur after assaults, accidents, operations or any situation where continued survival is in doubt. Drug-related hallucinogenic experiences where solid objects such as walls or floors appear to be moving and changing shape, or where music flows in visible waves, or parts of your body merge with the surroundings, can undermine our understanding of how the world is constructed. Meetings with spirit beings from other dimensions of consciousness, or dead people whose spirit fails to pass over, introduce the notion of a universe with a multitude of possible identities besides the physical body. The more welded we are to our identity in this lifetime, the more chance for fear of death and panic to result if anything threatens it. The question becomes 'How do I know if the person I know as "me" will exist any more in that expanded universe with this larger sense of "self"?' People find themselves in a world in which they don't know how to absorb the new information, and panic may follow.

In the case of night panics, the images that present themselves to the screen of consciousness during sleep occur at a time when the chakra system is most open. At night a person may be experiencing more than can be admitted to or acknowledged at a conscious level during the day, when the mind's censoring processes are in place. They find it confusing and worrying to wake from a terrifying panic attack without knowing what frightened them.

CHAKRA SHUT-DOWN

What dictates that a person's system will blow open or close down as a response to panic? Those who have been sexually, physically or emotionally abused have often developed the ability (unconscious wisdom) to close their chakras as a way of shielding themselves from the trauma, as a protective strategy. The sensory input, whether it is rape, repeated brutal beatings or rejection, is minimised by closing down on incoming energy. In this way the body is left to deal with it alone, and later on when it is safe to do so, the chakras may open again. Closing your energy system is like locking the windows and doors and pulling the shades to prevent any light getting in. In present life, whenever a memory of the past abuse crosses your mind, your system will reflexively close again, for example if someone acts in a bullying or intimidatory manner towards you. This might not particularly bother anyone else, but it will cause closure and the panic response in you, and you may have no idea why. This kind of pattern usually indicates a buried memory.

When your chakras are closed, you feel isolated and alone. The pulse of the life-force energy, that expansion and contraction, as the universal energy flows in and out of you, is diminished. Without it, you feel you can't breathe, because the synchronisation of body and breath is what defines human life. With its interruption, you have no sense of place, and don't feel you belong anywhere. The very thing that reminds you that you're alive is missing, so you think you're going to die. In the absence of external connections, whatever you are thinking really comes alive. You are trapped with whatever fearful imagery or thought-forms are in your field, reliving them. Feeling paralysed and unresponsive, you can't really hear the reassurances of others.

WORKING WITH PANIC ENERGETICALLY

The ability to notice the early signs of change in your chakra system is an essential skill. Most commonly, it is the third chakra that first picks up the signs of an oncoming attack, as it has the strongest connection to the fight or flight response. Physically this may mean nausea or uneasiness in the stomach. Emotionally you may begin to be aware of feeling helpless and out of control, and mentally your thoughts may shift to 'I can't handle this'.

Exercise 1 – Grounding Your Energy

There is a major energetic channel running through the body which gives us a sense of who we are in this lifetime. It runs from the tip of the tongue down the body to the genitals and into the first chakra. It functions like an 'on' switch to connect the body and spirit together as one, stimulating the 'surviving you' which knew that it could come here to this planet and be resilient and tough enough to face whatever was here. It is that protector part of your identity that looks at the proposed lifetime, the karma to be faced, the issues involved beforehand, and says 'I can handle this, this is not outside my realm of influence.'

With the onset of panic the connection with this stable identity is lost, and there is no sense of a 'self' that can handle the problematic situation or the stress. This first exercise stimulates this channel.

Place your right palm on your fourth chakra, and your left palm on your third. With the tip of your tongue behind your front teeth, slide it up to the ridge where the gum rises up into the hard palate. There is a trigger mechanism here that opens that channel if you stimulate it or push on it with your tongue. Breathe in, and as you exhale, push your tongue into that spot, and imagine your breath running down through the centre of your body into your genitals, down into your legs and grounding in the earth. This exercise redistributes the excessive energy to the lower end of the chakra system, and for that reason is excellent in paranoia and when the mind is in a frenzied state.

Exercise 2 – The Sound of Safety

The voice, and the use of sound, which is a pure energetic form, can be your best representative of the present moment during a panic attack, as your thoughts are loaded with the conditioning of past experiences.

Put your left hand on your stomach over your third chakra, and the right on your second chakra, and chant 'oh ah, oh ah, oh ah, om'. Do it with the 'oh' directed to the third chakra, the 'ah' directed to the second, and the 'om' directed to the navel point, your belly button. This is the point where integration of the physical and non-physical realms occurs. It has the effect of taking all the chaotic energy and putting some sense of order on it. It allows you to respond to your own voice, establishing a centre, calming the emotion at your second chakra, and soothing the desire to 'just make it stop' in the third chakra. It reassures that helpless urge and re-orientates you to your surroundings. It is like someone putting their arm around you and saying 'I'm here with you, this is what's going on, you're having a panic attack and although it feels overwhelming it is not going to be, you can deal with this.'

Exercise 3 – Help Is Here

These are exercises to help someone who is having an attack.

• Put the palms on each side of their third chakra. The person who does it may feel the heat coming off, running down them and into the earth, so it should only be done by someone who will not be unsettled by the panic, and can remain neutral, like a therapist or family member who is grounded. That person is trying to maintain a dominant safer reality than the one the panicker perceives. They need this to be protected in order for them to feel safe. It is a direct communication to the fight or flight response that says 'I'm here with you' and breaks through their feeling of vulnerability and loneliness.

- Put the palm of your hand on their sixth chakra, and the other palm on either their heart or their third chakra and channel energy into it. (To use this exercise you must have the awareness of being able to channel energy.) If their system is closed down, the easiest way to influence it is through their sixth or fourth chakras. This targets the panicker's mental processes, counteracting the feeling of aloneness, isolation and being overwhelmed, and establishes a sense of someone being here with them directly. It achieves more than you merely using your voice, because they literally feel energetically 'I'm present in your energy system'.

Gerard's company was modernising, and at the age of fifty-four he wasn't sure he could keep pace with the new computer skills required of him. He had thought he was cruising towards retirement, and was disturbed to find that he could possibly be asked to retire prematurely if he couldn't get up to speed. Weeks of insomnia had given way to the symptoms of irritable bowel, and then panic attacks. Eventually, feeling trapped and depressed, he saw his doctor, who recommended he take sick leave.

Although it was the first time he had taken a day off in years, he was no stranger to illness. Two of his children had cystic fibrosis and over the years he had found that constant vigilance and a healthy mistrust of doctors were his best assets regarding their welfare. More than once mistakes had been made by doctors and hospitals and one of the girls had been close to dying due to an allergic reaction to an antibiotic. At the first sign of infection, he always insisted on their speedy admission to hospital, and from then on monitored their progress with a degree of intensity that often alienated the staff. He wouldn't rest until they were home again, and even then, they were never far from his mind.

He hated to see them suffer, and made it his personal responsibility to get them well again. Although they were eighteen and twenty-one now, he felt he would never forgive himself if anything happened to them.

Now, with these panic attacks draining him he was at his lowest ebb ever. He knew that if one of them fell ill he would not have the energy to camp out in the hospital as he usually did. He was aware of skating on 'thin ice', and it terrified him to feel so vulnerable.

While on sick leave he decided to adopt the same proactive stance he had always taken with the girls' illnesses, and sought help for his panic attacks. Our first session focused on his childhood. His father had been a cardiac cripple, who frequently needed the assistance of the doctor at home. It was always a worry and, being the eldest, the job of cycling to the doctor's house fell to Gerard. He also knew that his mother drank secretly, and felt that it was no harm if he unofficially monitored his father's health. He was always uneasy away from the house since more than once on his return he had found his father in a distressed state, in pain and unable to breathe.

On the night his father died Gerard had been unable to locate the doctor and he cycled into town for help. Returning too late, Gerard never forgave himself for not having hitched a lift rather than wasting precious minutes cycling. He agreed that he had made himself the 'custodian of his father's health' at a young age. His daughters' illnesses had fed straight into that identity, as he became theirs also.

Stressful as that was, it never slipped out of his control over the years, and even though it was at great personal cost (he and his wife rarely got away from home for long), he refused to delegate the responsibility. Despite the fact that the girls themselves often found his 'guardianship' intrusive and claustrophobic, and had begun recently to resist this, he couldn't let go. Now with the stress at work he had reached breaking point – something had to give.

Looking at Gerard's energy field it was clear that the girls' health needs connected into his second chakra through an energy cord which all children have to their parents, and through which he registered their distress, just as surely as the doctor's stethoscope picks up the sounds in their lungs. He had learned to define himself through this caretaker role as a young boy, so 'custodian of the health of others' was woven into the personality of his second chakra and the way it expressed itself. The irritable bowel symptoms were a sign of imbalance there, as the lower bowel is the anatomical territory covered by that chakra.

His third chakra, the 'manager' and the one that makes things happen in our lives, had always worked effectively enough for Gerard, until recently. There was now too much challenge for it to process, and not enough resources to go around, and he knew he was at risk of losing control of things. Energetically, panic attacks are an expression of loss of control, where the energy fails to be contained and directed and instead 'blows out' in many directions.

Encoded in his first chakra, where our survival identity is lodged, he was running a script that says 'I stop caretaking and they die'. This chakra received urgent SOS messages from the third chakra whenever it felt that the caretaker identity was threatened, or when it looked like 'Gerard the caretaker' was about to be made redundant or cease functioning. Since Gerard would be unable to feel consistent without this thread, he effectively faced annihilation, so the fight-flight response was set in motion.

There is obviously an imbalance within the chakra system whenever survival is on such a knife-edge. The present situation was asking him to loosen the second chakra connections with the girls, and accept that nobody can ultimately be responsible for someone else's life. But the older guilt about letting his father down was ultimately driving the emotional pattern, and needed to be changed if it was not to re-create itself in another form, say if his mother or wife fell ill. The forging of a new identity, one that included 'responsible for my own health' and the ability to delegate without guilt, needed to be brought into being. His sick leave and psychotherapy provided such an opportunity.

John had always been a communicator and an innovator. Since he was a boy he had been writing articles for school magazines, putting on plays and doing spots on radio stations. 'Getting it out there' was a strong driving force for him. As an adult his interests became more and more socially based, with environmental, political and health issues preoccupying him. Although he worked for a computer company, he hoped to find employment ultimately in publishing, journalism or radio, as an avenue for his expansive ideas. He felt it almost his duty to 'inform and educate the masses' about all the exciting new developments in health, housing, consciousness, and any idealistic topic that he felt 'pushed the envelope' past the mainstream view.

His brain never stopped and, like a beacon, he seemed to attract people who were engaged in groundbreaking, progressive projects. His talent was in pulling people together and firing them up with enthusiasm, energising any project he came in contact with. When no opportunity emerged to allow him to work in the area in which his passion lay, at twenty-nine he decided to take the bull by the horns and start up his own magazine.

Within weeks he found himself in the middle of a cyclone of activity. He was overseeing the renovation of a building to work from, hiring new staff, brainstorming till the early hours about magazine layouts, advertising space, and all the millions of details he never knew needed to be attended to in the running of such a publication. However, there was one vital element that John lacked – experience. He had never actually worked in publishing and was now learning the ropes 'on the hoof'. His talent was innovating and creating, not follow-through and attending to the nuts-and-bolts of production, especially the finance end of it.

116

Months of work, during which time he was never happier, culminated in the launch date. As it approached, he became increasingly anxious. He saw his doctor for a burning pain in his stomach, which was treated as an ulcer, and had a series of severe panic attacks in the week leading up to the deadline. In the following months, as the fledgling magazine lurched from one unanticipated crisis to another, as teething problems emerged at every level, ranging from personality clashes in the office to financial deadlines missed and pasted over by borrowing from other areas, to subtle changes in the targeted market, John's dream turned into a nightmare. His rising adrenaline levels made it increasingly difficult for him to concentrate, to make decisions, to sleep, or to cope with hard-talking bank managers, printers and advertisers demanding money.

John's sense of life purpose is located in his fifth chakra, the one that governs our creativity, 'speaking our truth', and our public persona. All his life he had been driven by the script in his fifth chakra telling him to get information out to people. Now here he was on the launching pad. But the previous weeks had revealed something to him that he had never known before, that there is a huge difference between the airy-fairy world of idealism and fabrication, and the very concrete world of bank managers, employee salaries, printing deadlines, copyright issues, marketing strategies and the unpredictable temperaments of staff.

He began to doubt if it would work, or if he would be able to control all the variables. As his third chakra sensed that his skills didn't cover the situation, it became overwhelmed, and he got an ulcer. Finally his first chakra, receiving the messages that social annihilation was imminent, initiated the fight-flight response in an effort to rescue the situation, and panic attacks followed. What John needed was to have balance restored within his energy system. The idealistic 'up-in-the-clouds' approach that he had always been able to use until now, concentrating most of his energy in his upper chakras, needed to be countered by an increase in energy running through his lower 'down-to-earth' chakras, which contain the skills for living in the material world.

9

SUBSTANCE-INDUCED PANIC

With the increased use of recreational drugs such as ecstasy, cocaine, speed, LSD, marijuana and hallucinogenic mushrooms, panic attacks during or after a trip have become more frequent. The reasons for this vary with the drug, but the fact that it is very often kept private, and therefore inadequately treated, is common to them all.

EXPERIENCING THE BOUNDLESS

The concept of a *psychological boundary* is essential to understanding this type of panic. One of the earliest stages in the emerging consciousness of a small child is the sense of there being a difference between 'self' and 'other'. Our skin gives us the most basic impression that 'we' are contained within its confines and that everything outside it is reliably going to stay there and not start oozing into us, and that we are not about to leak outwards. Only 'you' feel your pain physically. Your thoughts and emotions reinforce that separation at the mental and emotional levels. It is only 'you' who feels your distress, and the privacy of your most secret thoughts allows you to feel secure and confident that there is always a central deep core place that is inviolably 'you', which cannot be penetrated and which will never disappear.

These concepts instil a sense of security that you will continue to be 'yourself' because *your identity as a separate entity is intact*. And also that the seat of your consciousness, the rudder steering your ship, the command post from which you direct operations, is within your control. This sense of containment is an essential source of safety and continuity.

Now picture a scenario where a person's daily existence is filled with fear, pressure or confusion. If 'living in your skin' is far from being a pleasurable experience, if your current identity is failing you and you can't seem to change it, if you would do anything to escape the contents of your mind because it seems to be pitched against you, you might welcome a break from being 'you'. Chemical substances will efficiently allow you to 'zone out', replacing your negative experience with a more positive one. Recreational drugs do just that. A new 'you' is created for a while, one that feels good, whom you like and who likes you, and for a brief time the business of living seems more bearable.

The ingredient responsible for much of this shift in perspective is the *ability of the chemical to generate a psychological feeling that your boundary is loosening*. It achieves this by literally 'spreading' the aura, the electromagnetic energy field surrounding the body, and opening the chakras. The advantage is a feeling of expansion, of more flexibility in ideas, less rigidity in the ways they have become linked to each other, a freeing-up physically, emotionally, mentally, sexually and spiritually. With hallucinogenic drugs such as LSD or magic mushrooms, perceptions change radically. The ways in which you sense the world alter in terms of depth, colour and sound. The entire 3-D experience can even expand to other dimensions of space-time.

Electromagnetically you can seem to be merging into and 'becoming' the pot-plant standing next to you, and the sound coming from the stereo approaches you from across the room like a wave along the ground, a tidal wave of sound that you can see! While research into these hallucinogenic experiences was eagerly carried out in the 1950s by Timothy Leary and others in an effort to explain the many facets of consciousness, it can engender terror in the uninitiated.

The disadvantage of any interference with what you used to know as 'reality' is that some people can find that boundless feeling terrifying. Unprepared, *such a dramatic shift can radically undermine their understanding of the basic principles on which reality relies, and engender fear instead of pleasure*. They may not even be conscious of their mind asking existential questions: 'If my senses, thoughts and even my physical being can seem to change so much, how do I know if I'll be able to change back? Who is in the driving seat if the person having these experiences isn't recognisable as "me" any more? Can I trust that perceiver? How reliable is reality anyway if a chemical can make it all look and feel so different? If there's no basic difference between me and a plant, then what's the point of working, going to school or doing anything? If I can pick up the thoughts of others, does that mean they know all of mine too?'

Much of the stability in your world view can disappear and you may feel terrified at the prospect of ceasing to exist as the identity by which you've learned to define yourself. In essence you may feel as if your sense-making mechanism is under threat of imminent annihilation, and the fight or flight response can kick in. Some individuals have a clear-cut out-of-body experience in which they 'see' themselves from a position floating above their physical body, which is still sitting in the chair, unaware of this occurring. There seems to be two of them, one observing the other. This poses the obvious existential question 'How do I define my identity now – which one of them is "me"?'

If it occurs during a trip, the ensuing panic attack may then be mistaken for an effect of the drug. If it happens a few days or weeks later, it may be *incorrectly* assumed (not without a tinge of guilt over the fact that an illegal and therefore 'dangerous' substance was responsible) that it is a sign that structural damage has been wrought on your neurons. Now your imagination runs riot – a life of limited potential since your brain will cease to function properly, opportunities such as going to college or developing a career lost, your chances 'thrown away'. Or worse – mental illness, medication, psychiatric hospitals! The fact that the symptoms are continuing many weeks or months later 'confirms' to many that they have done permanent and probably irreparable harm to their nervous system – an incorrect assumption.

Tragically for some, a diagnosis of paranoid schizophrenia can be incorrectly made at this stage. Such drug-related experiences often occur around the age when schizophrenia is most likely to appear; and the two can be confused. When a chakra system has been prematurely opened by a drug experience, many of the extreme changes in consciousness that follow can closely resemble the schizophrenic state. With upper chakra dominance there can be hallucinations, paranoia, a disconnection from the outside world and a breaking down of relationships.

Many are reluctant or ashamed to confide in parents or doctors because of the consequences. They dread everyone 'freaking out' and the inquisition that would follow – their friends being exposed, parents contacted, their social life monitored and policed. Such an action could spell the end of their social life. Why, they might lament, out of a group who all smoke joints regularly, do they have to be the only one who has an adverse reaction to 'getting out of their head'? If it occurs during adolescence, being set apart from the group for any reason, not being able to 'handle' the drug, can be a source of embarrassment, and so secrecy is their only defence.

Meanwhile, it can be a daily strain trying to explain why being confined in a classroom or school assembly has now become torture, as the panic attacks take hold. People have to invent excuses as to why they aren't joining their friends socially or going to concerts – since crowds have now become a problem. They can feel lonely, isolated and depressed. And of course, as the fears build, more and more panic is created, because the problem seems to be taking over.

Psychotherapy, if it is to be helpful, should ideally be done by those informed about the psychological and physiological effects of the different drugs. Panic is still a 'reaction to' an experience, and it helps if the therapist knows what the nature of that experience is. Some fluency with transpersonal and existential psychology, and the notion that we are spiritual beings having a human experience, is a particular advantage in the case of the more mind-altering substances, as many of these transpersonal experiences relate to the 'big picture', and our journey from the infinite perspective.

UPPERS – BUZZING UP YOUR METABOLISM

Ecstasy, cocaine and speed increase the 'revs' at which your metabolism works. They do this by stimulating a release of serotonin from where it is stored in the nerve endings into your bloodstream. Through its action, there is a speeding-up of the heart rate, more sweat is produced because of the increased heat in the body, and the muscles become restless for movement. For the percentage of people who unconsciously fear unexplained sudden or excessive physical sensations like these, their occurrence can precipitate a panic attack. If it is their first exposure to the drug they have no way of knowing that what follows is in fact a panic attack, thinking it to be the normal effect of the drug.

In the case of ecstasy, as much of the effect of the drug is in the body as in the head. The experience centres on the heart, both physically and psychologically. Ecstasy was originally used in California in the 1980s as an aid in marital therapy, and was a prescription drug until it was later withdrawn. It became known as the 'love drug' because of the effect it has in promoting loving, friendly feelings towards others. It is also the drug that fuelled the 'rave' culture because the speed of vibration of the drug and the resulting impulse to move the body seemed to match the tempo of the music.

As the drug 'comes up' and the heart rate speeds up, this sudden increase can create a fear that a heart attack is imminent, and a panic attack may then be triggered in those who have an excessive wariness of unexplained sudden physiological variation.

At the level of the energy system, all the chakras pop open, and take in much larger quantities of energy than usual from the surroundings, a desirable experience for most. For others, with no filter to screen out unwanted incoming frequencies, flooding occurs, which they find unpleasant. The inrush of environmental energy, particularly if there are variables in the environment outside their control, such as violent or aggressive interchanges, or being questioned by police or security, can set up a paranoia that they are unsafe, and trigger a panic attack. With the opening of the sixth chakra, the judgements and criticisms of others are registered, and projected to be about them, setting up the conditions for paranoia about their acceptance as one of the group.

ALCOHOL

There are many for whom alcohol is an easily available, effective, and culturally condoned anaesthetic for feelings of distress. These feelings can have their source in a wide range of life difficulties, from relationship conflict, low self-esteem, painful childhood traumas, to financial ruin, unfulfilled expectations, or bereavement. While the blood level is kept up the distress is less apparent, and many who have panic attacks misuse alcohol in this way. However, on the day after a binge, with more fluctuations in physiology occurring as the body tries to re-establish chemical balance, many find they are at their most vulnerable at this time to panic attacks being triggered. As in any toxic state, the senses are more on edge, the reserves lower, and the margin between well-being and distress is slim. Panickers often find that they haven't the energy to 'fight it', or to effectively use their usual tactics while recovering from the night before. By keeping records of when panics occur you may notice a similar pattern.

PRESCRIPTION DRUGS

Anti-depressants act by causing an increase in serotonin, thereby 'lifting' the mood. Like jump-leads on a car, they try to kick-start the system into action. However, in a person who already has too much adrenaline in their system, these 'uppers' can tip them over from high anxiety into panic, interrupt sleep and even remove their inhibition towards suicide.

PART TWO

PANIC NO MORE

10

CONTROLLING PANIC

KEYNOTE: A TOOLBOX OF SKILLS

One of the worst sensations in panic is that it makes you feel that it is in control, and that you're merely an unwilling passenger along for the ride. It feels like some huge beast is out of control inside you and you have no power to stop it. *Much of the fear stems from the feeling that you cannot influence the course of an attack.* This may have been your experience to date, but it isn't universally true that panic attacks cannot be controlled. Once you truly understand the mechanics behind an attack, you can then learn to intervene in several different ways to bring the adrenaline level down and end the cycle. This section of the book is about acquiring those skills. Our cave-dwelling ancestors wouldn't have had such fear of predators if they'd had today's choice of weaponry to keep them safe. In the same way, your defence against panic is going to be your toolbox of skills, and they'll empower you. Great advances in the understanding and treatment of panic attacks have been made in recent years. Professor David Barlow of the Center for Anxiety and Related Disorders at Boston University has successfully treated many sufferers of panic attacks with an approach described in his book *Mastery of Anxiety and Panic* elements of which I draw on.

Many sufferers report that they experience much less fear when they are assured that they can *learn to reduce the intensity of the horrible sensations* quickly, as opposed to having to endure them for an agonisingly long period. This makes them feel more in control. They report feeling less dependant on the presence of another person, and more relaxed about being on their own, if they can *learn to trust that their symptoms are harmless*.

When they begin to notice that many of their attacks happen under certain conditions – when they are pushing themselves beyond their limit, worrying too much what people are thinking, or spreading their energy too thinly – they can see that the attacks are in fact not so unpredictable and out-of-the-blue as they thought, but fairly reliably follow a certain pattern of thought or behaviour. This awareness makes attacks seem less inexplicable and mysterious, because they *learn to foresee the triggers* and can act accordingly to head them off.

Control skills can be learned through three different avenues, at the level of:

① *Thoughts*

- witnessing
- replacing fearful thoughts
- correct information

In some respects your body is like your TV; it only delivers whatever channel you choose, it doesn't pick them itself, nor does it have any agenda as to whether you should be calm or tense, it just follows orders from your brain. So you have to consciously decide that the 'calm channel' is what you will choose, rather than the 'panic channel', and move your thoughts (the equivalent of using your TV zapper) in that direction. The kind of thoughts people have who are caught in the state of vigilance are 'Something bad may happen at any minute and I don't know whether I can deal with it, but if I catch it coming in advance, I'll have a better chance of controlling it.' Those who are actually having a panic attack may be thinking 'I'm going mad/having a heart attack/suffocating/making a fool of myself.'

This chapter focuses on developing the ability to witness yourself, to learn more about your panic reaction by using awareness and attention as your first tool in deepening your understanding of its origins.

② *Physical Sensations*

- abdominal breathing
- relaxation techniques

By learning to manage your breathing pattern or your muscular tension, you move two of the fight or flight variables in the direction of calm, and since they always work as a complete package, that means you influence all the other symptoms for the better. These dampen down the sympathetic (emergency) nervous system response, and boost the parasympathetic (restoration) nervous system response. The next two chapters teach you how to do this.

③ *Behaviours*

- changing the avoidance tendency to one of approach
- experiencing the sensations as safe, rather than dangerous

With time people usually adopt a certain stance in relation to their panic attacks, as a method of coping. They either refuse to give in to them and stay put, or they instantly locate an exit and run for it, without even waiting to see if it is going to get any worse or if they can bring some control over it. Or they may start avoiding going to places where they think they might have an attack or have had one in the past, such as crowded shopping malls or cinemas. Very subtle escape or avoidance patterns begin, of which individuals are not fully aware, in order to reduce the chances of the feared bodily sensations occurring. They may attempt to prevent falling by always standing close to a wall or leaning on a bicycle or baby buggy, or head off arguments by becoming silent or leaving the room. These behaviours keep the panicky feelings to a minimum and ensure that they are within their 'comfort zone' all the time. This has advantages in the short term, but whenever they move back into the 'risk zone' it is just as bad as ever. The approach this book offers relies heavily for its success on *replacing this avoidance tendency with one of approach* in order to undermine (and ultimately invalidate) the belief that 'only avoidance will keep you safe'.

TRACKING BACK – IDENTIFYING YOUR TRIGGERS

If you kept breaking out in a blotchy red rash every time you ate Indian food, or all the electrical circuits in your kitchen blew whenever you turned on the washing machine, you would quickly link the two and a solution would emerge.

It is a basic premise of this approach that *all panic attacks are cued or triggered*. Although you may not yet be aware of these triggers, in time you will learn to observe signs that will point to them.

Looking for patterns is the first step in learning that *panic is a reaction to something, not the cause*. It is the end result, or effect. A chain of events precedes it. The implications of realising this are profound. When you view it as an automatic response over which you have no control, and which holds your life to ransom, with your future at its mercy, you feel powerless and vulnerable. If this continues for a long time the future begins to look depressing, and opting out can disturbingly become an option.

If, on the other hand, you see that panic is a reaction, *the end-point of a series of internal events*, then obviously if you know what those are, and can learn to react differently to them, you can bring control over the end result – whether a panic attack will occur or not. In the same way that an exploding bomb is the result of someone lighting the fuse, and of time elapsing before the flame reaches the dynamite, so a panic attack has a beginning, middle and end.

Tracking back from the moment of explosion, back along the fuse, you can learn to identify what triggers are starting it. Like a detective you must learn to be observant, paying attention to subtle changes in your body, and looking for clues in the details of your life, your thoughts, feelings and behaviours. When the trail becomes obvious, it is like completing a join-the-dots picture! One thing is for sure. If the bomb has exploded and you've had a panic attack, something must have lit the fuse; it's just a question of revealing what.

THE THREE DOMAINS

It makes it easier to gather information about your panic reaction if it is broken down into *three separate domains – thoughts, sensations, and behaviours.* Suppose you have a belief that 'getting through the shopping quickly and finding the shortest queue is the best way to avoid having a panic attack' (thoughts). In the supermarket, tensely gripping your trolley, and with jaw set, you're trying to get through it as quickly as possible. The meat counter, however, is short-staffed, and a chatty neighbour irritates you by pinning you down for a few minutes. Delayed, you now feel yourself breaking out in a cold sweat, and you can hear your pulse pounding in your ears (sensations). As you finally make it to the checkout, you almost lose it completely when the girl needs to change the reel on her cash register. Cursing under your breath, and with shaking hands, you fumble for your money and run for the exit (behaviours).

Now suppose you held a different belief, that 'avoiding a panic attack depends on my staying relaxed and not getting pressured'. Then you

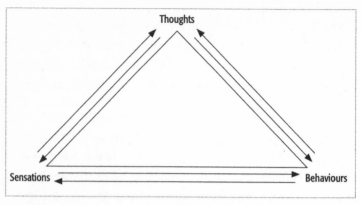

would make it a priority to keep your muscles loose and your breathing slow and deep as you peruse the shelves. Any time you felt a slight tensing of your muscles or quickening of your breath, you'd stop where you were and concentrate on slowing them down again, reassuring yourself that all was fine. By the time you got to the checkout you'd feel in control, calm, and above all safe.

Each domain has had a knock-on effect on the others, influencing the experience as a whole. In the first example the lead came from the thoughts, as is often the case in panic, and the focus on speed negatively influenced the entire sequence. At other times, it could be a behaviour that is the 'go' button, like not saying no to people's requests, which means you're then overloaded. Or by contrast, you could find your racing mind (thoughts) and tense body (sensation) instantly lead in the direction of calm by sliding into a steaming hot bath (behaviour) or finding stillness creep over you in the car to the sound of your favourite piece of music (sensation). Equally you could find that your sense of victimisation (thoughts) at the end of a long tiring week with an overbearing boss is immediately lifted by a phone call from a friend who makes you laugh (sensation) and who persuades you to join them for a movie (behaviour).

You can learn to control and minimise attacks by intervening in all three domains. The first essential tool is awareness – opening your own eyes to what's happening inside you.

YOU CAN'T CHANGE SOMETHING YOU'RE NOT AWARE OF

Sometimes we want to improve the way we do something, in order to get better results and become more efficient. At times, although we can plainly see that we're getting it wrong, we don't quite know why, while at other times we have a total blind spot and don't even realise we're making a mistake to begin with.

On these occasions it is useful to get feedback from someone who will act as a mirror, reflecting our mistakes back to us. Hopefully if we take in the new information and make the necessary changes, then learning occurs. Imagine if you were going for an interview or an audition and were wondering if your presentation was up to scratch. You might ask a friend or someone knowledgeable in the field to give you some feedback so you could tell where your weak spots were and brush up on those skills. That observer would be *paying attention to all aspects of your performance* – from your body language, the volume of your voice and your posture, to the appropriateness of your answers. If they took a video of your performance as you went through the trial run, you would get a lot of information from running through it with them and noticing all the things you were unaware of before. 'Do I really stoop my shoulders like that?' you might think. 'What a silly answer to give to that question, and what's with the nervous laugh?' Only now do these mannerisms become obvious to your awareness in a way they weren't before, and useful to help you change in certain directions.

WHY LEARNING TO WITNESS IS IMPORTANT

A witness is someone who 'looks at something happening'. It implies standing back and observing from a distance. The person who is the victim of a car accident is right inside the car involved, feeling the sensations, thinking the thoughts, playing the role. The experience of a witness to the accident is not so intense. From a distance, they can see the beginning, middle and end of the drama more clearly.

By developing the ability to become a witness to your panic attacks as they happen, to pull back and see what's happening from a more objective position, you can get a lot of helpful information. You're using feedback from yourself – your sensations, thoughts and behaviours. So *witnessing helps you see what's going on and also lessens the intensity of the unpleasant emotions.*

These informed observations are the first step to changing the pattern of panic. Through them you learn to be proactive and scientific about changing your reactions, rather than a helpless victim waiting for the next attack. Think about standing on the platform waiting for a subway train. Unaware of any timetable, and not paying attention, you suddenly find that the train has arrived before you found out the correct platform, without you having been able to catch what its destination was, or gather up your things in time to board. Contrast this with having observed from previous times that a train arrives every eight minutes during weekdays and every fifteen minutes on weekends; that platform 2 is for northbound trains and platform 3 is for southbound ones; that a gust of wind, a noise and a light at the end of the tunnel announces the train's arrival and if you listen, an announcement gives you ample time to notice the destination and move unflustered to the front of the correct platform. In the second scenario you are efficient, in control and calm, because you paid attention.

You can't change what you are unaware of. One of the most frustrating things about panic attacks can be that no matter how hard you may have tried to control them, they can keep happening in spite of your best efforts. Many of your efforts fail because you are *not fully aware of everything* that's happening during an attack. You zone in on certain aspects of it, say breathlessness or dizziness, and become convinced you'll pass out or choke if you don't get outside quickly. This deduction (false but understandable) increases your fear and pushes up your adrenaline, making your symptoms more intense. You have taken premature action (a behaviour), which was based on incorrect information and a partial understanding of what's going on (a thought). While this action may have eased your breathing (sensation), it wasn't for the reasons you thought, and in fact only serves to perpetuate the incorrect belief that 'getting out is the best way to prevent fainting' and reinforces your urge to run in the long term.

By focusing solely on your breathing and catastrophising about what would happen in the future, you didn't give yourself an opportunity to test out anything in the present. In the example above, by staying relaxed and breathing slowly, a new belief was given the opportunity to form.

STAY IN THE PRESENT

A prerequisite to change of any kind is *not to resist what is happening*. However, often the instant reaction at the first sign of a panic attack is 'Oh no! I don't want to have another one!' and every fibre of your being resists the fact that it is happening as you set about trying to avoid it, frantically grasping at the quickest short-term solution that comes to mind.

A necessary prerequisite to sorting out any difficulty is that you first *give it your full attention.* You 'attend' by being fully 'there', with all your senses focused, with your thoughts fully devoted to the present moment, and with an openness to take in new facts, to perceive 'the whole problem' in order to gain maximum information relative to a solution.

Just as your tape recorder cannot lay down new material while in fast forward, but requires you to press the 'stop' button first, if you want to find a new way of looking at your panic attacks, it helps to first *be still and do nothing but observe.*

Focusing your attention only on the present is essential. Only in this way can you become familiar with what is happening right now, rather than trying to prevent what you predict will probably be happening in five minutes' time. Much of the time our thoughts are not on what we're doing in the present moment. We drive cars, cook meals, hold conversations, and even make love while our mind is elsewhere. This habit will not help you rid yourself of panic attacks. You will need to 'school' your awareness to stay focused on all the sensations and thoughts coming up inside you. Within that maelstrom of overpowering emotions and the physical earthquake that a panic attack is, lies your solution. If your mind is somewhere else you'll miss it. At each stage there are choices that would work better than others, but you can only know what to use, and when, if you recognise each stage as distinct from another.

You want to become as adept as a detective in a whodunnit movie, re-running your mental video looking for significant clues.

- The beginning. Do the panic attacks always occur when you're alone? Do they only occur at work? Do they only happen on stressful days? Does any one kind of mood precede them, like being under time pressure, feeling out of your depth, or frustrated? You might notice that before an attack you were involved in a lively argument, or watching a sports event on TV. Or you felt hot as you walked into a crowded pub, got into a steamy shower, or took a lift in a car with the heater on full blast. Is there any one physical symptom that usually occurs first?

- The middle. What thoughts flooded your mind next? How did you respond to them? Did things change for the worse or improve? Were your choices informed or chaotic? For example, while it may be helpful to repeat certain reassuring phrases to yourself, these will not be very effective if you do them while at the same time frantically running to an exit! Your mind is now saying one thing,

'You're safe', and your body is doing the opposite, 'Run for your life!'

- The end. What finally ended it? Was it something external, like a pill, a phone call, or the arrival of a reassuring person? Or did being in a 'safe' place do it, like reaching home, or getting out of the meeting? If so, you'll always be vulnerable if those aren't an option. By placing the control inside yourself, you'll leave behind the sense of being a victim of your panic.

What Does Witnessing Involve?

I recommend that you photocopy the panic attack record (pages 138–139). After carefully witnessing *about five to ten attacks* you'll begin to see trends and patterns. If yours only happen once every few weeks or months, observe instead your level of anxiety in between attacks, noting what makes it go up and down, in what circumstances, etc. If they're night panics, observe what the preceding day was like. Keeping records will never be a waste of time – information is power.

As soon as possible after an attack is over is the best time to fill out your record form. If you wait too long you'll lose the accuracy, and since memories are notoriously coloured by mood, you'll look back at the event through 'anxiety goggles' or 'depression-tinted spectacles'. Then they'll seem worse than they actually were. Recent recall, as soon as possible after the attack has passed, is more trustworthy.

Note *details* like time of day the attack occurred, or when your anxiety peaked, with whom, and whether it was a situation in which you would ordinarily have expected to be on edge. Note whether the attack was expected or 'out of the blue'. Rate its level of intensity on scale of 0 to 10.

PANIC ATTACK RECORD

Date: _____

Time: _____

Duration: _____

Where were you, and with whom (Family, friend or a stranger?)

Were you under stress or relaxed at the time? What mood were you in?
(pressured, worried, depressed, upset?)

Were you expecting to get a panic attack, or surprised?

Were you tired or rested?

Were you asleep before you panicked?

Were you feeling hot or cold?

Rate your fear level: 1 – 2 – 3 – 4 – 5 – 6 – 7 – 8 – 9 – 10

                         Mild   Moderate   Severe

Check off which symptoms you experienced and circle the first one in the
sequence:

Difficulty breathing   ❏

Numbness/pins and needles   ❏

Dizziness/unsteadiness ❑

Feelings of unreality ❑

Hot/cold waves ❑

Racing/pounding heart ❑

Choking sensations ❑

Sweating ❑

Trembling/shaking ❑

Nausea/abdominal upset ❑

Chest pain/tightness ❑

What fears did you have? ❑

    Fear of dying ❑

    Fear of losing control ❑

    Fear of going crazy ❑

    Other fears ❑

Specific thoughts:	e.g. 'I'm going to lose my job over this' or 'what will I do if it doesn't go away?'
Behaviours:	e.g. pacing restlessly, smoking, frantic phone calls
Background concerns:	Any extra challenges, deadlines, tasks, demands.

It helps to observe your *first symptom*. For example, suppose this is always 'difficulty breathing'. In time it may come to your attention that you always have a series of fearful thoughts following this, such as 'I won't be able to get enough air and that would be very dangerous'. That pointer would help you zone in on that misleading information specifically. Also, if you've noticed that breathing features early on in the attack, you might begin to notice that, without realising it, you were in fact breathing faster for a few hours before then, and unwittingly setting up the ideal internal climate (of high adrenaline) for an attack.

MOODS

High levels of anxiety, and moods such as depression make a difference to the likelihood of having an attack. On certain days you may be more preoccupied with fearful, worrying thoughts of the future, such as when several bills arrive together, or when you feel particularly out of your depth at work, with looming deadlines and your boss breathing down your neck. At other times the predominant mood may be anger or frustration, when you feel you've been treated unfairly or been misunderstood, or when despite all your best efforts things still don't happen the way you'd planned. The past may consume your thinking other days, with regret, sadness and depression predominating. These may all be trying to break through into your awareness, nudging you to seek help in sorting out underlying emotional issues.

People often say 'But I wasn't thinking anything when the attack started!' What they mean is that they weren't *aware* of thinking anything – there may well have been impressions or vague subliminal perceptions that fleetingly passed through their consciousness without them realising it fully. Have you ever lost your car keys and could have sworn on a bible that you left them on the hall table? Yet when you retrace your steps you find that in fact, *without being aware of doing it*, you had opened the boot of the car to lift something out and left them hanging from the lock.

Your conscious memory, initially denying any irregularity, had to be prodded to retrieve that information. In panic there are many thoughts that you may not realise you're having, but which are responsible for raising your fear level, and it helps to identify them and eliminate them. The presence of these 'almost thoughts' can be highlighted with practice and their contribution to the beginning of many panic attacks revealed and nipped in the bud.

Many moods have a fear component to them, which will raise your adrenaline and make panic more likely. For example, fear can underpin anger, sadness, frustration, physical exhaustion or depression. Keeping a record of the level of these emotions on a scale of 0 to 10 will reveal any connection. Over a number of weeks you will see trends emerging, and this feedback will help you to track down the specific origins.

In terms of your beliefs, if you have a recurring one such as 'I'm having a heart attack', it gives you a pointer that such gross misinformation needs dismantling. If certain counterproductive behaviours are generating fear, such as being constantly under time pressure, the record will indicate the need to look at why this is a recurring feature in your life and whether there's anything you can do to ease it.

Take the records that Deirdre kept. She was a 42-year-old mother of three who began having attacks after a benign breast lump was found and removed. The first attack occurred on the day before her follow-up appointment, one month after the biopsy. Since then she had been having a few a week, mostly when out in public. Her first symptom was invariably dizziness and 'jelly legs'. She noticed from her records that there were certain days when she found her mind dwelling on her mother, who had died from cancer eighteen months previously. Deirdre had nursed her for the two years before, and her death left a vacuum. Her mother had been her closest friend, and caring for her had provided her with a role vacated by her children, who were now adults and needed her less. The diagnosis of cancer had been a shock, as her mother had been perfectly well.

Deirdre noticed that on these 'moody' days she panicked more. Ultimately she realised that she had a deep-seated anxiety about her own health, and feared that her symptoms of dizziness and unsteadiness might be signs of a brain tumour, which she felt would ultimately kill her like her mother. She had general background anxiety with panic occurring if her adrenaline got high enough. When she made this connection Deirdre came for therapy which helped her address these concerns by giving her correct information (that dizziness does not indicate a brain tumour) and encouraging her to explore her fear of death and let go of her apprehension at the slightest sign of ill-health.

To those who have been panicking for years, and who have resigned themselves to the fact that their panic will be with them for life, it may hearten you to know that I haven't found a correlation between the number of years a person has been having panic attacks and an inability to recover. And to those who think that the cure for their panic lies outside themselves, who have been looking for a pill that 'suits them', or the right time to change – I would encourage you to give up waiting. That dependence keeps you vulnerable and disempowered. If your position is 'cure me but don't ask me to change', this approach may not suit you.

In order to end panic you must be prepared to practise the exercises, to change how you think, to take some (calculated) risks, to explore your mind, and to become an active agent in your own healing.

Are you?

11

BREATHING CALMLY

T he core aim in the campaign to eliminate panic centres on *calming down the fight-flight response and reducing the number of adrenaline molecules in your bloodstream.*

Of all the physical components of the fight-flight response – faster heartbeat, shallow breathing, increased sweating and tensed muscles – the two most amenable to change are those that are the easiest ones to become aware of, your breathing rate and your muscle tension. Changes in these are relatively easy to pick up, and since you can't learn to change something you're not even aware of doing, they're good places to begin learning control skills.

HYPERVENTILATION

Hyperventilation or over-breathing is a state that affects 50 to 60 per cent of people who panic. Often panic attacks can be controlled solely by eliminating this important contributing factor.

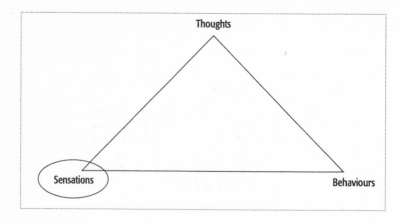

You are hyperventilating when you have a sensation of not being able to breathe normally, of choking or smothering, of tightness or even pain in the chest, or of not being able to get a 'deep enough' breath. This can be happening quite separately from a panic attack, whenever you're feeling stressed or upset. Or it may only develop when a panic attack is already under way, as part of an overall fearful reaction to either a thought ('I'm losing my mind!') or to another worrying symptom such as a racing heartbeat. It is therefore important for you to establish now whether you are hyperventilating or not, because if you are, learning to slow your breathing gives you a very useful tool to use to ease an attack. If you're not, you will still benefit from the exercise in this chapter. This is because slow breathing has a calming effect on heart rate and all other aspects of panic, and is a powerful way for anyone to dampen down their nervous system response.

Hyperventilation is not something to be worried about. It is really just a bad habit – *you're breathing too fast and too shallow*. As such, the problem is that you take in too many breaths every minute, none of which are completely filling your lungs. Shallow breathing is a disorder of rate and rhythm; nothing is the matter with the lungs themselves. This is why, whenever your doctor listens to your chest, he finds nothing wrong, because it all sounds normal to his stethoscope when he asks you to take in 'a big deep breath'. He's not to know you're not normally doing so. No X-ray will pick up anything either, because only actual disease in the lung tissue shows up there, and your lungs themselves are clear. This can lead to misunderstandings, and many people end up wondering if their doctor is missing something.

Hyperventilation can be acute or chronic. The acute form is distressing and uncomfortable, and only happens in short bursts, such as for a few hours, after which it passes. It is obvious to you and sometimes others too. In other words, you would be aware you are doing it.

The chronic form can be going on round the clock, even while you sleep, and while it can be mildly uncomfortable, you may be relatively unaware that you are doing it. It may be a pattern of breathing that's been in place for years.

ARE YOU HYPERVENTILATING?

Do you often feel as if you are unable to take a deep enough breath, as if you can't fill your chest satisfactorily?

When you are worried, pressured or feeling frightened, do you ever hold your breath, or breathe faster and more shallowly?

Do you ever feel as if you're going to suffocate or choke?

Do you occasionally have chest pains or chest tightness?

Do you experience numbness, tingling or 'pins and needles' in your hands and feet?

Do you ever get cramps in your calves?

Have you been yawning a lot, or taking big deep sighs or gulps of air?

If you answer 'yes' to several of these questions, then you're a hyperventilator and this chapter is very relevant to you.

HOW MUCH IS HYPERVENTILATION CONTRIBUTING TO YOUR PANIC?

The following test will show you whether hyperventilation is contributing to your panic symptoms. Sitting comfortably, start breathing very fast, as if you were jogging. Make the in-breaths deep, right down to the base of your lungs. And when you exhale make them forceful, as if you were blowing out candles on a huge cake each time. Keep going for at least a minute and a half if you can, unless you feel you can't go on, in which case don't push yourself, just stop.

When the time is up, close your eyes and let your breathing slow right down, for another two minutes or so.

Were any of the symptoms like the ones you get during your panic attacks or whenever you're really stressed? If you are in the category of people who become afraid the moment their breathing goes out of control, your fear level may have risen to the same level as during an attack. You may have even been afraid to do the exercise at all, or aborted it early on out of apprehension.

Obviously because you knew you were bringing on these symptoms yourself during this experiment, there would not be quite such a high level of fear as there would be if the hyperventilation had begun spontaneously, for example if you awoke during the night gasping for breath. Nonetheless, ask yourself if the symptoms were in any way similar to those of a panic attack. If they were, then hyperventilation is playing a part in your panic attack, and you will get a lot of relief from retraining your breathing to its original slower, deeper rhythm. If you're in doubt repeat the exercise, but for two or three minutes this time.

WHY DOES IT BEGIN?

Supposing some time in your past you were very afraid or extremely stressed. Your adrenaline would have risen and your breathing become fast and shallow. Your mind may have created a conditioned response following that experience, so that whenever your breathing quickens now, fear may automatically accompany it, just like it did that first time. Fear has been twinned with fast breathing, so from that point on if you have one of these sensations, you may get the other too.

In which kind of experiences do fast breathing and fear occur together? Possibly the journey through the birth canal, having an asthmatic attack or pneumonia, or following an abdominal operation or an episode of pain, where it is agony to breathe deeply, and breathing is short and panting. Or any smothering experience, such as when children playfully put pillows over each other's heads or hold each other underwater. Any frightening or traumatic experience, particularly in childhood, can lay down a memory trace of this kind, without you being aware of it.

William had been off sick from work for six weeks. He had been finding it harder and harder lately to force himself to go in. He operated a crane, and spent most of his day in the cabin high above the site. In recent years, being in the cabin distressed him; he felt trapped and tense, as it wasn't easy to get down quickly.

As he sat in my office he was pale and visibly trembling, and kept looking anxiously at the door. His breathing was laboured, like someone with emphysema, and punctuated by the odd huge sigh. He told me that he had first experienced something amiss about thirteen years previously, when he began having episodes of feeling dizzy, disoriented, 'spaced out' and sweaty, and feeling he was going to die. He was convinced he had a brain tumour because nearly all his symptoms seemed to be 'in his head'. It would come and go, and when he began to experience pins-and-needles in his hands, and sometimes a numb feeling in his face, his fears escalated, and his doctor sent him for a brain scan to reassure him. Over the years he had nine of these done, all negative. Still, because the symptoms persisted, the doubt lingered that something was being missed.

He had tried medication for his anxiety, but found that it made him 'woolly-headed' and didn't relieve the unpleasant sensations in his head at all. His wife told me how he had changed over the years from a gregarious, fun-loving man who loved the countryside around their house, walking the fields with the dogs, to a quiet homebody who rarely went out, and who seemed to prefer his own company nowadays. She felt he had aged greatly and although he was only fifty, he had the attitude of an elderly man waiting for death to release him. In the last three months he had deteriorated the most, arriving home looking grey and exhausted after a day fighting off the urge to walk off the site. Since he took sick leave, she often found him up at night making tea, unable to sleep. It was she who had insisted he see me, but he had no real optimism that anything could be done: 'Thirteen years is a long time, doctor.'

I asked him if he would try the hyperventilation experiment, explaining that I felt his breathing might have something to do with his symptoms. Politely cooperating, he began to breathe faster as instructed. Within one minute he was feeling dizzy, and the trembling increased. Terrified, he insisted that he had to stop. I explained to him that this showed that he was hyperventilating, and had been since the whole thing began thirteen years ago. I enquired if anything unusual had been going on that year, anything that might have been particularly stressful or worrying. He drew a blank, nothing unusual at all. I asked him to think about it, and instructed him in slowing his breathing and fully expanding his chest right down to the bottom of his lungs. He found this difficult to do as he was accustomed to using only his upper chest to breathe, with no movement whatsoever going on in his abdomen. But he was impressed at how similar his panic symptoms were to how he felt when he had deliberately hyperventilated, and agreed to practise. In addition I suggested that a relaxation exercise would help him and perhaps improve his sleep.

One week later I saw a different man. The trembling had completely stopped. He had colour in his face, and was smiling broadly. He had practised daily and felt much less dizzy, and in addition felt excited that he might have identified the source of the problem. The year it began he had changed from driving smaller cranes to the taller ones because the pay was much better. The first month on that job happened to be March, and the winds were the highest he could ever remember. After a few days he told his boss that he thought he'd have to stop operating the crane because he was convinced they were heading for a serious accident in such dangerous conditions. The reply was that they had a deadline to meet, and so he endured the following weeks swaying high up in the cabin, terrified and very stressed, but with no option but to continue. This was the initial identity threat, with his very survival on the line. His wife reminded him that he had felt so shaken after that job finished that he was unable to join the family on holiday. He became too nervous to fly (another enclosed space that he would have been unable to leave), something that had never happened before.

I saw William on four more occasions and each time he reported returning more to his former self. By learning to breathe differently he had carved a new groove in his mind. He could now notice his breaths as they began speeding up, during the early stages of a panic attack, without automatically feeling afraid as they did so. This change, plus the reassurance that he did not have a tumour, broke the conditioned response, and with no juice to fuel it, his panic attacks ceased. On the last visit he delightedly told me that he had bought himself a mountain bike, and would be touring during the summer, his first holiday in years.

INFORMATION IS POWER – WHAT'S HAPPENING WHEN YOU OVER-BREATHE?

Since panic is underpinned and fuelled by fear, it is essential to root out any fears about breathing that are unfounded. Information about what's really going on when you hyperventilate can move the entire experience from ominous to temporarily uncomfortable. By removing your fears through having the correct information, you reduce the number of adrenaline molecules in your bloodstream, and so reduce the possibility of a panic attack occurring at all. Even if you're not at all afraid of the experience of hyperventilation, a knowledge of how chest breathing affects panic through changing your internal chemistry can help make sense of why it is essential to stop doing it.

When you inhale, you take in that substance so essential to survival – oxygen (O_2). It enters the lungs and is taken from there into the bloodstream where it is transported around the body. The haemoglobin molecules carry it to wherever it is needed and release it at the site for use by the cells. All cells use oxygen and the waste product of that activity, whether it is a skin cell, a digestive cell in the gut, or a muscle cell, is carbon dioxide (CO_2). This is sent back into the blood by the cells for removal, from there to the lungs, and then exhaled out of the body.

As with any ecosystem, there must be a balance maintained between materials taken in and used, and the waste produced. The normal rate of breathing at rest is around 10 to 14 breaths per minute. For every O_2 taken in, a CO_2 has to be exhaled out of the body. Obviously if you breathe more frequently you increase your O_2 levels and lower your CO_2. Likewise, if you breathe more slowly, you decrease your O_2 and allow your CO_2 to accumulate. So we keep the ratio of O_2 to CO_2 at the appropriate level by slowing down or speeding up our breathing.

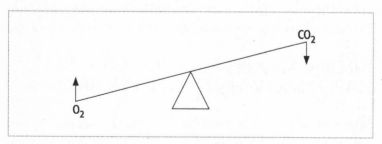

FIGURE 11.1

Hyperventilation is defined as *'a breathing pattern which is too fast and which is providing the body with too much oxygen for its needs'*. There are times when the body needs to take in more O_2, and is producing more CO_2 to be eliminated, such as during exercise, and at these times your breathing becomes faster to cater for this. If less O_2 is needed and less CO_2 produced, such as during sleep or relaxation, then it is fitting that your breathing slows down.

Most of these adjustments occur without your awareness, automatically and unconsciously. The same can be said for the increased rate of breathing that adrenaline causes if it is flooding your bloodstream. You are breathing faster without even knowing it, because your fight or flight response is preparing you for a challenge.

Since hyperventilation is a protective response, it cannot harm you and is not dangerous.

However, unlike the response during exercise, this one can be brought under voluntary control, just like when you breathe faster to blow up a balloon or hold your breath to swim underwater.

The rise in O_2 that results from over-breathing can't do you any harm. However, the corresponding drop in CO_2 leads to the blood becoming more alkaline, and this is what causes many of the unpleasant symptoms, even though they don't harm you. This state is called *respiratory alkalosis*. The changes that occur include:

- Narrowing of blood vessels, including those going to the brain, so less blood is being delivered there.
- With less O_2 reaching your brain cells, you can experience light-headedness, dizziness, confusion, blurred vision, lapses in concentration and memory, difficulty making decisions, and feelings of unreality.
- Haemoglobin becomes more reluctant to release its O_2 for use by the cells when it does reach them. This is called the Bohr

Effect and is the reason why we can feel fatigued over the smallest physical demands. If our cells aren't getting what they thrive on – O_2 – they can't do their job.

- The brain receptors whose job it is to monitor whether the O_2 level is sufficient now pick up a slight drop in the blood level, and *step up the fight or flight response* hoping to rectify it. Result? A panic attack.

Some facts are important here.

- These chemical changes are totally harmless.
- Although you may feel as if you are not taking in enough air, or as if you are choking or smothering, this is not what is actually happening. In fact, you already have too much 'air' inside you as a result of over-breathing.
- You will always be able to take in air, even if it feels like this breath is your last. Even those in a coma continue breathing, although they may have lost consciousness. So even if you fainted you would *always* go on breathing.

If you're hyperventilating at a chronic rate all the time, or at an acute rate on and off over the course of a day, you're going to be tired much of the time. People often find it hard to understand why they have so little energy, but what they fail to take into account is all the extra physical activity involved in faster breathing. They are also using the chest muscles between each rib to increase the breathing rate, rather than their diaphragm, usually the main muscle of respiration, which lies below the ribcage.

As a consequence, the intercostal muscles can become tired and sore, like any overworked muscle. This can feel like a tightness across the chest, or a stabbing pain between the shoulder blades. You may even experience chest pain or pain going down the arm. This is called referred pain and is not originating in your heart, but because these muscles use the same nerve supply as the heart, when they are overused the pain is felt along the shared nerve distribution.

The habit of yawning and sighing (often to the extent where others begin asking if you're bored with the conversation or if they're keeping you up!) has a chemical purpose. It is an effort to readjust the CO_2 imbalance. It is harmless and will disappear when the balance has been restored naturally through breathing retraining.

If you've been hyperventilating for years, your symptoms can be less obvious. That's because your body has developed subtle ways of compensating for marked drops in CO_2, while keeping the blood pH value stable and within normal range. This compensation means that fewer symptoms are produced – in other words they are being masked. Like the heating thermostat in a house, your body is set to a lower CO_2 than originally. Now, whenever even a slight rise occurs, such as happens during a yawn, or when your muscles are at rest standing still in a long queue, it can set off a period of over-breathing, and an unexpected panic attack may follow. The common feeling of claustrophobia in crowded, enclosed places could be because of the subtle change it causes in your CO_2 level.

CALMING THE BREATH

The hyperventilation habit may take a few weeks to change, but most people feel some of the benefits of retraining in the first few days. In the meantime, whenever you notice it, it is best to regard it merely as an uncomfortable nuisance which is there for a logical reason and which will soon be gone. By eliminating any fear of not yet being able to control it, you prevent your adrenaline rising, and reduce the chance of a panic attack.

Healthy breathing is slow and deep, and fills the lungs right to their base, with most of the movement happening in the abdomen. Stressed, fearful breathing, on the other hand, is fast and shallow. It only fills the lungs to about one-third of their capacity, pinched off by too-tight abdominal muscles before the breath can fill the chest properly.

The adrenaline drive calls into action the intercostal muscles as back-up, although they wouldn't normally play much of a role in bringing air in and out of the lungs. That job usually falls to the diaphragm, the muscle lying between the chest and abdomen, which acts like a piston, moving the air in and out. When we are stressed for any lengthy period of time, we get so unused to full deep breaths that our diaphragm, like any rarely used muscle, becomes lazy. On the other hand, our chest muscles suffer from unaccustomed overuse. This pattern of 'upside-down' breathing, where the upper chest is overused and the lower chest underused, is what we are trying to correct by breathing retraining.

The daily practice will require motivation, so remember why you're doing it:

- to control physical symptoms during your panic attacks, such as breathlessness and dizziness;
- to eliminate any unconscious triggers of attacks to which you are sensitive, and afraid of;
- to lower your adrenaline level and move you to a state of relaxation and calm.

Practise the following exercise *twice every day for at least five minutes each time, lying on a bed initially*. Many people find it convenient to do this before getting up in the morning, and just before settling down for sleep. Do it in a quiet, comfortable place where you won't be disturbed. Sitting or lying, breathing through nose or mouth, it doesn't matter.

BREATHING EXERCISE

- Breathe in for a count of 4, then breathe out for a count of 4 (each count being one second on the clock).

- Your breaths don't need to be any bigger in volume than normal, and try to keep the rhythm smooth and fluid. Think of the air as flowing or 'oozing' in and out, rather than being suddenly hauled in or forcibly ejected.

- Allow your abdomen to gently expand as you breathe in, and flatten as you breathe out, keeping the chest as still as possible.

- If this is comfortable, after a few days' work on stretching the breaths, making each one longer. Breathe in to a count of 5, then breathe out to a count of 5. Whenever it becomes comfortable, lengthen the inhale and exhale to 6, then 7, and finally 8.

- Continue until you're confident you have changed your breathing pattern to abdominal and each breath lasts longer.

Some people find that when they begin to pay attention to, and count their breaths, the very fact of focusing on their breathing makes it speed up and feel more uncomfortable. It is as though the moment they tune in to their breathing they become more aware of it as this uncontrollable and unpredictable force that has begun to dominate them, determining how 'good' or 'bad' a day they're going to have. This conditioned response will fade with practice if you think 'calm' as you count your in-breaths and 'relax' as you breathe out ('calm' 2, 3, 4, 'relax' 2, 3, 4).

It is always difficult initially to focus exclusively on the breath, so if you find your mind wandering, don't get fed up or berate yourself – this is normal. Just begin counting again. Concentration comes with practice.

Do not make your breaths bigger than usual. Remember, you are already taking in too much air, so you don't want to over-breathe on your exercise to eliminate over-breathing! Taking in a 'deep' breath doesn't mean sucking in as much air as you possibly can as though to dive under water for a few minutes, while sticking out your chest and holding in your stomach as though you were in an army lineout. It means that the breath travels deeper down to the base of your lungs, but in a natural way with no unusual effort. Nobody should even notice you doing it.

BEFRIENDING YOUR BELLY

The focus of your awareness should be on your abdomen rather than your nostrils or chest. All professionals who make special use of their breathing as part of their work, such as opera singers, dancers, TV presenters, martial artists, or those who play a wind instrument, put their concentration here. Look at the little pot-bellies children have, before the cares of adulthood make their breathing reactive and irregular, as chest breathing tends to be.

Just as the sea always has a gently swelling undertow below even the choppiest of surfaces, so you can access a calm, rolling centre in your abdomen below the agitations of your thinking mind, which you can always call on in order to re-establish calm and balance. In this way your breath can function as an anchor, allowing you to drop below the surface into calmness. The surface worries may still be there but by using this exercise you can learn to leave them there like the little white horses the wind creates, and drop below them. The perspective down deeper is entirely different; you don't have to be tossed and thrown about by every passing thought. Looking from that part of your mind that is calm and stable (your witness) allows you to see more clearly and act from a point of balance. In this way you can begin relating to your belly as an ally.

- Place one hand on your chest and the other on your abdomen around your belly button. Is there any movement going on under your abdominal hand? Or is it all under your chest hand? Try to prevent the chest area from moving more than the belly. Imagine that with each breath you are bringing air in and watching it travel via a tube going from your mouth, bypassing the chest, to fill up a 'balloon' in your abdomen. This is a passive exercise, no force is needed. The air should really inflate the balloon without any help from you. On the inhalation you allow the balloon to fill, and the hand on your abdomen to rise; on the exhalation you watch it deflate and your hand fall, keeping your chest fairly motionless.

All the action is down where the balloon is filling and emptying. You must allow your abdominal muscles to loosen like the child's pot-belly. A 'holding in' attitude would be the equivalent to the balloon being prevented from expanding with the incoming air. (The main cause of the Victorian woman's tendency to 'swoon' was the tightness of her bodice, which prevented her taking in adequate-sized breaths.) By allowing more space for your breath to travel right down to the base of your lungs, rather than being pinched off further up by tight muscles, your in-breaths will take longer and subsequently your out-breaths also. The full cycle lengthens, and over the course of a minute you'll be taking fewer but longer breaths.

If you are a habitual chest breather, this relaxing of the belly muscles and slowing of the rhythm may initially feel uncomfortable for you, and you may find yourself wanting to take a big gulp of air. If you have to, take your gulp and return to the exercise. This urge will decrease with practice. Or if you find yourself breathing in a jerky 'staircase' fashion, it is simply because your diaphragm has been out of action for a long time. This too will become smoother with practice.

If you find it impossible to get the feeling of air going down to the abdomen while keeping your chest still, try this other position. Lie on the floor on your stomach with your forehead resting on your hands. This makes it easier to still the chest.

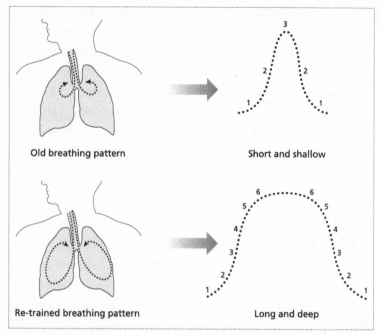

Old breathing pattern

Short and shallow

Re-trained breathing pattern

Long and deep

FIGURE 11.2 ABDOMINAL BREATHING

It can feel unnatural and laborious learning to be aware of a process that should be on 'automatic pilot'. Some find it tiresome and difficult to pay attention for any length of time. If you are one of this group, I would ask you to remember what it was like when you first learned to drive. Paying attention to so many variables seemed impossible, yet within a short space of time you were hopping into the car and going through all the steps without even realising it. It had become automatic. The same will happen with breathing re-training. The day will come when you'll find yourself doing it automatically and without trying.

Once the exercise is familiar and easy for you, start extending it to other locations, while sitting or walking. Do it during the ads while watching TV. Or waiting at red lights in the traffic. Observe whether you're breathing fast or slow periodically during the day, by checking it whenever you do certain regularly occurring activities. We all use the bathroom several times a day, so check if you've been chest breathing in the space of time it takes to walk down the hall. Or during the few minutes it takes to make yourself a cup of tea or coffee. Or let the phone ring one more time and in those few seconds ask yourself if you've been shallow breathing. If you find you have been, just shift it to abdominal. Gradually see if you can weave the notion of 'remembering your breath' into as many aspects of your life as you can so it becomes second nature.

BREATHING DURING A PANIC ATTACK – SWAPPING FLIGHT FOR FIGHT

Of course, aside from resetting the CO_2 thermostat over the course of your weeks of practice, the skill will come into its own when you feel a panic attack coming on. Instead of your thoughts racing with fearful predictions, you now have a method of controlling the symptoms you're so afraid of. With your awareness zoning in on something different, you feel you have another option when panic begins, rather than going the old route and being thrown off balance by your own conditioned knee-jerk reactions. *Make your breath act like a path that you can follow to lead you out of confusion to safety.*

As the symptoms begin, just focus on counting your breaths and nothing else. Anchor yourself to it and you'll find the symptoms subsiding. Also remind yourself:

- Although you may feel as if you are not getting enough air, or as if you are choking or smothering, this is not what is actually happening. In fact, you have more than enough 'air' inside you as a result of over-breathing.
- You will always be able to take in air, even if it feels like this breath is your last. Even those in a coma continue breathing, although they may have lost consciousness. So even if you fainted you would always go on breathing.

• The chemical changes in hyperventilation are totally harmless.

In order to really have success with abdominal breathing, an important commitment has to be made within yourself which changes everything. The decision *to stay and face the panic* is a crucial step, instead of doing whatever you would normally do, like running for the exit, or pacing up and down, or beginning to drive home. *It means trusting* in a manoeuvre which you don't yet know will work. There is no way out of taking these steps if you really want to gain control over this condition that's crippling you. However, look at it this way. You've placed your trust in the flight side of the fight or flight equation so far, by always running out of the situation, or avoiding it, and where has it got you? Your panic is still there! So why not try the opposite position – deciding to stay and face it. Give it a try at least, you won't be sorry. Just by taking that stance you make an internal statement that declares 'I'm not quite as afraid as I was before', and that alone means less adrenaline already!

Abdominal breathing can be much more easily done during an attack if you've already practised it a number of times at home, and are familiar with it. When an attack begins, just stop where you are and begin counting your breaths, with one hand on your abdomen to make sure the air is reaching all the way to the bottom of your lungs. If your chest is still heaving, it means you're not breathing slowly enough.

Stay in the present. Do try to stay focused on counting the breaths. You're in the future if you're trying to figure out where the exit is, whether this disorder will be with you for life, or what people will think. By changing your O_2/CO_2 balance you will send important messages back to your brain that 'all is well, no more adrenaline is needed right now', so the supply stops and the level drops. It is counterproductive to the breathing exercise if you're thinking fear-loaded thoughts at the same time, rushing for the outside or driving fast to get home sooner, since these all raise adrenaline further and your breathing can't have much effect. So give it a chance, stay still, count, and trust that your chemistry is changing and that it will soon be over. The feeling of success is fantastically morale-boosting and makes you feel much more optimistic about the future.

Add an affirmation – on the in-breath you could say 'I'm breathing in calm' and on the out-breath 'I'm breathing away fear'.

12

MUSCLE RELAXATION

KEYNOTE: LOOSENING UP AND LETTING GO

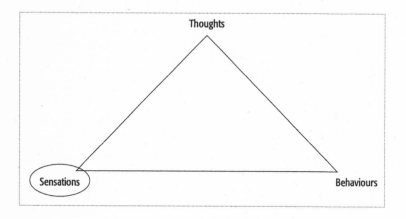

Thoughts

Sensations

Behaviours

You may find that when you panic there is not much change in your breathing pattern. It may be other symptoms such as a racing heart or a 'spacey' feeling, trembling or sweating which affect you more. Learning muscle relaxation is a very effective way to calm down your sympathetic nervous system and reduce all these sensations. It also activates the relaxation response, an expression of the parasympathetic or restoration wing of your nervous system. This directly helps panic symptoms because by taking one single aspect of the fight or flight reaction – muscles primed for action – and moving them towards calm, you change all the other variables in the package (breathing, sweat and heart rate). Since the response also includes your thoughts, these quieten also, and things begin to take on a calmer perspective, with fewer fearful bulletins flashing up on the screen of your mind.

To prepare for action, muscles must become a lot more active and energetic. This is referred to as 'tension' and has an obvious survival value. It is difficult to imagine running for your life or fighting off danger if your muscles are in a relaxed or laid-back state. Your muscles brace themselves once your brain, which has picked up an incoming threat, gives them the 'go-ahead'. Whenever we're worried about something, we often hunch our shoulders, fidget, pace around or screw up our facial muscles into a frown. A body on alert looks and acts very differently from a calm one!

Constant bracing of the muscles in this way can lead to headaches, jaw problems, shoulder aches, back trouble and, of course, extreme tiredness. In the caveman scenario, his battle with a wild animal would have been time-limited. The adrenaline accumulated in his muscles would have been burned off in the course of the chase, leaving him relaxed once more when it was all over. Since our modern-day threats are not so cut and dried, we are frequently awash with adrenaline around the clock as one crisis blends into another, and our muscles never really go 'off duty'.

In such a climate it is hard to distinguish a relaxed muscle from a tense one, because they're in 'go' mode most of the time, and an appreciation of what relaxed feels like is lost. For this reason learning the skill of 'turning off and tuning out' benefits almost everyone, but particularly panickers, who will only be having attacks because their adrenaline is already running high. These exercises *make you aware of tension as it is building up*. Once you spot it, you now have a new choice. Whenever you feel anxious, way before you reach the threshold for panic, you can use your awareness of rising muscle tension to alert you to triggers from outside influences, and in that way head off attacks by dampening down the response before it really takes hold.

If the state of tension begins to be less frequent, and your physiology in general is calmer, this means there are fewer instances when you have to endure the sensations that you fear, and which start the panic reaction. For those who have a conditioned response in play from the past, where tension symptoms have always been 'twinned' with a feeling of fear even when no real present-day threat exists, then by learning to voluntarily calm your body whenever you feel tense, you lay down a new groove in your mind.

LEARNING TO FLOW

There are many situations in which we cannot gain control by struggling, or putting up a fight, since by its nature our opponent cannot be controlled. Difficult people, bad weather and unpredictable events fall into this category. Likewise, there are many situations from which we cannot flee, although we might dearly love to. The more appropriate tactic for these situations is to learn to flow along with them, and ride out the turbulence until it is over, keeping your body calm and not wasting your energy on something you can't influence anyway.

> As a philosophy, relaxation is encouraging an attitude of choosing, at times, to neither fight nor flee, but to flow.

DEEP MUSCLE RELAXATION

Some points before you begin:

- For learning any new skill it is best to have optimum conditions at the beginning. This exercise will take 15 to 20 minutes, so don't stress yourself by 'squeezing it in' under pressure, or when you're expecting a phone call right afterwards, or someone to call to the door. Your antennae will be primed if this is the case and you won't learn a thing; you will only waste your own time. Better not to do it under these conditions, as you'll likely make the interpretation that 'relaxation doesn't work' and go back to thinking that you'll never be able to control your stress, a victim stance that could have been avoided by practising this exercise properly.

- Don't do it while you're doing something else at the same time. You wouldn't expect to learn to play the piano at the same time as talking on the phone, so devote yourself solely to the exercise by not combining it with, say, driving or child-minding. (Yes, people do. One patient of mine wondered why it wasn't working well and on enquiry I found that she had been doing it while she was ironing! So I emphasise this point now.) Initially, lying down or sitting in a comfortable chair works best, *by yourself in a quiet place behind closed doors* where you won't be disturbed.
- The attitude to adopt is one of *passively allowing, rather than trying to make something happen*. Deep down you remember how to relax, even if it was as far back as when you were a child. So you're not really learning a new skill, but rather re-familiarising yourself with one you once knew. Effort makes your muscles active, and you're seeking the opposite effect. So if you are a person who feels that 'anything can be accomplished if you try hard enough', you'll find an exception here. Fostering a passive attitude helps also when it comes to managing an attack, because 'making it work' smacks of meeting a challenge, and an implicit fear should you fail. This raises adrenaline, the opposite of what you're aiming for. 'Allowing', on the other hand, implies a certain acceptance, or agreement to experience whatever happens, to flow with that, and this has a flavour of courage and the security of knowing you can withstand it, a lower-adrenaline stance.
- If your body has been 'braced' or 'on guard' for a long period, maybe even years, when you find your muscles relaxing it may feel to you that you are leaving yourself open, vulnerable and unprotected. It is as though your bodyguard has momentarily abandoned you, and this provokes anxiety in a very small

minority of people. If this happens, just stop for a minute, remind yourself that you are in fact safe, and that it is just an old protective habit that's about to become extinct. Then start again. With time this will happen less, as your body feels reassured that it is OK to loosen up.

- Many people find it useful to have a recording of this exercise, which they then play back to themselves. They feel they can relax better if their eyes are closed, and all they have to do is listen to the tape. It also becomes a portable aid which they can do in a variety of locations such as a parked car, on a plane, or on the subway. In situations of particular challenge, such as one you've been phobically avoiding, it can provide a familiar and reassuring anchor, reminding you how you've been successfully reducing your fear at home.
- Rate your tension on a scale of 1 to 10 (10 being the worst) before you begin, and compare it with your level of tension when you've finished. By quantifying it, you become more specific and less likely to use meaningless, vague terms like 'awfully high' or 'terribly bad'.

DEEP MUSCLE RELAXATION EXERCISE

Lying or sitting in a comfortable chair, close your eyes. Take a nice satisfying deeeeeeep breath … and as you do so be aware that you are leaving behind the outside world. With your body no longer involved with external things you have made the commitment to go inward, to disengage from the all the struggle and striving happening in your life. Give your thoughts permission to take a break from problem solving for a while and instead to travel with your muscles through this exercise. Take another nice deeeeeeep breath … Feel yourself sinking down into the bed or chair beneath you.

Lightly place your attention now on the top of your head, and all the muscles around your scalp. Imagine loosening a tight headband around that area, and feel the muscles relaxing and stretching out, letting all their tension drain away. Take another wonderful deeeeeep breath … and as you let it out, breathe away some of the tension you've been holding. It feels soooo good to let it leave.

Now place your attention on the area around your forehead and temples. Feel the furrows in your brow relax, and realise how good it feels to have your eyes closed, your lids heavy as your eyeballs feel like they're dropping back into your head. Take another nice satisfying deeeeep breath … and as you let it out, feel your body becoming heavier and more relaxed.

Going down now to your cheeks and facial muscles, feel them go slack and loose, and let your jaw drop open a little to release any tension on the joint. Another nice deeeeep breath … and as you let it out you're sinking further inside, to that place deep within you that is always at peace.

Put your attention gently now on the muscles at the back of your neck, particularly those places that shoulder all your burdens; imagine a pair of hands massaging them, working in deep, circular movements. Take another nice deeeeeeep breath … and as you let it out, feel these muscles becoming like jelly, letting go of all their tightness. Feel those massaging hands easing away any knots where tension is being held. It feels sooooo good to let down the load for a while. Feel your body get heavier and heavier as you sink deeper into the bed or chair.

Now travel in your mind down your arms, allowing your muscles to become as loose and floppy as the arms of a rag doll. As you do, imagine the air coming in through your mouth and swirling down both arms. On down past your elbows, your arms are completely off duty now, not planning on doing a thing, limp and loose. Take another nice deeeeeep breath … and as you let it out, feel yourself sinking further, dropping down into that calm centre inside which is always at peace, always there for you to retreat to in order to know that 'the essential you' is OK.

Moving down to your hands now, let your wrists and fingers become heavy and loose also. Feel the weight of them resting against the bed or chair, be aware of them having no need for tension or activity of any kind at this moment. They're not planning on doing a thing, completely off duty. Take another nice deeeeep breath ... and as you do so, see the breath swirling down into your hands, as though filling a pair of empty gloves. Your arms from the shoulders down are feeling heavy, relaxed and warm.

Place your attention lightly on your chest, and as you breathe in, see the air filling the top, then the middle and then going right to the base of your lungs. Just allow your chest to fill itself, don't try to force air in, and be aware for a few breaths of the wonderful rhythm of 'in and out' that occurs, supporting you every day. Peaceful breathing is slow and satisfying. Let it carry you to that place of inner stillness.

Now move your mind's eye down to your abdomen. Take another nice deeeeeeep breath ... and let go of any tightness or holding-in there. Feel your gut relax. This is the centre where we process our emotions, so with each breath allow them to feel soothed and eased. Let the breath be like a healing ointment bringing comfort to any area that needs soothing.

Move your attention round now to your back, and become aware of how nice it feels to be supported. You can let the muscles flop, as they relax back into the bed or chair, allowing it to take your full weight, feeling heavier and more relaxed all the time. Another nice deeeeeep breath ... You are so relaxed and loose now.

Follow your backbone all the way from your neck down into your pelvis, and allow the large muscles in the buttocks to go loose and slack. Then move your attention on down into the thigh muscles, and allow the breath to swirl down past your knees and into your ankles and feet. Register how they feel leaning against the bed or the ground, how restful it is not to have to be going anywhere at all. Take another nice deeeep satisfying breath … Your body feels so at peace, so aware of its need to let go.

To intensify this feeling say it in words to yourself now:

> **'My mind and body can be relaxed and calm. I can know peace and stillness whenever I choose.'**

A mini-version of this can be done if you're on the go and feel a moment of tension which you want to dissolve.

- Stop what you're doing, be still, and close your eyes.
- Imagine a waterfall of healing white light pouring down on your head from a point above you. As it covers your head and face you feel your racing mind being soothed, and your facial muscles loosen. Visualise it pouring over your shoulders, running down your arms, and covering your chest. As it does so all the muscles in its path go loose and slack, and your breath slows down. As the waterfall of light reaches your abdomen, any tight or held-in muscles go limp. Flowing down past your legs, it relaxes all in its path, and as it reaches your feet, you are aware of your entire body feeling calm and peaceful.

HOW TO USE THESE EXERCISES

You are learning this skill *to instruct your body, anywhere and anytime, to calm itself* – in other words, to achieve control. The exercise becomes a tool that you can use when you are facing any increase in your adrenaline, either when you're stressed and tense or when you've just detected one of the early symptoms of an imminent panic attack.

As with the learning of any new skill, your expectations must be in line with what it takes to acquire it. For example, you wouldn't be surprised if after your first piano lesson you couldn't play the 'Moonlight Sonata'. You'd agree that it takes a series of lessons. Relaxation is child's play compared to learning the piano, but there are some who, if they don't get the instant control they were hoping for on the first few tries, stop doing it, saying it 'doesn't work'. If you are finding it difficult to relax, it is more than likely simply an indication of how long your body has been tense, and how ingrained that habit now is. Or it can mean that you're trying to force a result instead of trusting that it will happen. (This may even be an aspect of your personality that creates stress for you.) By no means does it mean that you can't learn it or should give up.

The full-length exercise should be done *at least once a day*, more if you are very anxious. Make the time. If you find you can't get fifteen minutes to do something important for your health, this may also be an indicator of your overall problem. The more frequently you return to that calm centre within you, the more reluctant you will be to allow external circumstances and thoughts to push you off course and away from it. With repetition the ability to relax comes more and more rapidly. Once you're aware of what it feels like to fully relax, then, by contrast, you'll recognise instantly when you've moved into tension. That's why it is important to practise often, so that the appreciation of the contrast is kept sharp and you can more easily pick up the very first early signs of tension, rather than detecting it at the last minute, just as the panic attack is upon you.

Remember the story of the frog in the pot. If a frog is thrown into a pot of boiling water, it will struggle to get out and then pretty quickly die. However, if it is put in a pot of cold water and the water heated up one degree at a time until it eventually reaches boiling point, a different thing happens. The frog doesn't struggle at all, one minute you look and it is alive and the next it is dead. Boiling point came upon him suddenly, without giving him time to jump out. The motto is that if the rise in heat – or in your case tension – is subtle enough to escape the radar of your awareness, you won't have the choice to do anything about it. Suddenly it'll be too late, and you'll find yourself in the throes of a panic attack! The point of this exercise is to increase your awareness, so that it doesn't creep up on you, and you will have the opportunity to intervene early on from a position of *conscious choice rather than last-minute desperation.*

FROM QUIET CUL-DE-SAC TO RUSH HOUR TRAFFIC

Learner drivers perfect their three-point turns and parking skills in a quiet cul-de-sac or car park before taking that skill out on the road and into the challenges of the rush hour traffic. In order to use relaxation as a tool to battle daily tension, and panic in particular, the same applies. If you have done your practice for a week or two in a quiet place, where you've gained confidence in achieving the relaxed feeling, then it is time to move it out into daily life. If you try to use it too soon, before you have achieved some proficiency at it, and if it fails to eliminate a panic attack because you're not adept enough at it, this may leave you disillusioned. So try to familiarise yourself well with it first.

Obviously the level of relaxation you'll achieve when you're at your desk or walking along cannot be the same as when you're stretched out on your bed, but many of the principles are the same. You are still lowering your adrenaline level and that's what counts, because you are then keeping it below the threshold for a panic attack. The main thing is that you've developed the concept that *you can consciously choose to relax your muscles* anywhere, anytime. By doing so, you're sending a strong statement to your brain that 'things are fine down here in my body, there's no emergency, so don't put out any more adrenaline'. With no continued supply there is no fuel for a panic attack.

Awareness of your level of muscular tension as you lie with eyes closed should then graduate to awareness of it occurring in the course of your day, when your body is active and on the go. It can be laborious remembering to check how tense your muscles are. That's because relaxing is something that usually happens automatically without you having to oversee it. The thing is, your body has forgotten how to use the 'calm' button itself, so you have to re-train it. It helps if you piggyback your monitoring on to some routine activities that we all do a few times every day – brushing your teeth, having tea and coffee breaks, taking phone calls, visiting the bathroom, waiting at traffic lights, sitting through the ads on the TV. Whenever you're doing one of these, take ten seconds to ask yourself – 'On a scale of 0 to 10 (10 being the worst), how tense have I been in the last hour?'

If you find you've let the tension creep up, then do something about it. Take a few seconds, nobody need even know, and do the mini-version of your relaxation exercise to bring it down. If you need to, you can always make some excuse to go outside, to get something from the car perhaps, or take a few more minutes in the bathroom. Review what ways you've been moving, thinking and breathing for the last while and see if you can do it in a more relaxed way. You'll also begin to notice themes with your scoring, such as the fact that all the high scores are in a certain context or when a certain person is present, or when you haven't slept well or if you have a hangover. It is all information to allow more informed choice-making.

For example, you may notice that you have a regular tendency to run high scores whenever you have to go out socially. You may then connect these high scores with the fact that often a panic attack occurs later on during that evening. This information – high muscle tension coupled with socialising – can help you to seek help with whatever it is about mixing with people that puts you on edge or challenges you. It also gives you an opportunity to see whether bringing down the tension in your body would reduce the likelihood of having an attack, and in future times help you feel more in control when you're out.

Remember the reason for trying to achieve control of physical symptoms. It is to *gradually reduce the intensity of the arousal of the nervous system,* not to 'make it stop now' or to prevent 'dire consequences' occurring. These smack of magical and muddled thinking, and should not be applied to the practice of methodically learning a skill. If executed properly, with persistence and commitment, these exercises will achieve the results you want.

13

CATASTROPHIC THINKING

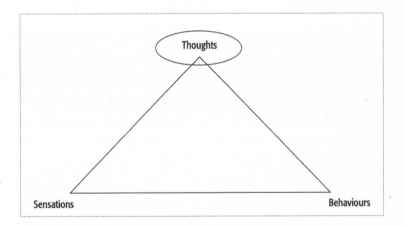

As a result of keeping records of your panic attacks, you will begin to notice patterns emerging. For example, you may see that a spiral effect occurs where, following the original trigger or cue, say a hot sweaty feeling or uncomfortable breathing, what follows is *an interaction between your thoughts, bodily sensations and behaviours that spirals upwards into more fear*. Each thought has a knock-on effect on sensations and actions, which results in a sequence beginning, where each component 'ups the ante' on the last one, like falling dominoes. These sequences or patterns are the first step in showing yourself that *panic is a reaction – not some automatic response over which you have no control.* Calling it a reaction implies that you can become familiar with what you're reacting to and learn how to interrupt the spiral.

Take Tina's Story. It is a busy week in the office, and there's an important client attending a presentation today. Over the last few weeks Tina has been feeling tense and irritable because things haven't been going that well with her boyfriend. He's been out with his own friends a lot more than usual, which she has found worrying. She didn't sleep well last night and the train was packed on the way to work, something she always hates. As the time approaches for the meeting her boss tensely inquires if she has all the figures. 'This meeting is an important one, Tina, so let's make sure it goes OK.' Tina thinks to herself *'I simply cannot mess this up, she'd give me hell.'* Shortly afterwards, as the meeting begins, a hot, sweaty wave passes over her. Her mind races looking for ways she could excuse herself, but there are none which don't involve a major loss of face. Her chest is tight now and there seems to be very little air in the room. Thinking *'I'll faint if I don't get out'*, she bolts for the door.

Let's review the record she made of this attack to see what we can glean from the sequence of events that led up to it, and how the various aspects interacted to spiral into an attack.

PANIC ATTACK RECORD

Date: *10 November*

Time: *11 a.m.*

Duration: *5 minutes*

Where were you, and with whom? (Family, friend or a stranger?)	*At an important meeting with my boss and a new client.*
Were you under stress or relaxed at the time? What mood were you in? (pressured, worried, depressed, upset?)	*I felt my boss was impatient with me, as I'd taken a few sick days the previous week. I knew my help was crucial to provide the figures, so I felt under pressure.*
Were you expecting to get a panic attack, or surprised?	*I wasn't surprised since I was so tense that morning.*
Were you tired or rested?	*Tired. I hadn't been sleeping lately.*
Were you asleep before you panicked?	*Awake.*
Were you feeling hot or cold?	*I was hot and flustered from the moment I got to the office.*
Rate your fear level:	1 – 2 – 3 – 4 – 5 – 6 – 7 –(8)– 9 – 10
	Mild　　　Moderate　　(Severe)

Check off which symptoms you experienced and circle the first one in the sequence:

Difficulty breathing	❑
Numbness/pins and needles	❑
Dizziness/unsteadiness	❑
Feelings of unreality	❑

Hot/cold waves	❑
Racing/pounding heart	❑
Choking sensations	❑
Sweating	❑
Trembling/shaking	❑
Nausea/abdominal upset	❑
Chest pain/tightness	
What fears did you have?	*Fear of fainting*
	Fear of losing control
	Fear of ultimately losing everything, job, boyfriend, etc.
Specific thoughts:	*'I'll faint if I don't get out for air'*
	'I'll die of embarrassment if I lost control.'
	'I'm going to lose my job over this.'
	'Why is this happening to me?'
Behaviours:	*Escape. Then wait to face my boss when the meeting is over.*
Background concerns:	*Relationship strain*

This is the first boyfriend Tina has had for many years. At school she was agonisingly shy and missed out on all the usual fun that her sisters enjoyed. In her opinion her shyness ruined her childhood. Over the years she had managed to gain some confidence and had a few boyfriends. She got a few panic attacks after smoking dope at a party six months previously, and ever since then she has been edgy and nervous of having more attacks, and sometimes avoids going out. This feels very reminiscent of her childhood pattern of withdrawing and then missing out. This has been making her irritable, and her boyfriend thinks she's cooling about the relationship because she has felt too ashamed to tell him about her nervousness socially. The extra pressure this morning is only the tip of the iceberg.

The sequence:

1. Extra work to be prepared for meeting.   (behaviour)

2. Tense, hot and sweaty.   (sensation)

3. Thinks 'I can't panic here'.   (thought)

4. Chest tightness.   (sensation)

5. Thinks 'I'll suffocate – I must get out'.   (thought)

6. Escapes.   (behaviour)

This chapter looks at the contribution made to panic attacks by fearful thoughts or beliefs. If Tina had been able to think differently at stage 3 or 5 of the sequence, the spiral might have ended right there, and she could have gone on with the meeting. If she had realised that although she felt uneasy and it wasn't a pleasant feeling, there was no actual threat to her, that she was safe, then the adrenaline cascade would not have been activated at all, and she would have felt what we all feel from time to time, slightly nervous, but not panicky.

If Tina had learned to control her physical sensations, she might have stopped the sequence at stage 4, because she could have felt enough in control of her breathing to see the meeting through. She could also learn to confront her fears by changing her behaviour, staying put long enough to see if it was possible to lay down new empowering experiences and beliefs, instead of automatically running.

IDENTIFYING THE THOUGHTS THAT WIND YOU UP

If you tell yourself incorrect information about panic, these thoughts will frighten you and cause the panic sequence to begin. In this chapter you are going to learn more direct techniques for modifying these self-statements. If you bring your fear level down a few notches, you reduce the amount of circulating adrenaline, which is the very engine behind panic.

Correcting what you tell yourself is in effect undermining the very structure that panic is built on.

Most people find that it is easier to reassure themselves with the correct facts at a time when they're calm, but when they're panicked it is much harder to believe the same facts; it really does feel as if they're about to collapse, faint or die! This shows the strong connection that exists between emotions and thoughts. When we're sad and depressed it is difficult to access any happy thoughts, and when we're afraid, it is difficult to have any safe thoughts.

The reason for this is that thoughts and emotions are all part of a hormonal reaction which is happening in your bloodstream.

Here's an analogy. If you drink alcohol, as the molecules flood your bloodstream you find your consciousness changing, which is the very reason why most people like it. Life seems subtly a little less harsh and your stresses more manageable and less worrying. If you take a small amount, say one or two drinks, you notice only a minimal change. You're still very much in touch with reality, which is now slightly 'coloured' by a more relaxed frame of mind. If you've consumed, let's say, ten or twelve drinks, your consciousness will have shifted dramatically.

Looking at someone in this drunken state, you marvel at how it is like talking to someone from another planet, their perspective is so different. They really do sincerely believe that they are still capable of driving their car, that the attractive blonde across the room is flirting with them, that their jokes are the funniest ever heard, or that another guy is trying to pick a fight with them! Looking on, we can all see that none of these is really true. However, from their alcohol-loaded viewpoint, *what is appearing on the screen of their perception is indisputably true*. Next day, when the molecules of alcohol have left their system, they may cringe in disbelief as others recall the antics they got up to. 'Where was my head?' they might wonder. It was involved in a molecular event that dictated what thoughts they would and could have.

Now let's relate this to panic. The first difference is that the source of the molecules is inside you rather than from a glass. The second difference is that your consciousness moves in the direction of fear rather than enjoyment. So in the initial stages you notice only a few worrying thoughts and a slight restlessness that makes your body feel a little more on edge and tense. Basically though, reality is still the same, although perhaps not quite as user-friendly. With a sizeable increase in the number of adrenaline molecules floating round your bloodstream, you begin perceiving an entire world that others do not. You feel self-conscious, think that you'll make a mess of whatever you're doing, that you're stupid, your job is on the line, your future looks grim, if you haven't died from a heart attack, etc. To you this is the indisputable truth. It will remain so as long as the molecular blood level of adrenaline stays high. You know how you feel after the attack is over? Don't you often feel disgusted with yourself for having bought into such ridiculous, irrational thoughts, made such a panicky phone call home, or let yourself down by running from the room? That's because your perspective has changed back to normal as the adrenaline level drops, just like the drunk the morning after.

The point is, you need to learn to place less faith in these catastrophic thoughts, and stop confusing them with truths. Since they come and go with the molecular level, they can't be relied on. Truths remain no matter how high or low our molecules go.

TRACKING DOWN THE CULPRIT – PINPOINTING FEARFUL THOUGHTS

You might be saying to yourself 'I don't tell myself anything when I panic, except to wonder what on earth is happening to me!' There are occasions when you will be unaware of having had frightening thoughts, because *they were obscured by the physical sensations which were happening at the same time*, and which were taking centre stage. So in the middle of coping with your heart racing or your head swimming, you may not have been aware of the influence of your thoughts on the situation. This has been called *automaticity* and implies that the thoughts appear as automatically as your hand would shoot out in front to break your fall if you tripped on the rug. You would not be aware of your arm moving as it was doing so, only afterwards. It is the same with the thoughts that try to alert us to danger. In the same way that you wouldn't want that arm shooting out reflexly in inappropriate situations (like during meetings at work or when out socialising), you need to learn how to control those fearful thoughts, so they stop setting off false alarms, and causing panic attacks in neutral, non-threatening settings.

These almost subliminal thoughts may vary with the situation. One time they may warn you not to draw embarrassing attention to yourself, another time they may warn you of the dangers of being alone or too far away from medical assistance if you get an attack. So sometimes you have to search quite hard for the specific content of the fearful thoughts. With practice you'll learn to go from 'I wasn't thinking anything' to 'I was afraid of my boss's anger', like Tina earlier, and with this shift you now have unveiled a concrete belief or set of thoughts to work on changing. For example, Tina can now go on to examine why she places such emphasis on her boss not getting angry, and the predictions she makes of what that would mean. This might lead her to connect it all back to the shyness in her early years that prevented her learning to assert herself and put forward her point of view with confidence. Perhaps she might see that if she had told her boss and her boyfriend that she was feeling panicky, they would have been supportive and she could learn that it is safe to show your vulnerability, rather than hide it and withdraw (as she did in her childhood), causing misunderstandings.

BOTTOM LINE BELIEFS

With a bit of detective work you can work your way past the superficial thoughts and beliefs that contribute to an attack getting worse, right down to the source or bedrock fears that you may never have acknowledged to yourself before.

Saying 'I felt awful' or 'I felt terrible' is far too global and isn't specific enough to challenge. Ask yourself to unpack the term a bit – what precisely was so horrible about it? What aspects made it terrible? What exactly did you envisage happening? What is so frightening to you about losing control? Constantly seeking clarification as you move through the surface layers, you eventually reach the culprit, the *source belief* that underpins all the others.

Let's ask Tina

Tina	'My biggest fear was that I'd have to leave the meeting suddenly, which I had to do once before.'
Question	'What do you predict would have happened if you had stayed?'
Tina	'I try not to think about that, something terrible I guess, that's exactly why I leave, to prevent it.'
Question	'Prevent what exactly, do you know?'

Tina	'No, it makes me uneasy even thinking about it.'
Question	'Imagine yourself back in the meeting, right before you left. You are feeling scared and trapped, but you can't leave. Run the video. What happens to you?'
Tina	'I'm not going to be able to breathe in that hot stuffy room, and that'll feel awful.'
Question	'What do you mean exactly when you say that not being able to breathe is awful? What's awful about it?'
Tina	'Well, it would terrify me'.
Question	'Why?'
Tina	'Because of not being able to take in enough air, and…'
Question	'And what do you see happening then?'
Tina	'I suppose, well if you don't get air in you die of suffocation, don't you?'
Question	'Is that what you see when your mind runs the mental video?'
Tina	'Yes, I imagine I'd fall to the ground, clutching my throat, and gasping my last breath…dying.'
Question	'So basically behind your warning to yourself that if you don't leave you'll feel "awful", are images of terrible things happening to you, ending in death, for which there is no medical evidence, and which you feel were prevented happening by leaving?' *(Source belief)*
Tina	'Well yes, because when I get outside it eases, so it does work.'
Question	'What about the feeling of losing control? What exactly do you mean by that?'
Tina	'I don't really know what it means, just that anything could happen and I'd have no way of stopping it.'
Question	'What kinds of things might happen? Run the video for me.'
Tina	'Well, that I wouldn't be able to stop the feelings getting stronger and they might overwhelm me.'

Question	'And then?'
Tina	'Then I'd lose it, go blank, freeze up and everyone would think I was weird. After that I'd never be able to face anyone and I certainly wouldn't get my job back!'
Question	'So when you warn yourself not to lose control, you're making fairly specific predictions about what would happen, which are not in any way based on fact or medical evidence. (*Source belief*) Is it possible that your escape behaviour is guided by the belief that losing control is a very strong possibility when in fact it is not?'

As you can see, Tina needed to elaborate on and tease out which specific thoughts she was frightening herself with, before she could challenge them and replace them with sound factual truths that could make her feel safer. Chapter 5, Myths about Panic, deals specifically with the kinds of threat-filled beliefs that lead people to make inaccurate predictions about aspects of panic, and explains the real facts behind them. See if you hold any of these counterproductive beliefs:

- you could have a heart attack
- you could stop breathing
- you could lose control and do something irrational or dangerous
- the panic attack might not stop
- you might go mad or lose your mind.

Remember, thoughts aren't facts. A belief is only an opinion or preference, which is very different from a truth. Just because it feels real to you doesn't mean it is actually based on fact. It is a much healthier choice to reassure yourself with the truth instead of frightening yourself with false information.

'WHAT IF' THINKING – OVERESTIMATING AND CATASTROPHISING

As the level of adrenaline rises in your bloodstream, the number of thoughts of a 'what if?' nature rise also, encouraging you to *overestimate the danger* and begin rehearsing for catastrophe. This exaggeration seems to have a survival rationale, in that if you take over-the-top measures, you can better ensure your safety. All very well theoretically, but as you learn to trust that you are in fact safer than you realised, you will see that this catastrophising is unnecessary. Part of the dampening down process is learning to identify and then disempower these thoughts, much like turning off a house alarm that won't stop by punching in the 'cancel' code.

We all overestimate and catastrophise when we're anxious, and we all know that most of the time the dreaded result never happens or isn't as bad as predicted. Ask yourself how many of the events you predicted about panic have ever happened. What does the answer tell you? You may feel that you realise afterwards that these things are unlikely to happen but at the time the possibility seems much more likely. Why, in spite of it occurring dozens of times without you going crazy or losing control, do you still fear it? Why do you continue to overestimate and catastrophise despite repeated disconfirmation?

One reason is that you may believe that it was just 'lucky' that the worst didn't happen during this attack, but that it could still happen – next time. Instead of realising that the reason it didn't happen was because your original prediction (that you could faint) was simply incorrect and nothing to do with luck, you have fed yourself an inaccuracy. This false belief in luck only serves to make you feel totally at the mercy of a force beyond your control, rather than instilling trust in your own ability to keep yourself calm, a more empowering (and true) belief.

Here are some examples of incorrect and damaging beliefs:

'If I hadn't managed to get my husband on the phone just in time, I would have collapsed.'

'I don't know how I would have survived that one if the doctor hadn't arrived so quickly; I really had nearly stopped breathing.'

'It was a miracle that the train stopped at the station just when it did or I would have passed out for sure.'

All of these are typical self-statements that ignore real evidence or distort it to fit into the (inaccurate) theory that there is real danger. *Although the danger feels real it is not, and the truth is that you survived not because of luck or rescue just in time, but because you were never in any real danger in the first place.*

Another reason why these fear statements continue despite repeated disconfirmation is that they have become part of the conditioned panic response, and being part of that package they slip in without your even being aware of them. You might not logically believe them at times when you're feeling safe, but when the panic begins they appear to be true. *In order to uncouple these thoughts from the rest of the response, you have to first isolate them, and then challenge them* to logical analysis of their accuracy.

Just because a thought comes into your mind doesn't mean that it is any more accurate than if it never came into it. Worrying about losing control doesn't mean you will lose control, any more than worrying about dying means you are going to die. We all know this applies to other areas of life. Just because we fear failing the exam doesn't mean we will, and being afraid we'll miss a deadline has no connection to whether or not this will happen, except to worry us enough to take the appropriate measures to ensure that it doesn't.

We know well enough in these situations that after we've taken what measures we can, the best policy is to ignore these promptings. Learning to objectively evaluate these thoughts before automatically believing them is a useful skill for heading off panic attacks and also diluting worry in general. By doing this you will be stopping the sequence at an early stage and preventing it from spiralling any further by introducing a counter-belief – that you are in fact safe.

In Tina's case, as soon as she became aware that the reason she was afraid of the sensations in her chest was that she saw her breathing eventually stopping and death following, she realised that this prediction was outrageous! It was overboard, because her attacks, like most people's, although uncomfortable, had never led to any danger to breathing. Also, she could see that she was connecting her childhood dread of being publicly awkward to the possible consequences of a panic attack, and intensifying her fear.

BELIEVE IT OR NOT – QUESTIONING YOUR THEORIES

Learning to change your reaction to your fearful thoughts, and the credibility you give them, centres on questioning the evidence on which your judgements are based. It is important here to distinguish between a truth and a belief or theory. A truth is something that is based on accepted fact, describing something as it really is. It is therefore a truth that 'some children grow taller than others'. Anyone would agree. However, if I were to state that 'tall children are better than short children', or that 'they grew tall because they ate more greens', these would be beliefs that not everyone might share. Truths state facts; beliefs are merely opinions, or preferred ways of thinking.

If you learn to regard thoughts as guesses or theories, rather than as solid facts, and decide that before you make a judgement you will examine the evidence for thinking that way, they will lose their power.

Like many a dogmatic thinker whose theory is subjected to a rigorous exploration of alternative opinions and their value, fearful thoughts begin to show themselves as the dictators they are – anti-change and anti-growth.

PREDICTIONS – WHEN TWO PLUS TWO MAKES FIVE

In order to evaluate the evidence for a prediction you may be making, you need to consider all the facts, rigorously asking yourself – What are the real chances of this happening? Has it ever happened to you or anyone before? If not, then what makes you think this time will be any different? For example, you may be assuming that a friend who is abrupt with you is annoyed over something you did. What you may overlook is the possibility that they could be angry with someone else or be exhausted after their day, besides the fact that you have done nothing to displease them. You've made a snap deduction without looking at all the angles of the situation – and the result is all it could be, inaccurate. Two plus two equals five.

In the case of panic, you may assume that feeling dizzy and unsteady is a sign of a brain disorder, while editing out the fact that apart from these symptoms, your brain seems to be functioning normally, and that this feeling has been happening on and off for years without ill-effect, not a pattern characteristic of brain disorders. Certainly Tina is overlooking the evidence that none of her past attacks has ever caused her to be completely unable to breathe, and that her boss and boyfriend are usually very understanding people.

Negative predictions may also be made based on a limited set of past examples. You've had two panic attacks, both in shopping malls. Now you're telling yourself 'I know I'm going to panic next time I go to a mall'. You are relating to a possibility as if it were now a certainty, and your anxiety has to be higher if something you dread is a definite rather than a maybe!

The very fact that you challenge these theories for evidence means you've done something different, broken the cycle of emotional reactivity. *You're less likely to be 'carried along' or controlled by the fear if you decide to make a choice about allowing yourself to be frightened or not.* By doing so you also stop the reaction from spreading to involve sensations and behaviours, preventing them from being drawn into the spiral which may end in a panic attack.

Such questioning may seem a bit artificial at first, but don't be put off if it doesn't immediately result in a reduction in panicky feelings the very first time. Thinking exercises need practice just like the physical ones, because learning to replace an old habit with a new one is achieved through laying down new tracks, and this requires repetition. Your tenth piano lesson is going to sound better than your first, and psychological change is no different.

FROM CATASTROPHE TO COPING – ADRENALINE FOLLOWS ADJECTIVES

You are catastrophising when you describe an event to yourself as 'insufferable', the consequences of it 'disastrous', the effect on you 'unthinkably horrible, I would never recover'. If the event is ever examined realistically, such superlatives are usually not accurate. You do actually manage to suffer and survive another one, and although far from pleasant, no disaster follows, and against your expectations you do recover. The point here is that *your anxiety level will follow your adjectives*. The more awful your mental description of what is to come, the higher the adrenaline you'll need to cope with it. This is the equivalent of zapping the 'catastrophe channel', and then complaining that all the movies are about disasters! If you want the 'tranquillity channel', then you'll have to consciously decide to choose it.

Perhaps in your case your worse nightmare did once happen, you fainted or vomited or a panic attack began while you were driving your car. You still need to be rigorous with yourself about the probability rating you're giving of that recurring. If you're giving it a 50 per cent chance of happening any time you panic, then ask yourself if it has indeed happened every second time you have panicked, to deserve such odds. If it has only happened once in twenty panic attacks, that's only a 0.5 per cent probability and you're paying a high daily price for something that has such low odds of happening.

'I'm so frightened of slipping back into the way I was several months ago when I was panicking more frequently – I couldn't stand to go through that again.' This is a pretty catastrophic statement and it is only natural that if that's what you're looking at on your inner screen, then you'll continue to be distressed. On the other hand, you could decide to concentrate on the fact that you're panicking a lot less than you were before, and generally feeling safer and more optimistic nowadays about the future. Remember, you choose the channels that appear on the screen!

What if the worst were to actually happen and your hands began to shake uncontrollably while pouring a cup of tea, or you drew a blank when giving a presentation, or you had to get up and leave a room because you felt trapped? You might think 'I simply couldn't stand that'. But have another look at the whole picture, at other possible outcomes, and the disaster could be cut down to size.

For example, if you really examine how much influence the opinions of strangers have over you, you might realise that you've left their mind within a fairly short time, just as they leave ours. If the 'disaster' were to happen in front of friends, they're still going to like you afterwards, maybe all the more so because they see you're human and have problems too. If you yourself witnessed a person having a panic attack, your response, like most people, would more than likely be to offer sympathy and assistance rather than to shun or judge them. (Some catastrophisers I have met have even visualised people stepping over them as they lie in a faint on the ground!)

Using this approach reduces the experience from 'horrendous' to 'unpleasant but manageable'. Adjectives matter a lot in the realm of thought. Some feed the beast and keep the beliefs alive. Others starve it and it eventually dies.

CATCH YOURSELF IN THE ACT

Remember being caught as a child doing something you shouldn't have been doing, such as drawing on the wallpaper? Your mother might have immediately disrupted the activity, reprimanded you for the behaviour, and maybe sent you to your room to 'think about what you've done'. The first step to changing your fear-mongering thoughts about panic is to catch yourself in the act of thinking them. But they can escape detection if you're hurried, tense, or if your mind is always running on to the future. You won't be able to really notice and challenge them if you're simultaneously looking for the nearest exit, or pacing the floor frantically phoning for help.

> So if you're beginning to feel slightly panicky, you will only detect the catastrophic thoughts if you stop what you're doing and be still.

This is the central theme of mindfulness training, encouraging you to be present with all aspects of your experience – the sensations in your body, your thoughts, your urge to take certain measures – taking it in as it is, the reality happening in this moment, rather than what you fear it will turn into, the illusion in the future. Such 'grounding' particularly applies to those who have a tendency to dissociate, and works to reconnect them in the same way the string operating a kite prevents it flying off. The essence of learning to disempower catastrophic thoughts is in moving the emphasis from fear to safety. In this way you starve them of vital energy. There are several ways:

① *Deflate the Danger – Use Coping Statements*

> 'I know I don't have to fear my heart beating strongly.'
> 'My breathing is only uncomfortable because of my fear, not because there is anything wrong.'

'If I breathe slowly I will feel calmer.'

'I am safe at all times.'

'I can survive the judgement of strangers, and I can explain to those who know me, so I have nothing to fear.'

'These are just thoughts – I can let them go.'

'These sensations will soon pass.'

② 'So what!'

After you've frightened yourself with 'What if...?', answer it back with 'So what! So what if I appeared shaky, apart from cringing with embarrassment, nothing happened! So what if I look foolish in that meeting! I might not like it but I'll still survive'. It is not that you want to negate your fear by trivialising or rubbishing it. It is just an attempt to jolt you into looking at different versions of what it would be like if it did happen, to roll the entire mental video rather than stop it at the point where the catastrophe is all that's on your inner screen, as if this was the only possible conclusion to the story.

If your only options are 'Plan A or die', then obviously when you see Plan A (avoiding an attack) vanishing, and it looks like you might be about to have a panic attack, then your fear level will escalate. On the other hand, if you can be flexible and move to Plan B, you reduce your fear and begin adjusting to that option, as you emphasise to yourself that there are other safe alternatives besides Plan A. For Tina, Plan B could have been to say she urgently needed to leave the room, for reasons she would explain later, but that it would only be for a very short time and she would return quickly.

Obviously, it is inappropriate to use this response in all cases. You can't answer 'So what' to fears that you'll die, have a heart attack or stop breathing. A more useful technique in that case is challenging the possibility of it happening in the first place, rather than saying it wouldn't matter. When you go to the toolbox, try to pick the right tool for the job.

③ *Thought Stopping*

Remind yourself sharply that what you're doing is just a bad habit and destructive, and to 'stop it!' It is like a mental slap on the hand, and if it is a habitual thought that you know from old, which you've examined many times before, but now you just want to cease doing, then it can be like 'zapping' off the 'catastrophe channel'. Rather than expecting your mind to go blank, switching to another set of thoughts helps, like planning what you'll cook for dinner every night for the next week, or trying to remember how you celebrated your birthday for the last five years. Alternatively, you could move into a behaviour that starts off a different train of thought, like defrosting the fridge, or cleaning the car. Or you could bring on a feeling that runs contrary to distressing thoughts, like relaxing in a bath or listening to music.

Once Tina began thinking like this she could clearly see that her 'what ifs' were increasing her anxiety. When she questioned herself as to what would be so embarrassing about panicking at the meeting, she realised that it was that she would appear so obviously afraid that everyone would know how she felt, and would therefore think that she was weird – a social annihilation which she felt would be just like the feeling of being ostracised from her peers in her painful schooldays. She was helped by her psychotherapist to realise that she was overestimating the chances of people either noticing her reaction, or judging her so harshly. She could also appreciate that she was no longer a powerless child. These were people that she could explain it to afterwards, and who would, unlike her childhood peers, be mature enough to be sympathetic and helpful. If she felt she really needed to, she saw that she could also change her job, a choice she didn't have at a younger age when she had to continue suffering the ridicule for years.

Identity plays a central role in all this. It is the one thing our personality is always trying to preserve at all costs. At a survival level Tina was aware of a possible transition from 'accepted by the group' to 'rejected because I'm different' if she had an attack during the meeting.

Some find that as they begin to delve into deeper psychological perspectives of situations, their anxiety can increase. This can be due to the fact that up until now they might have been trying to avoid thinking too deeply about past events that were painful, or future events (such as death) that are disturbing to them. Only by running these 'disaster videos' will you be able to see what has really been frightening you. It may be time to begin working with a psychotherapist to help unpack some of the issues, as it is never easy to ask yourself questions of a sufficiently challenging nature. This will also provide support as you confront any fears that the insights stir up.

MEDITATION – TRAINING YOUR MIND TO BE LESS REACTIVE

There are many types of meditation. Some have the objective of helping you to concentrate and focus your mind, others to calm it. Meditations can be done sitting still in the one position, or while doing some activity. Their common goal is to train your mind to be in the present with whatever is happening, without reacting to it. This means that if thoughts appear on your inner screen, you let them pass through without becoming emotionally involved with them or planning what you'll do later about them, or even trying to stop them occurring. Such skills are particularly useful for those whose minds are too busy or who worry excessively.

The following exercise can be piggybacked onto your breathing exercise if you like, since it substitutes the breath as a focus for the mind to follow, instead of thoughts. You can do it lying or sitting, with your eyes closed or open, and for as long as you like. Obviously you make it easier for yourself if you are in a quiet room, without any distractions. Ten or fifteen minutes is a reasonable time to spend, but if you find you keep putting it off because you can't find the time, then even three minutes a few times a day is better than not doing it at all.

When you begin watching your own thinking, you begin to see that most thought processes happen in chaotic reactive patterns of association, contriving fantasy worlds, endlessly analysing its own content, and replaying strands over and over again. Thoughts with a high emotional charge tend to most easily magnetise you away from the present moment into useless fretting. When you get used to looking at them without being interested in their content, you become freer from that pull, and are less often sucked in. The discipline of meditation is to 'see and let go', 'see and let go', 'see and let go', nothing more.

Meditation on the Breath

- Bring your attention to your belly, feeling it rise and fill up on the in-breath, and fall on the out-breath.

- Keep the focus of your awareness on your breathing, 'watching' it travel all the way from your nose or mouth, down your windpipe, into the base of your lungs. Try to 'be with' each breath in the fullest way, feeling the sensation of the air coming into your nostrils or mouth, and aware of your ribcage moving, your abdomen filling, and the air leaving again as you exhale. Ride the wave of each breath alternating with the next.

- Every time you notice that your mind has wandered off the breath, *label the thought or feeling*, and then gently return to the feeling of your breath coming in and out. For example, you might label the distraction as 'hungry', 'too hot', 'impatient' or 'phone-call to be made'. Simply label it and then let it go off your screen again, do not become involved with its content, like what you'll eat when you're finished, why you're impatient, or what you'll say on the phone.

- Even if your mind wanders away dozens of times, your 'job' is to bring it back. Don't give yourself a hard time over this; even the minds of experienced meditators keep producing thoughts. Your goal is not to empty your mind but to prevent it being so choicelessly reactive.

- In time you will see thoughts as merely 'events' in your mind, which you can choose to interact with or not. This enhances your ability to witness, and gives you the power to distance from distressing sensations or thoughts, reducing their intensity.

Jon Kabat-Zinn, in his book *Full Catastrophe Living,* outlines many other methods of meditation that have been used in the Stress Reduction Clinic in Massachusetts General Hospital in Boston, where he treats every kind of stress, including panic attacks, with meditation alone.

14

BRINGING ON THE PANIC

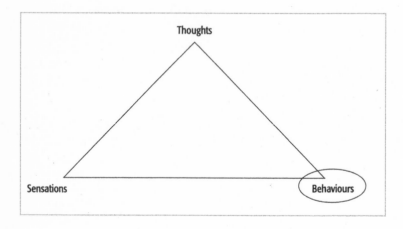

Once you have gained some confidence in controlling the physical sensations of panic, through slowing your breathing, loosening your muscles, and replacing your distressing thoughts with safer ones, you can move on to this next very important step. It is for this reason that it is left to the end, because some people find it difficult to do.

If you were trying to persuade a child who was terrified of water to swim, you could try reassuring him as you both stood at the poolside. You could ask him to observe how much fun his friends were having, and to question whether they'd be laughing if water was the harmful substance he predicts it to be. You might draw his attention to the fact that nobody was drowning, as he seems so certain he would. You might even get him to begrudgingly admit that his belief that 'the water will harm me' is illogical and has no basis in fact.

But these arguments may still not convince him that he won't drown. The clincher is going to be when he gets in the water and experiences safety there. This means the physical sensation of safety in his body rather than any theoretical mental argument. *The primitive part of our brain that looks out for our survival can sometimes be impressed more by experiencing safety than by verbal reassurances.* When it comes to life and death issues, cold logic is often ignored by our primitive brain in favour of raw sensation, which intuitively strikes a deeper chord. When our swimmer feels safe, he'll believe he is.

If he does agree to venture in, he'll be more cooperative if he is given some shred of control, and not flooded with fear. So rather than throw him in at the deep end, it would be wise to introduce him to water by having him sit on the steps of the shallow end. You would also give him safety aids like a rubber ring if you wanted him to stay long enough to give the venture a chance. These give him a feeling of security as he faces his demon. Ultimately, as fear gives way to a more neutral feeling, and finally to fun, you would be able to 'up the ante' and encourage him to learn to stay afloat himself by using certain strokes. But he won't entertain these thoughts if he stays feeling unsafe deep down; a certain level of trust in his own experience is necessary first.

In this way his initial position, 'terrified of the water', gradually gives way to 'don't mind the water too much' and finally to 'this stuff is OK'. This chapter is about moving you through similar stages of fear of certain panic sensations.

THE SHALLOW END OF PANIC

You've been learning that panic is an exaggerated fearful reaction to sensations and thoughts – a false alarm. This section encourages you to test out that reactivity, to 'put a toe in the water' and to learn to dampen it by using your new skills. The difference to the previous chapters about control is that, rather than waiting until a panic attack starts before using your skills at dampening down the sensations (the deep end), this time you're going to first *bring them on yourself, and then make them go away.*

Below is a series of exercises that will produce sensations similar to those you might experience during an attack, the only real difference being that you choose when to produce them, rather than waiting for them to 'strike', catching you off balance.

Their goal is to decrease or eliminate your fear of bodily sensations by repeatedly confronting the sensations that frighten you. In doing this you will finally break the conditioned response that means fear automatically follows certain feelings in your body. As with anything you fear, whether it is spiders, heights or thunderstorms, it is only banished by repeatedly facing your fear, preferably in bite-sized pieces. The more you practise a particular strategy, the better you get at it and the greater is your confidence that you'll be able to use it when you confront that feared sensation during a panic attack. These exercises are especially useful for

- those who have intellectually taken in the information that these sensations can't harm you, and who understand that panic attacks are not some mysterious out-of-the-blue magical process or disease, but who still feel intensely afraid of them. Doing these exercises establishes beyond doubt the fact that you start and stop all panics yourself; luck has nothing to do with it. Experiencing is believing.

- those who get such infrequent attacks, say one a month, that they have not had much practice at dampening down the sensations, and therefore have not been able to demonstrate to themselves that the tools they've learned work.

- those who learn more if their skills can be tested out in low-risk situations first, rather than only high-risk, such as during an attack. These exercises are done in the safety of your own home, so you can push the boundary of your comfort zone more because you know you can stop any time and feel safe again pretty quickly. The presence of this safety net can paradoxically encourage you to endure the fearful symptoms and persist with your new skills for longer.

- those who have particular problems with one symptom mainly, like dizziness or a racing heart. With these exercises you can go over and over the one that emphasises that symptom until you're sure you can control it.

Ciara first noticed her heartbeat change during her pregnancy. She and her husband Jeff had been trying for a baby for some years, and she was delighted to finally find herself pregnant. However, early on during one of the routine ante-natal visits it was discovered that her heart was excessively rapid, which happens in a certain percentage of pregnancies. From then on she felt anxious and began to dwell on her health and whether the baby would be all right. At one point she had to spend the night in hospital for 24-hour monitoring, and found it difficult to accept the reassurance that it was not serious and would go away after the delivery, which is what happened, and her baby was born healthy.

However, the worry remained that something was wrong with her heart, and whenever she was nervous she noticed that it got faster, and even skipped the odd beat. Again, reassurance that her own doubt was actually bringing it on, and the fact that she was constantly focused on every little bodily change, was to no avail. She began to tense up at the slightest sign of irregularity, then began to feel her knees 'go wobbly', and in time she had her first full-blown panic attack. After that her life gradually changed in subtle ways. Socialising became a burden and she began staying at home a lot more. Initially her excuse was that getting reliable child-minders was difficult, but finally she had to tell Jeff. Her dependence grew when he took over the shopping, and accompanied her if ever she had to go into town.

She kept a packed bag by her bed, 'ready for the hospital' if she had a heart attack at night, and would never agree to holiday anywhere too far from an emergency unit. Finally her dilemma caught up with her when their son, then aged five, wanted to venture farther afield than their backyard, to play with friends a few roads away. He couldn't go unless she brought him and walked back alone. What if something happened to her on the way home, and she was all alone? Her fear of limiting his development outweighed her fear about her heart, and she decided she needed help to overcome the problem.

She proceeded swiftly through the initial stages of learning relaxation and breathing abdominally, and she began feeling a lot calmer. Intellectually she accepted the adrenaline drive behind all panic attacks, and could see what effect her thoughts were having in escalating her fear levels. However, she still felt much more afraid of panicking when she was on her own than when she was with Jeff, or even when other people were around. She felt there was a safety factor about having somebody to call the ambulance. Clearly she needed to change her reaction to the sensation of her heart racing, because there was a disparity between her intellectual understanding, one of acceptance that this was harmless, and her emotional reaction of terror and 'knowing' it might kill her if it occurred while she was alone. Only by actually orchestrating a safe experience and disproving her inaccurate belief would she be convinced.

SENSATION EXPOSURE EXERCISES

Exposure involves practising specific exercises and exposing yourself to what follows. The goal is to fully experience the sensations that the exercises bring out, such as dizziness or sweating, and then to practise your new skills to dampen them down. If you like, have someone with you the first time you do the exercises.

The point of them is for you *to find the ones that best mimic your panic sensations*, since everyone's panic is different. You must try them all, and settle on those that do this most accurately, because these are the ones that create your greatest opportunity for learning. *If more than one is very similar to when you panic, start with whichever of them generated the least fear.*

① *To Bring On Dizziness*

- Shake your head from side to side for thirty seconds.
- Put your head down between your knees for thirty seconds and then quickly lift it to an upright position.
- Spin around in a chair for sixty seconds. A desk chair is ideal, and if someone can spin you around that's even better. Otherwise, while standing, turn around and around quickly to make yourself dizzy. Have a soft chair handy to rest in when sixty seconds are up.

② *To Bring On Chest Breathing*

- Hold your breath for thirty seconds.
- Breathe deep and fast forcefully for sixty seconds while seated.
- Breathe through a straw for sixty seconds, while holding your nose.

③ *To Increase Your Heart Rate*

- Do step-ups on the bottom step of the stairs or on a stool. Repeatedly step up and down for sixty seconds at a fast enough rate to notice your heart beginning to pump more quickly.

④ *To Increase Sweating*

- Sit in a hot stuffy car with the heater on, or in front of a hairdryer, for sixty seconds.
- Turn up the heat until you feel yourself getting uncomfortable.

These exercises are designed to be *repeated until your fear level comes down and you are in control again and out of danger*. Here's how to use them:

- When the first sensations are noticed, it is important to continue with the exercise for at least ten more seconds for breath-holding and head shaking, and thirty for the others. Remember to distinguish between unpleasantness, which can be experienced and tolerated without being afraid, and anxiety.

- Next *identify any anxiety-provoking thoughts* that you find yourself having as you're doing the exercise. Write them down. Be particularly aware of statements such as 'I'll have to stop, these feelings are getting out of control'. This is a prediction you're making based solely on fear, not fact (you can in fact tolerate them and continue the exercise, as you're about to show yourself). Now is your opportunity to demonstrate that you *can* bring control yourself, and gain confidence in doing so.

- Now *begin to use all the techniques you've learned* so far to control the fearful sensations and thoughts – diaphragmatic breathing, relaxation, and reassuring thoughts rather than catastrophic ones.

- Repeat the exercise as many times as necessary to feel you're back in control and any danger has passed. Your goal is to get your fear rating of the experience to drop to less than 2, on a scale of 1 to 10. On each repeat wait until all the physical sensations have abated and the fear has subsided before repeating it again.

- If your anxiety does not subside and some sense of safety does not return within five trials, then wait until the next day to have another go, or you'll exhaust yourself. Once you've achieved this, even if it takes several days, move on to the next most challenging exercise, until you have control over your fear of that one also.

- If the sensations continue to be unpleasant, but the fear has gone, then congratulations! Now you are reacting the same as anyone else. The exercises are not designed to eliminate all sensations but to control the fear of them, and any subsequent wish to avoid them.

- It is important that you *fully* experience the sensations, before jumping in to dampen them down using your strategies. It is only through allowing them to build to a reasonably challenging level that you learn through experience that they will not harm you. If you bail out before they even get threatening, you will only reinforce the belief that they are intolerable. By 'lasting it out' until the recommended time has elapsed, you can show yourself that you can in fact tolerate them. This means that in the future if you feel them coming on, you won't catastrophise.

- Don't be too cautious in doing the exercises. Do them strongly, and try to elicit a decent reaction in yourself. The importance of experiencing the sensations intensely cannot be emphasised enough. For example, during the step-ups, you have to make the pace fast enough to bring on definite cardiovascular symptoms.

While hyperventilating you should breathe in and out with some force, like you would if you were jogging. With the spinning, it needs to be continuous if it is to create dizziness, so don't stop and start or you'll defeat the purpose.

If none of the exercises produce fear, even though the sensations are very similar to the ones you get when you panic, then one of the following is happening:

- You feel too safe. Not enough anxiety is being created with which to practise. If you do the exercises with someone there, but feel that you couldn't do them while you were alone without feeling a lot more nervous, then you have exposed one of your inaccurate assumptions right there, that 'I would be in danger if I were to bring on the sensations without help at hand'. Wrong. The fact is *these exercises are not dangerous at all, either alone or accompanied. Only by actually practising them alone will you show yourself that this is true.*

- The sensations are not as frightening since you've brought them on yourself, and know exactly where they came from (your own actions). This is another of your false assumptions unveiled, namely 'Spontaneous panics are more dangerous because there are no specific triggers for them.' Wrong. *All panic is triggered by something you fear, either a sensation or a fearful image or thought. The only difference with spontaneous panics is that you may not be aware of the trigger before it has acted, but that does not mean there wasn't one.*

Go back over the reading material about levels of awareness of the triggers until you're sure you are not putting spontaneous panics in a different and more frightening category than these exercises. It all boils down to your reaction to the sensations, and even sensations whose origins you cannot account for are still only sensations and as such will do you no harm.

Ciara found that the hyperventilation exercise made her a little anxious, but she reduced her fear without much difficulty, since she had always found that slowing down her breathing made her calmer, and this strengthened her trust in it more. However, she found it took her almost a week to reduce her fear of the step-ups to less than 2/10, even though she had Jeff by her side. She could see that she really wasn't giving the relaxation or breathing techniques a chance to work with these exercises, as opposed to when she was using them to reduce tension. At the first sign of her heart rate rising she began running her mental video of collapsing, needing an ambulance, and getting to the casualty department. Each time she did the exercise it was an enormous challenge to her to stretch it out for another ten seconds. Initially she found it hard to visualise herself continuing for an entire minute. She worked at substituting her catastrophic thoughts for more reassuring ones without denying her feelings of discomfort – 'Although this feels unpleasant I know what to do to make it less so.' 'I have made my heart speed up myself, and I can reduce it myself.' 'I know I can finish this exercise because I'm safe at all times.'

During her second week she went on to try it without Jeff in the room. Her fear score went up to 10/10 the first day, as she faced her worst fear. She again realised that her mind was so taken up with rescue plans that she was giving herself a strong message of danger, one that would completely negate any dampening down effect her techniques could have. But by the third day it had fallen to 6, and by the end of that week it was 3.

The last stage was for her to do the step-ups while Jeff was not even in the house. Again the scores climbed to a maximum, but after day three she had them down to 4. The greatest shift in her thinking was her appreciation that she had been making a distinction in her mind between panics she would get with someone there (bad but not life-threatening) and those she might get when alone (definitely life-threatening because of lack of assistance and presumed death). She could see now that both are the same, an experience that, while frightening, she could survive and manage alone.

With regular practice, you'll begin to find in your day-to-day life that when these symptoms occur, you will be less afraid of them as a result of doing these exercises. This will have two important results – in any subsequent unscheduled panic attacks, the sensations will be less intense, and you will also feel more in control, simply because that's what will have been happening during your practice.

It is important to learn, like the fearful swimmer, that although the symptoms may not be comfortable, they are tolerable, not unbearable as you may previously have been suggesting to yourself. By seeing them through, you will be laying down a new track in your mind – one that emphasises safety rather than fear, borne out by your own experience. If you always try to suppress or run away from the early symptoms of panic, you are in essence telling yourself that you can't handle what is happening. You must practise every day if you really want to benefit from this section of the programme. And remember to use all your self-statement strategies along with the breathing and relaxation techniques each time.

- Do all the exercises and decide which of them creates sensations most similar to when you panic.

- Start with the exercise that seemed to generate the least fear (low risk). As you let the sensation build, write down any specific fearful thoughts you had.

- Use your breathing and relaxation techniques to bring control over the sensations, and to reduce your fear level back down to under 2/10. As you're doing these, challenge any fearful thoughts with the facts, putting safety thoughts in their place.

- Repeat the exercise up to five times in any one day, or until you're experiencing the sensations without fear. Then leave that exercise and move on to another one.

- Do the exercises every day, working through each until you are below 2/10 on it. If that happens very soon, say within three days, keep on practising anyway twice a day for a full week.

15

WHEN PANIC TURNS INTO PHOBIA

KEYNOTE: STAYING SAFE AT ALL COSTS

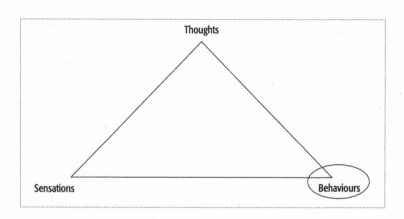

A phobia is the avoidance of a situation or place because of fear or panic when no real danger exists.

BIRTH OF A PHOBIA

One of the many functions of your human brain is its preoccupation with your continued survival. With this as its primary agenda, as we've seen, it scans constantly, mostly without your awareness, for potential danger. A noxious experience which occurs once, or even twice, may be ignored, but once a pattern begins to emerge, like a submarine with an unidentified blip on its radar, your mind is on the hunt for helpful clues to piece together a profile of the problem in order to formulate a solution. Like a highly efficient computer, it starts cross-referencing, linking things up, looking for trends that could be predictive for the future, tips-offs in advance of the event which might provide you with that little edge that would warn you to avoid it in time.

Policies form quickly. So a few dodgy tummies after certain types of spicy food, one let-down too many by a certain person, or one inefficiency too many by a certain travel agency and your mind has the solution – avoid. Not for anything would you put yourself in the way of that again. A sensible decision, most would agree. This avoidance policy is the basis of how phobias form. A panic attack, or even the lead-up anxiety, begins to be firmly associated with a certain situation or object as the trigger – lifts, dogs, spiders, the sight of blood, dental work, heights – the list is endless. If the experience is repeated often enough, you develop a dread of it occurring, and you begin to divide your world up into safe or dangerous places, depending on the likelihood (according to your mind's reckoning as opposed to reality) of encountering the triggering situation.

Research shows that phobias come into being by three possible pathways.

1. Direct conditioning – first-hand experience, such as being repeatedly terrified by panic attacks, or bitten by a dog, or nearly drowning.

2. Vicarious or observational conditioning – witnessing another person experience an attack by a dog, or repeatedly watching someone who becomes paralysed with fear when they see a spider.

3. Information/instruction conditioning – being cautioned about thunderstorms, or warned to be vigilant of creepy-crawlies lurking in the long grass, or reading information suggesting that dogs can be prone to attack without reason.

Such programming, which suggests 'it happened before so it'll happen again' casts experiences in stone, with the past impressions (inability to breathe properly while a dog was barking at you, or you were under water) dictating how you relate to the present which is occurring right now. Your mind makes them out to be the same – 'all dogs are dangerous' – and your interpretations become clouded and inaccurate to the point where you truly almost 'see' the dog in front of you barking, even though it's not, only the dog in your memory is, and you 'see' yourself blacking out, despite continuing to be fully conscious.

Despite all these horrible mental scenarios, you hang on to one thing for reassurance – that if the worst happens, and you end up having to confront your worst fear, that you'll always be able to run to safety. But what if running wouldn't be an option? Then you'd be facing your worst nightmare, being forced to feel every inch of the fear as it spreads through you, without any hope of escaping those terrifying sensations it brings with it, and the even more sinister realisation that you wouldn't be in control any more. For you that could mean having to look 'certain death' in the eye as your 'overloaded heart packs in', expecting to collapse unconscious on the ground, or suffering the excruciating indignity of being shunned (as you predict) by others when they see you shaking and trembling with panic.

It is these situations, those from which escape would be impossible or difficult, which now become your obsession, and reaching this stage can be seen as a fork in the road. For if escape is ruled out, you feel there's no option but to fall back on the only other manoeuvre possible to protect yourself – avoidance. So you devote vast amounts of energy to plotting, planning and strategising to this end, resulting in some cases in a life lived 'safely' behind closed doors for years. A 'little life' far smaller than you deserve.

BULLETINS FROM THE EDGE

It is the intensity of the fear in certain specific contexts which creates the edges of your comfort zone, with alarm bells sounding the moment you pick up that you're not as safe as you were. There are several factors which determine how severe panic sensations can get, and therefore dictate the safe/risky interface.

- Controllability over sensations is greater for most people in their own home where they can lie down, drop what they're doing, pace around, or divert their attention to other things. It's harder to concentrate on your techniques when you're also trying to pay a bill quickly, act 'normal' and hide your reaction from others, or continue a conversation.

- Unpredictability escalates in the outside world. You can't always know exactly how crowded a place will be, how many people will attend a function, how slow a queue will move along, or what mood your boss will be in.

- Your resources at the moment the panic attack hits. Virtually all panickers find that the day after a few drinks is hard going, the reason being that your physiology changes as your body clears the alcohol from your system, and such minute deviations from normal, a tiny rise in heart rate, sweat or muscle tension, is spotted instantly by your paranoid internal bodyguard. All unconsciously of course. Likewise, during times of strong emotion or lack of sleep, you may be triggered more, and feel less like bothering to use your techniques.

- Memory influences where your edge lies. If you've panicked before in a certain situation, or were embarrassed in front of certain people (even as far back as the classroom) you'll have been thinking about that before you even leave the house, or perhaps since you woke that morning, or possibly since the invite arrived a month ago! In terms of adrenaline molecules, this means your handicap is higher than usual.

- The option to avoid is compromised in many places outside your safe zone, essentially leaving you with no protection at all (until now) in the face of an attack.

Experience tells you that panic attacks which occur away from your safe zone are somehow in a different league of seriousness than others because of the factors above. 'Fuzzy logic' has crept in, where deductions are being made which aren't true. Yes, you breathe easier when you get off the bus, when the meeting is over, when the shop isn't crowded. But it's not for the reason you think. It's not because you're safer then, it's because your thoughts change and are lower-adrenaline in nature – 'I'll be fine now, it's over, I won't get an attack'. In contrast, in the above situations you're more likely to have high-adrenaline thoughts such as 'There were too many people for me to deal with / I couldn't use the breathing because I had to get through the checkout at the same time / there simply wasn't enough oxygen so I had to get out!'

A con is happening now where your mind persuades you to avoid using logic that it doesn't find convincing enough, creating a distorted conviction which cements in place the conditioning that perpetuates the habit. It tells you:

> Having a panic attack in certain situations would have disastrous
> consequences, therefore the best way to stay safe and in control is to avoid.

A distorted belief is like a plant – you can feed it or starve it. If you met someone who believed pigs could talk, you'd want to call their bluff by a visit to the farmyard, and you'd be pretty suspicious of someone who, once you got there, began making excuses like 'the pig doesn't feel like it today', or 'it has laryngitis', or 'it can't think of anything to say'. Yet this is what you may be doing yourself, reinforcing the misperception that the sensations of panic will overwhelm you and cannot be endured, so you avoid staying and calling its bluff, the surest way to keep the belief alive.

The capacity to feel safe and in control is inside you, not in a certain place. If you avoid every time, you never realise this. If you've developed a phobic element to your panic, this is not an indication that it has reached a more serious level or is unlikely to resolve. It simply means that your belief system still has a gremlin in it which needs more work, misinformed ideas and fears which perhaps only surface in certain situations.

THE TRAPPED FEELING – PANIC IN DIFFERENT SOCIAL SETTINGS

In claustrophobia, the entrapment is literal, when the escape route in the event of a panic attack could be physically ruled out as an option such as in:

- Lifts
- Planes
- Buses
- Trains
- Motorways
- Car washes

Others feel trapped by social conformity, where escaping seems out of the question because of their prediction that social humiliation or negative consequences would follow, such as loss of professional standing, or the good opinion of others. The dread is that, in being seen having a panic attack, you might be judged to be a 'person who has problems coping' or who is 'odd or weird' and is at best to be pitied or at worst exposed to ridicule and shamed. That state of extreme vulnerability can arise in:

- Office meetings
- One-to-one conversations
- Dining out in restaurants
- Cinemas and theatres
- Church services/weddings and funerals
- Supermarket checkouts
- Hairdressers or barbers
- Dentists
- Shopping malls
- Queues

While the above are examples of places where you might be subjected to the 'gaze of the other', there are some rather particular situations where that scrutiny is even more intense. It 'ups the ante' considerably to feel you will be scrutinised while performing a specific task at the same time. It is one thing to be privately fighting inwardly with panicky sensations while sitting in your seat on a plane, but another altogether while 'on show' where your concentration is likely to be needed for the task in order to carry it out without mishap. This ingredient is what earns the term social phobia, and situations with this added pressure might include:

- Giving speeches or presentations
- Performing on stage
- Sitting exams

- Urinating in a crowded men's room
- Writing your signature in front of a bank clerk
- Controlling a shaky cup or glass during a meal
- Performing duties such as bridesmaid, or godparent
- Sex involving a pressure to succeed

Those who have difficulties with the above types of situation must not be confused with those whose personality in general has a tendency towards nervousness when being introduced to new people in any setting, or meeting people in authority, both of which may require little more than shaking hands or saying hello, but can be an awesome task for a person who has always been socially hesitant by nature. In contrast, most people who have newly become socially phobic because of panic attacks, although some might admit to having been slightly on the shy side of the extrovert–introvert continuum, were previously perfectly capable of socialising in most of the normal ways until their first experience with panic began to shape those experiences, adding fear to the equation where it wasn't there before.

After the attacks began to take over, you may have found your confidence in your abilities undermined to such a degree that you hardly recognise the person you've become, with your mind over-run by fearful and hesitant thoughts and worries. Depression often becomes a travelling companion to this socially isolating state, since it's the natural response to any situation where you lack control, feel defeated or helpless to change things for the better. A more in-depth look at how the relationship between panic, anxiety and depression can be found in my book *Depression – An Emotion not a Disease* (co-written with Michael Corry).

Medicating such a response, while it can dissolve some of the feeling of being on your own with the problem, can for some people serve to hammer home that you've crossed the line from being a normal coping person, to one unable even to ease their own distress without the aid of a 'crutch', and this can further diminish your fragile self-esteem and cause you to lose faith in your own ability to be the one to get yourself well.

In all these phobias, the core of their treatment is helping a person deal effectively with their panic attacks, so that they feel safe enough to expose themselves to the social events that trigger them.

Aileen was fifteen when she had her first panic attack. One morning during maths class, a subject in which she excelled, her head began to swim and she couldn't see the figures on the pages of her textbook. Her tummy felt like heaving, and prickles of cold sweat broke out down her back. Glancing around to see if anyone had noticed, she put her hand up to ask to be excused, and fled to the bathroom. She had barely got there when a wave of diarrhoea gripped her, and it was some time before she felt composed enough to leave the cubicle. It was with relief that she heard the bell for the end of class, but when she entered the next classroom for English, a subject during which you were often asked to read aloud, she decided she couldn't be sure that it wouldn't return, quickly gathered her things, and went home.

Months of school refusal followed, and Aileen changed from a sociable, athletic, well-adjusted teenager to a virtual recluse. Different approaches were pursued, such as sessions with the school counsellor in an effort to unearth any bullying, academic problems or conflicts at home. Finally a consultation with a psychiatrist was arranged, depression due to a 'chemical imbalance' was diagnosed, and medication prescribed. There was no improvement. The dose was increased, then the brand changed, and finally, after six more wasted months, Aileen's mother decided to phase out the drugs. This cycle repeated itself again, a course of cognitive behavioural therapy was tried, and nutritional adjustments made to Aileen's diet. Another newer anti-depressant was given a trial, this time with a weight gain of fifteen kilos, another nail in the coffin of Aileen's self-esteem, but still there was no return to the classroom.

Patience in the house was wearing thin when, two years after the initial panic attack in the classroom, her mother rang me. Unfortunately Aileen couldn't travel to see me, she said, as she hadn't so much as sat in the car to drive down the road in the last three months. My first question on hearing the story of this so-called school phobia was if Aileen had ever been instructed in handling panic attacks. Her mother expressed surprise, and enquired what panic attacks were, and what they had to do with Aileen's problem?

No one had ever discussed with Aileen the physical symptoms she had experienced that first time. If they had, she would have told them that she remembered the time some four years before when her older sister had been in a near-fatal car accident, and spent a week in a coma in intensive care, although finally recovering fully. Every day at assembly the whole school would pray for her recovery, and the other kids would avoid Aileen, not knowing what to say. There was an air of drama, and she'd felt like a freak, set apart, the nuns asking all the time how her sister was, making it worse. The feeling she'd had that day in class was that if she had to ask permission more than once to go to the bathroom, she'd be attracting the same kind of unwanted attention through being 'different in a bad way'. Aileen had witnessed others being teased for less and was not prepared to risk it.

Neither was it a coincidence that her panic attack followed her mother's discovery of a breast lump, which although diagnosed as benign, had caused Aileen to have a few nightmares and her parents to remember that she had always found separations very distressing as a child.

Adolescents will do anything to blend in, but no one was giving her the one thing she needed, the tools to deal with what made her different that day, the panic attack sensations. To add to the problem she then had to deal with her peers enquiring why she wasn't at school. To answer 'because I have a psychiatric problem' seemed like a death knell to her already diminished social life, and she gradually stopped going out rather than deal with such enquiries and the inevitable judgements they would elicit.

Jim had been a member of the police force since he was a young man of twenty. Since the internal modernising of the station's office had occurred, he hardly recognised it as the one he used to oversee in the past. The place now buzzed with computers, and all the new recruits could put him, now in his fifties, in the shade with their 'techie' skills. He tried his best, but found the new world of technology very daunting, with less emphasis, or so it seemed to him, on good old-fashioned people-skills.

A period of stress occurred in his family life – his father hadn't been coping since his mother's death three years before, and the question of getting good care for him during the day was weighing on his mind. And his eldest son was looking at courses of study in the UK for which, coupled with the accommodation costs, Jim knew it was going to be difficult to find the money. With these issues on his mind, he hadn't been sleeping well, and with less and less enthusiasm for socialising, was spending more time in front of the TV trying to get his brain to switch off.

One morning, after a long and intense family meeting the night before, he noticed his hand shaking as he made himself his mid-morning cup of tea in the station. It puzzled him, but beyond that he forgot about it, putting it down to the times that were in it. However, shortly afterwards, a young woman came to the cubby-hole to make a complaint about an attempted mugging which she had succeeded in escaping by eliciting the help of a passer-by. The assailant has still managed to make off with her handbag and she needed to report it.

This kind of task was routine for Jim: after twenty-odd years of dealing with distressed people it was something he could have done in his sleep. Yet, as he reached for the required form and lifted his pen to begin recording the details, to his horror he noticed his hand shaking again. He slid it out of sight. Within seconds he found his mind flooded with thoughts – Has she noticed? How can I take the complaint if it continues? What excuse can I possibly give – me, an experienced officer, shaking like a girl! If I can't do it I'll have no option but to ask someone else on duty to do it in my place, but how can I explain that to them?

Furtively, trying to look casual, he used the pretext of the pen being dry and walked very slowly to his desk, glancing round to see who could cover for him. The shaken girl cried softly at the opening, and he felt bad for being so seemingly off-hand when she was so obviously shaken. The other two on duty were out in the yard, and he knew of no believable excuse he could give them, so he did the only thing he could think of. Trying to sound as authoritative as he could, he told her that just as she'd arrived an urgent call had come in which had to be responded to instantly, and that he would have to call to her house later to document the complaint, adding that very few handbags were ever retrieved in such cases unless they turned up in bushes or bins, in which case she'd be better off getting her friends out helping her to look. He was counting on someone on the next shift having to deal with it if she rang later on, and hoped she might forget the whole incident once she got home and felt better.

Jim put things off that day, but it was not the end of the shake, and some weeks later, worn out by trying to come up with more and more novel avoidance strategies, he sought help for the problem from a psychotherapist.

DEGREES OF 'DANGER'

In each of the above examples, the 'danger' factor is decided by each individual based on their own unique perception of their ability to endure the awful sensations and prevent them 'escalating out of control'. One person will be reassured enough to drive if someone else is in the car with them, yet others have the trapped feeling unless they're alone driving, when they'd be able to control all the variables, such as taking alternative routes to avoid the motorway, stopping the instant they need to find a bathroom, or even cancelling the trip altogether without having to cringe in apology!

Likewise, the edge of the comfort zone varies – for one person a not-so-full supermarket, or a three-mile drive, may qualify as just about safe enough to tackle, but a crowded shop or a ten-mile drive is deemed completely and utterly out of the question. On the other hand the exact same scenario can be safe for one, but dangerous for someone else. I found this in one group I ran in which the subject of public transport was being discussed. One woman dreaded full train carriages, feeling under pressure the more people were there to observe her (negatively of course) if she got an attack, yet another was aghast at this, because she felt more vulnerable in an empty one, and found the very same crowds reassuring, because they would take the necessary measures (pulling the communication cord to stop the train, and organising the ambulance, etc). Notice the personal stamp on each individual 'logic'? And the very definite demarcation in their mind of where safe ends and risk begins, their vigilance kicking in when they see some external 'evidence' of the level of threat having just risen a notch, as in the transition from a minor road to a motorway, or at the moment the lift doors close. Perversely, the same stretch of road which instils unease on the outward journey is always a doddle on the way back – why? Because on the home stretch there is less perceived risk ahead and you're thinking safe thoughts.

AGORAPHOBIA

The terror of a panic attack leading to your heart 'not being able to stand it', or of blacking out and being without the necessary access to help, may mean that for you, being alone at home is on the same scale of threat as being in the house with an assailant holding a gun to your head. Many will pay whatever price is required in their relationships to see they are never left alone. Sometimes that price is exceedingly high, leading to endless conflict and even divorce, as a partner's patience wears thin, their life becoming impossibly constrained by the dependency.

By comparison, others fear leaving the safety of the home base, where, if symptoms arose they'd feel able to deal with them in their own way, unobserved by others. Agoraphobia is the medical term originally meaning 'fear of leaving a safe place, or venturing into crowded places'. This definition is consistent with the original derivation of the term from the Greek word *agora* meaning 'marketplace', and its aptness is never more true than today, with so many fearing the shopping mall as one of their most frightening situations. The term can be misleading, however, because it can give the impression that it is a person's difficulty with the public arena which is the problem, with its exposure to the judgement of others, when in fact it is their fear of experiencing panic sensations at all, ever, anywhere, which is the basic problem, their main solution to that being to stay where that's least likely to happen, at home.

It is recognised now that the core of agoraphobia, and all other phobias, centres on the threat that comes from within – 'the fear of experiencing the fear', also known as 'interoceptive avoidance'. Putting excessive attention on one or other external trigger can tend to detract from the one central point.

Phobics will do anything to avoid feeling the sensations, because they see that experience as intolerable, the only solution to which is to avoid it.

Therefore, not only will they avoid being away from their safe place, but it is also extremely common in agoraphobia to find avoidance of activities and scenarios even inside their house which will increase their arousal levels, such as heated angry debates, exciting movies or sports events, stuffy rooms, lifting heavy objects, sex, standing up quickly, or steamed-up bathrooms. Even though none of these would be traditionally associated with 'fear of open spaces', the common denominator is a fear of the sensations being triggered. In helping those with all phobias, this fact holds the key to the goal of treatment – reality-testing the symptoms in order to put them in the same category into which non-panickers do, unpleasant but tolerable, and in no way dangerous.

PHOBIAS WHICH ZONE IN ON SPECIFIC SYMPTOMS OR TRIGGERS

It can happen that over time you get to feel more threatened by some sensations, while others bother you less. For example, driving or using public transport may illicit the usual cluster of unpleasant fight–flight symptoms, but it may become the bowel sensations – cramping, gurgling noises, etc. – or the breathing difficulty which you become particularly intimidated by and zone in on.

Gerry was travelling with other family members in the car at the head of his father's funeral cortège on the way to the cemetery in a small country town. Without warning, he became aware of feeling decidedly queasy and unwell, finding it difficult to breathe, and of the urgent and unquestionable need to empty his bowels. Feeling there was simply no alternative, he asked the driver to stop, and despite the angry protestations of his brother, ran in behind a wall and did so.

In the ensuing months, with his mother's increasing dependence and feeling unsupported by the other family members, he began having more panic attacks, but to him the most distressing aspect of them became the bowel sensations, which he could experience anywhere. Whenever they arose, his policy was to waste no time in seeking out the nearest toilet, and on many occasions he would comment that he 'barely made it in time, before my bowels relieved themselves in no uncertain terms!' The only situation where it was sometimes impossible to practice this safety manoeuvre was the car.

As time went on, the routes he took became more and more tightly defined, all centring on heading off the predicted 'bowel explosion', which he would reluctantly admit had never actually happened. He held an unshakeable belief that it 'would definitely have occurred had I not prevented it by reaching the toilet in time'. The sense of embarrassment and shame he might bring on himself should that occur in the presence of others was unthinkable to him, and he went to great lengths to avoid occasions on which there was even the slightest risk it might.

Soon it became his policy never to travel with anyone but close family, given that strangers, or even friends and acquaintances, might find it difficult to understand why he might suddenly need to make a detour to find a toilet rather than simply wait until they reached their destination. Always having access to a toilet became the sole goal, therefore public transport without any, such as subways or buses, were out of the question but planes and trains posed no problem. His wife joked that every trip was mapped out more by the scenery inside the toilet than the actual route.

Gerry had developed a firm conditioned response in which 'access to a toilet' meant 'safety', and since 'not getting there in time' was paired with 'danger', any potential obstacle to that manoeuvre became a trigger, and was avoided. Heavy traffic which hemmed him in, tight deadlines which could not allow time for any detours, driving after a heavy meal, or unexpectedly having to share a taxi or car with others were on his list of situations to avoid.

Maggie became anorexic during a period of major transition in her life. Although her aversion to eating differed very little from other anorexics in terms of outward behaviours, the main dynamic operating for her was not a body image distortion, but rather a terror and phobic avoidance of vomiting. Food in her stomach gave her a 'full feeling', a danger sign for her because of her prediction that the uncontrollable impulse to vomit would follow if she dared continue past that point.

She had no traumatic memories of vomiting, or of feeling in danger during any illness during which she had felt severe nausea, but simply the thought of it happening filled her with dread, although she couldn't articulate exactly why, aside from the sheer unpleasantness of the experience. Her nose would wrinkle in disgust at the very thought of being so out of control.

Medically, at times her low body weight was concerning, but like all anorexics, Maggie was caught in a double bind – psychologically, for her, 'eating leads to danger' and 'avoiding eating keeps me safe', yet physically the opposite was true. Like many other anorexics, if Maggie had to choose between preserving her emotional identity, her sense of selfhood, at the expense of her physical identity, her body, there would be no contest, she would let her body die. The only avenue of treatment would have to involve disabling the powerful conditioned response she had which made vomiting in some way dangerous, and reinstating it to the category most people feel it belongs in, highly unpleasant but endurable, and essentially harmless. In doing so she would have to be helped to unseat the culprit linking the two – the erroneous belief that 'a full feeling in the tummy is a warning sign preceding vomiting'. In other words, calling her own bluff through exposure to the phobic trigger, in a way that gave her the experience that such an action, although highly anxiety-provoking and unpleasant, is tolerable, and holds no danger.

NOW, OR NEVER?

'Freedom's just another word for nothin' left to lose' – Kris Kristofferson. Once your life has reached the stage where panic dictates all your

movements, deciding where you can or can't go, with phobic avoidance strategies ruling your future, you have become a slave. It always seems to have the upper hand, and you can feel virtually powerless to act differently even though you may want to. A crucial turning point, which I call the point of no return, in getting to grips with this tyrannical presence in your life is the moment when you acknowledge that the price you're paying by using avoidance to stay in control has become far too high and must stop – no matter what.

It's that last phrase which holds the problem, because for many, the idea of staying where you are when the sensations begin to get strong, and learning to endure them rather than running out to 'safety', can seem like lunacy, putting you at risk either medically or socially. But what about the risk of continuing the way you have been? Is that not a far greater risk? To have your life slowly slipping away unlived, precious opportunities missed, days wasted keeping yourself 'safe'? It may seem as if you're weighing up safety/status quo on one hand versus danger/risk on the other, but if you really think about it, in truth both are a risk, with one crucial difference between them – one holds the potential for change, while the other can only deliver more of the same misery. One patient of mine, who after years of living in this half-dead limbo decided to take the bull by the horns. He would repeat to himself:

If you always do what you've always done
You'll always get what you've always had

So, do you keep on using tactics which aren't working for you, or confront your fear, no matter what? There are several important differences between these two stances, avoiding or staying, which sometimes make it hard for people to find the motivation to switch, differences which often reflect a person's fundamental style of coping with any difficulty, proactive or reactive. Proactivity implies a 'can-do' approach, where an effect is imposed by you on something. Reactivity suggests that the effect is being imposed *on you* by something external and would be a common theme in avoidance situations.

Reactively avoiding requires much less effort, while learning to master your nervous system arousal requires time input, courage, and perseverance. It also means that you get to stay safely inside your comfort zone most of the time, whereas self-mastery only comes about through braving it out in the risk zone and learning to tolerate the unpleasant feelings you feel there. Reactively avoiding means you don't have to feel entirely responsible for how events turn out – such as when you have to leave a situation. 'What could I do? I can't help it if I get panicky in supermarkets (need to get to a toilet quickly, get away from a nearby dog etc.), can I?' Through learning to face down the sensations by staying, you learn through first-hand experience that it is only you who is ultimately responsible for the sensations reaching such high levels of intensity, through the beliefs about them which you hold to be truths, and the efforts you do or don't make to reduce them. And that it's you who is ultimately responsible for how narrow your horizons have become.

This principle applies to any change we're trying to bring into our lives, whether that's losing weight or saving to buy a car. The reactive stance focuses on short-term gratification, whereas the proactive approach invests in the long term. So the longings the delicious cream bun or the enticing clothes shop window instil in a proactive person are fully experienced, their effect registered, but a decision ultimately made to ignore them because they conflict with their long-term goal. They aren't prepared to forfeit their future goal by being seduced by here-and-now sensations.

Before reading on, and in order to deepen your commitment to ridding yourself of your panic and/or phobia, it can be sobering, if painful, to make a list of all the ways in which it curtails your life. Put down everything from the literal restriction on freedom to go where you want, whenever you want, to the emotional price you pay in terms of relationships and self-esteem, to the financial effects such as loss of earning potential or promotional prospects. Most importantly, and frequently left out of such a list, is the soul-shrinking effect, the down-sizing of what could have been a much bigger life to a lesser, compromised version. Also include on your list the effect on those closest to you, especially children, in terms of missing out – holidays which are out of the question because of your fear, social occasions unattended or un-enjoyed by you but perhaps significant to them, and of course your company in those everyday parts of their life where you couldn't follow, such as dining in restaurants, shopping, going to the cinema. The purpose of this exercise is not to make you feel more miserable than you were, although it may, but to prod you out of your denial which allows you to convince yourself that living such a life is your only option. It's to help you realise that it is not the only option, either for you or them, so place your list somewhere prominent, and read it often.

Any person with a phobia who is hoping for some other way around it needs to let go of that illusion now. Phobias rarely simply miraculously fade away, and waiting for some new medication to come on the market while your life ticks by is a tragic waste. Freedom from phobias can best be achieved by regular controlled exposure to the dreaded triggers themselves, and to the panicky sensations it generates. Then at last the conditioning which links sensations to inescapable danger can be broken, and your cycle of fear interrupted for good. Also, the good news is that once overcome, phobias rarely return, so you only have to take this leap of faith once.

A word of comfort to those of you who are still doubtful about facing those dreaded sensations without running. Paradoxically, although it may seem that staying and allowing sensations to get stronger would mean more fear hormones, the opposite is in fact most often what happens. Your body believes every word you tell it, so alerting it to 'flee, run away, escape at all costs!' is followed by a corresponding surge in adrenaline. An attitude of 'stay and face it, ride it out' is reflected in a subsequent drop in adrenaline and in the sensations, because in order for your mind to even entertain for one split second the proposition of staying as a viable option, it must have convinced your body that it was going to survive the sensations safely.

Whenever you opt for fleeing in order to 'get to safety', remember the triangle governing the three domains of being – thoughts, sensations and behaviours – and how interlinked they are. As the old song goes, 'love and marriage ... go together like a horse and carriage ... you can't have one without the other.' It is referred to as entraining when certain behaviours automatically call up specific emotions, ones which may not have been there to start with. A side-splitting laugh at a great joke can shift you from gloom to glee in minutes. Or a couple of hours of digging your garden can gradually bring a feeling of calm your hurried week had robbed you of. Likewise, fleeing is a behaviour which, if you commit to it and begin to give it energy (planning your escape by checking out the exits, restlessly watching for the right moment, making agitated phone calls) intensifies those emotions normally associated with escaping, fear and dread, and encourages thoughts of a catastrophic nature – just what you don't want. One of the laws of consciousness is 'whatever you focus on expands' so if you focus on staying, you'll get more and more of a feeling that you could manage it.

16

FROM FLIGHT TO FIGHT

KEYNOTE: FACING DOWN YOUR FEAR

This chapter is about taking up the challenge to venture beyond your comfort zone, knowing that it will involve confronting instead of automatically running from the unpleasant feelings, through:

- learning to distinguish unpleasant sensations from dangerous or unendurable ones, and choosing to stay and tolerate the unpleasantness
- learning not only to endure and tolerate the sensations, but eventually to eliminate them totally through the use of specific tools
- laying down new 'grooves' of knowledge in your mind so that you can keep yourself 'safe' by means other than avoiding, making your phobia unnecessary.

This new learning will take commitment and perseverance, because some of the activities involve going out in public, and they may also take longer to complete, like going to a shopping mall. Or the occasion may not come around spontaneously too often, like going on a train or travelling some distance from home, so you may have to deliberately set up opportunities to challenge yourself. One of the ways in which I gauge a phobic person's ambivalence about change is when I hear rationalisations like 'I couldn't practise taking the bus because I was offered a lift in to work', or 'the bad weather kept me from getting out to the shops', or 'I don't have any dog to practise the exposure exercises with'. If you're serious about recovering, you can't wait any longer for the occasions to arise spontaneously – you have to seek them out.

INCH BY INCH, MILE BY MILE

The task of this chapter is to target a certain phobic situation, such as going on the bus or to the supermarket, and making it your goal over a number of weeks, to cease avoiding it by fleeing at the first whispers of nervous arousal. In order to prepare yourself for the task ahead, certain adjustments to your thinking help.

You must start by expecting to experience unpleasant sensations, and accept that these may be pretty intense when the time comes to do each practice. Just as with the activities such as spinning and step-ups in the previous chapter, it's deluded to hope that 'with a bit of luck' you might not feel too anxious, and 'cross your fingers and hope for the best' is certainly not advice you'd give to someone sitting an exam or playing in Wimbledon. Luck has nothing whatsoever to do with the outcome, and everything to do with the preparatory groundwork you've put in.

The plan is to deliberately allow the very sensations that frighten you to begin, and, against all your instincts, to intensify, so you can have opportunities to practise dampening them. So if your task is to go to a shopping mall, remind yourself that you can expect to feel light-headed or nauseous, but that instead of trying to resist the sensations when they begin to arise, you're going to witness them start, and when they're as intense as you can handle without running, you will begin using your strategies to bring them down. The goal each time is to reach a stage beyond the point where you would have used avoidance measures before.

So the attitude 'I hope going there doesn't make me feel dizzy or shaky' doesn't make any sense if you want new learning to happen. How can that kind of reactive wishful thinking lead to a feeling of competence? That's like going out to a golf match or a driving lesson hoping you won't have to hit a ball or meet another car! Can you appreciate the difference in attitude between 'Hopefully I'll get through the activity without panicking' (said with fingers crossed) versus 'I know I'll be nervous but I'm prepared to feel it if it helps me permanently lose my fear of it'? One is doing it while still internally avoiding it, thinking all the while of short-term escape. The other is deciding to face it squarely, and proactively see it through, in the interest of long-term progress. This stance is very different from avoidance, because you are actually prepared to feel anxious, and if you've been taking in most of the information you've been given in the other chapters, the sensations should not terrify you to the same degree as before. It means you're at the point of really deciding to go for it – no matter what.

This new attitude must also apply to how you relate to the anxiety-lowering strategies you've learned. Your objective shouldn't be to 'prevent at all costs any sensations whatsoever'. That thinking still implies you're terrified of them ever, ever happening. The techniques you've learned are not designed to prevent 'dire and dangerous consequences' but to dampen down a nervous system over-reaction. By doing this they are attempting to change your conditioned response to the sensations from 'they overwhelm me and I can do nothing to stop them' to 'as they occur I've learned that I can dampen them down so I don't need to feel out-of-control and fearful of them'. Do you see the difference?

RETREAT RATHER THAN ESCAPE

If you couldn't conceive of staying and sitting out your phobic urge to escape, perhaps because it's been so long since you did, then retreat is a good half-way house measure. This means going to a point past your previous comfort zone, and if the sensations get too strong, then temporarily exiting the situation with the intention of returning when your anxiety has subsided somewhat. This is slightly different from escape because it implies that you are merely taking a break away from the intensity of the feelings rather than bailing out entirely. By retreating you are saying 'I need to take the space to reduce my sensations before I return to the challenging situation' rather than 'I need to get out to safety and I won't be coming back'.

Very few situations have absolutely 'no exit' as you may have been suggesting to yourself. Such all-or-nothing thinking can sabotage you by filling your mind with obstacles, persuasively rationalising that it would ruin things for others if you had to go home, that people would be offended that you left, etc., suggesting that if you can't last through an entire social event you're probably better not going at all. Retreating is a way of showing yourself that there is more than one version of escape, and if you get used to using it, sometimes even a couple of times during the event, it can allow you to tackle the challenge of staying by degrees instead of all in one go.

Retreating might mean pulling your car over on to the hard shoulder for a while to slow your breathing before going on, rather than trying to keep going the whole way till your destination. Or leaving a meeting 'to use the bathroom' and returning quickly after easing the sensations somewhat. Or it could mean briefly absenting yourself from a dinner table to 'make a phone-call' or 'get something from the car', and then returning. In these ways you can stop urging yourself to 'get home quick!', and in doing so abandoning the entire situation, complicating things by the guilt of having to let other people down, feeling later that you've missed out, etc. Don't throw the baby out with the bathwater by being too all-or-nothing: much can often be gained by the middle road.

SETTING A PACE – WALK BEFORE YOU RUN

Although it's important to fully expose yourself to the sensations in your chosen situation, it makes sense also to keep it within an achievable range. A success, however humble, is preferable to feeling a failure because you set your goal too high. If going to the supermarket is your task, you must stay for at least long enough to get the sensations going. It's important to be firmly outside your comfort zone, so you can feel the old familiar feelings of anxiety rising. Only there are you creating new pathways, learning grooves in your mind, presenting opportunities to practise your skills. So there's no point in staying only a few minutes and then leaving because 'nothing happened'. That just means you were still inside your comfort zone. As you begin to feel the sensations build, by repeatedly reassuring yourself that 'no matter how uncomfortable I may feel, I am not in any danger and can tolerate it', you are extending it. Remember, actually getting the shopping done is not the task: losing the sense of risk, that is your priority.

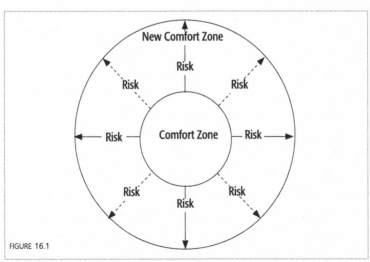

FIGURE 16.1

233

With all situations, pace the exposures. You may find too that if you take it at your own pace, you can tolerate the sensations for longer than you thought. Rather than letting someone pressure you into lasting out the whole evening in a hot pub, travelling the entire journey in a stuffy car, or actually petting a dog, if the exposure was long enough to have genuinely challenged you, and generated a level of fear beyond what you're used to, then it's OK to quit while you're ahead. Each time see if you can lengthen the activity by a few minutes. In the same way, step up the level of challenge – from going into a shop with someone, to tackling it alone, from walking past a garden containing a dog in the company of someone, up the scale of 'risk' to going on your own to the park, without your mobile, where dogs run free. If having someone encouraging with you helps you to endure the sensations for a bit longer, then arrange it. However, much as most of your learning to drive a car took place once you were on your own, remember it's you who has to learn to endure the situation and still know you're safe, so don't hang on to people as a prop indefinitely.

If you have the experience of being challenged, feeling frightened and having to bail out, don't be hard on yourself, because there is still much information that can be gleaned from such an experience, so it's never a waste. A good sports coach will review videos with you of the matches you lost, as an aid to learning what went wrong. Spend some time evaluating your effort to analyse the feelings and your response to them. What were the elements of the scenario in terms of triggers? What sensations did you experience? What kind of self-statements were you running, supportive or sabotaging? Were there any defeatist beliefs running through your mind that you allowed to sabotage your efforts, and discourage you from giving your full attention to the techniques? If you go back over the experience you'll find that somewhere along the line something you may have thought or done contributed to raising your own adrenaline (an own goal) or preventing it from falling. If it isn't immediately obvious what it was, then keep looking – some fearful image from the past, an old habit of thinking or unconscious action crept in below your radar and spooked you into your old patterns. That's how conditioning works, by twinning one thing with another in a way we're rarely aware of.

LADDERING – ONE RUNG AT A TIME

Decide on the hierarchy of difficulty from least to most. Confronting the situations in a repeated and controlled manner is the best method of changing your reaction to them, and breaking the phobic conditioning. Small children learning to swim, or even adults learning to drive a car, do so more efficiently if the process is presented to them in bite-sized pieces that are manageable. Throwing them in the deep end of the pool can work for some, but for many it can turn them off swimming for life.

Next, try to be really specific about what it is in each situation that makes it particularly trying for you. Witness the thoughts you are having. For example, you may find that you feel OK on minor roads but that motorways are out of the question. Why is this? Have you convinced yourself that it's less easy to pull over if you panic on a motorway, whereas you could easily do so on a minor road? Or have you rationalised that nobody would stop to help you on a motorway because they're going by so fast, but would on a side road? Or is it because there are usually houses on minor roads that you could go into, whereas on motorways you can go for miles without seeing a house (and in your mind you'd be long dead by then!)? It's important to flush out and question such rationalisations so you can see through them, and instead, when they start filling your mind with 'what if' thoughts, argue it out in as bolshy a manner as you would in the face of any other line of rubbish someone was trying to put over on you. Your sense of safety does not depend on any of the flimsy excuses offered above, but on your ability to believe that it is only an illusion that you can't cope simply because certain bodily sensations are present.

Specify the rungs of your hierarchical ladder. Design tasks that are a genuine challenge and sufficient to get your adrenaline up, so you can practise lowering it. So for example, if driving within five miles of your home is something you could manage, but driving any further away from home would be something you would characteristically avoid, then pick a ten mile exercise, because only then will learning occur. Simply deciding to 'go out driving' is not specific enough. Or if losing your terror of dogs is your goal, then be specific, don't just go out 'to meet dogs', because those you come across could be on leads and so won't challenge you. If that's a level you're comfortable with, go one step up the hierarchy and make sure you meet some dogs running around off leads, by going to the beach or the park.

Likewise, sitting at a movie may be tolerable (and therefore not sufficient challenge) if you have an aisle seat, but anxiety-provoking if you are sitting in the middle of the row. Shops may be manageable first thing in the morning when nobody is around, but unthinkable during peak hours. Always go for the exercise that holds more challenge, otherwise you're not changing the fearful beliefs that say there's a difference between one situation and another. Never forget, the sensations will never overwhelm you, even if your mind tries to convince you otherwise.

Beginning the exercises is rather like going swimming in really cold water. Some people like to submerge themselves by the 'inch by inch' method, pacing themselves by starting small and working up. If shopping alone is your challenge, you could begin with, say, ten minutes and work up to thirty, the rationale being that each experience of success, however small, inches you towards your goal of demonstrating that you can survive these situations.

On the other hand, others find that jumping in at the deep end works better, and they opt to take the bull by the horns and go for it, attempting the most challenging item first. This is known as flooding, and involves a greater leap of faith, preparing to allow the sensations wash over, surrendering to them, and finding out if you can survive them. It produces results faster, but both routes bring you to the same destination in the long run, as long as you keep motivating yourself to try harder and harder challenges.

Planning is important. It can act as an incentive to tell someone like a family member or your therapist what your plan is, so that you'll be less likely to duck out at the last minute, and gives them a role as a motivating force from the sidelines, while not necessary accompanying you.

It really is essential to follow through with your plan in a structured and controlled way, otherwise learning is patchy and inconsistent, and you can slip back into complacency, pleading 'but I tried, it just didn't work!' rendering the entire approach unscientific and with a greater chance of failing, like cheating on yourself while you're following a certain diet.

① *Make a list of situations which you want to stop avoiding.*

② *Specify your initial goal.*

Driving on a motorway for ten miles alone.

Shopping in a crowded supermarket alone for an hour.

Lodging money in the bank during their busiest time.

Visiting a house where there is a dog.

③ *Specify the steps, if you've decided on the gradual approach.*

Driving for four miles accompanied then alone, eight miles accompanied then alone, ten miles accompanied then alone.

Shopping for ten minutes, then twenty, then thirty, then forty-five, then one hour.

Standing in line at the bank with one person ahead, then with three people, then with ten.

Being in the dog's presence on the lead with someone there, then with the dog off the lead alone.

④ *Visualise the experience before going into the situation.*

⑤ *Allow the anxiety to build as much as you can tolerate*, and then begin using your strategies to reduce your fear. Practise this as many times as you need to, in order to inch closer to your goal. Try to do the practice frequently and not leave long gaps, since that reinforces the old beliefs in avoidance and your new learning is forgotten.

VISUALISATION – REHEARSING SUCCESS IN YOUR IMAGINATION

To do this, while seated or lying, close your eyes and 'see' yourself going through the entire exercise. Start from before you leave the house, imagining how you might feel, what thoughts you might be running, based on past experience, which sensations might be likely to have started coming up. Witness yourself as though in a movie and make the picture realistic, filled with your initial habitual fearful images and escape-oriented self-statements. Next, watch yourself apply the various strategies you've learned, relaxing and breathing slowly, and countering any catastrophic thoughts. Visualise the fear levels subsiding as you bring control over your adrenaline level, making yourself feel safe without having to run.

The visualisation works best if you can conjure up a fairly convincing fear reaction followed by a successful dampening down of the physical sensations. It should end with calm being restored, with you feeling pleased to have had the courage to face the feelings, and optimistic that you no longer have to avoid in the future. These 'dry runs' will prepare you for the real thing, and may be the first time in a while that you have had an opportunity to inhabit the 'stand and face it' position with positive results.

Ciara had begun to avoid situations in which she felt 'trapped' and unable to easily escape. In particular this included the hairdresser's, where she felt she would die of embarrassment if she had to leave in a hurry, and for which she insisted that Jeff park the car out front and wait for her (in readiness). Also the supermarket check-out, where she knew some of the management (she would always feel better in one further from home than their local one). The parent–teacher meetings at the school were becoming a problem lately, and her godson's graduation looming up was on her mind. She decided to target the check-out first because she could practise more often.

On her first three tries she brought Jeff, having him wait outside in the car, and found that she never even made it to the desk before she had to run out to him for reassurance. As she did with the exposure exercises, she noticed that her thoughts were all taken up with her mental catastrophe video of collapsing and attracting a crowd of people round her. She also admitted that her approach had indeed been one of 'fingers crossed and hope for the best' rather than acknowledging that her reaction had nothing to do with luck, and that hoping that no distress whatsoever would result was unrealistic.

On the fourth attempt she began to truly commit to staying, and thinking out the consequences in a more realistic way. She allowed herself to visualise becoming distressed in the queue and how that might feel. The exercises in the sensation exposure chapter familiarised her with the concept of letting the feelings become intense, but it seemed harder to concentrate on applying her techniques when out in public. The thoughts that kept preoccupying her were all to do with people's disapproval or ridicule if they saw her on the ground, presuming she was drunk or on drugs. Social death! She had never realised that it was so important to her. She decided to counter them with an affirmation – 'I believe in the sympathy and kindness of others' and visualised the response of the check-out girl being one of understanding and helpfulness if she did indeed have to make an excuse and run. She decided to relate to her vulnerability with compassion rather than impatience and criticism, and found that this encouraged her to stay a few minutes longer each time.

Once she was confident of being able to survive the queuing and complete the entire task, she tackled it without Jeff being somewhere close by. Again, her anxiety rose as she confronted her fears about collapsing in public without someone who 'cares enough about me and who I could trust' to get medical help. She observed that at the first whisper of distress, right on cue, she began running a video of the staff not realising the seriousness of her situation (that she had not merely fainted but was at risk of dying of a heart attack) and failing to act quickly enough. This time, however, the thoughts were much easier to discredit because she saw them for what they were, a bad habit, and also that they did not bear up to testing, because despite the sensations getting stronger than ever before, she hadn't ever collapsed. She visualised herself becoming anxious but reminded herself that her reaction was no different from when she was doing the exercises at home without Jeff, that just being out in public didn't automatically make it more risky. Her mantra became 'I am safe wherever I am because my heart is normal and healthy'.

From there Ciara used the same tactics at the hairdresser's. More and more she could see that her confidence in the capacity of others to appreciate and understand her difficulty was very low. This would intimidate her into trying to prevent it happening at all costs, which she realised was putting her under undue pressure. Once she was comfortable with the notion of assertively stating that she was unwell and needed to leave, no matter what they thought, she didn't feel so trapped, and paradoxically the drop in adrenaline level meant that she was not as prone to panic as often. As her godson's graduation approached she decided to honour her own needs for once, and to give herself the option of missing the reception if she wasn't up to it. She visualised the actual ceremony many times before the day, emphasising to herself the inherent safety in the situation, while still acknowledging that she might feel a little distressed out of habit, but also making no distinction between the ceremony and the other situations she had successfully managed. In the end she made it, but allowed herself to retreat outside the hall a few times in order to bring down her anxiety enough to stay for the whole ceremony.

SOME SPECIFIC PHOBIAS

- dogs
- public speaking
- social phobia
- flying
- exams
- blood.

Fear of Dogs

In some phobias there may be only one specific trigger for the panic response, and it's often the case that this is the only single area in which a person experiences panic, and the usual watchfulness for imminent attacks of anxiety do not occur in their life in general. There is, however, the very same instant response once the trigger is spotted, such as a dog, and all the steps towards learning to control those sensations apply. The conditioned response was Dog = Danger = Fight–Flight sensations, and the task is to restructure that complex into Dog = Safety = No sensations.

Mary and I met some years ago when I was asked to take part in helping members of the public who rang in to a certain TV show to overcome their phobia. She had been phobic of dogs since the family dog, a little King Charles Cavalier, had jumped on her at the age of four, barking, knocking her over and licking her on the face until hauled away by her mother who heard her screaming. Subsequently the dog was given away, and she had always related to that incident as a very dangerous one.

Thirty-eight years later, having been terrified of dogs all her life, Mary was now a mother of two small children, unable to bring them to the park or the beach, and would even drive down the road to her sister's house six houses away rather than risk meeting a dog on the footpath. Recently, their first holiday by the sea had been a disaster, with every minute spent on the lookout for dogs. So, desperate to find a way of tackling her problem, she had contacted the programme, and prepared to reveal all to the nation in a bid to push herself towards her goal. If we were successful, the plan was for her to show a dog in the National Dog Show five weeks from that meeting. Since she lived at the other end of the country, I knew there was not going to be much opportunity to see her beyond one or two sessions at most, and the first time we met, for all of forty minutes, in less than ideal circumstances in a hotel foyer while the camera crew were setting up, was barely enough to get the abridged version of her story. I wondered how we were going to manage her recovery at long distance.

In any case, before we parted we discussed the general principles of what she had to do. First, she would read about panic so she understood all about what was happening inside her when the sight of a dog got her fear up. Second, she would begin practising the breathing and relaxation exercises every day for a few days until she felt confident she knew how to use them once she became nervous. (When you first learned to drive, you practised your skills away in a quiet car park until you had them perfected. You certainly didn't try them for the first time in rush hour traffic!)

Third, she would arrange to spend time in the presence of a dog, planning a step-wise increase in how long and how near to it she would get. Petting it did not have to be the goal, nor becoming a dog-lover, but simply to be able to be in its presence without fear taking her over, and without running away. Co-incidentally, her brother-in-law had a small dog, the same breed as the dog from her childhood. Initially when she had mentioned her project to her family, it emerged that in fact her memory of the incident had some inaccuracies in it, because in her child's mind the dog she recalled had been very large, when in reality it wasn't, and the reason the dog was got rid of was not because it was sent to be put down for being dangerous, but simply because it she was too nervous around it so they gave it to a neighbour.

Every day for at least an hour Mary went to her brother-in-law's. Initially, the dog had to put it out of sight while she entered the house, then gradually began bringing it into the room she was in, on the lead, at the far end to her. The first few times, even before it came into the room, Mary was so tense that she could barely breathe, and stood with a wall behind her and a chair between them. But she worked hard at gaining control over the sensations, remembering to unclench her hands, slow her breaths, and most of all repeating to herself that in spite of her mind suggesting to her that she was in danger, in reality she wasn't. Her mantra was 'feelings aren't facts, feelings aren't facts' and during the sessions she said it over and over to herself (while never taking her eye off the dog!).

Mary's fear was in relation to a memory, not to the dog in the room. We talked on the phone once a week during this time, and I kept emphasising that so much of the task is matching the reality in front of her (a docile older dog on a lead, who most of the time wasn't even looking in her direction, showing no signs of aggression) with her traumatic memory which to a four-year-old child was in fact dangerous, a true alarm (a young barking dog she couldn't control, who jumped right up on her). Mary began noticing how many of her thoughts were about what she predicted might happen – 'he'll bite me, he'll bark, I won't be able to get away' – in spite of the fact that no such thing was in fact happening. This realisation gave her more courage to overlook the short-term urge to run away, because she could see now the tricks her mind had been playing on her.

Gradually over two weeks she graduated to being in the room with the dog off the lead, then without its owner, then out in the garden with it running around. The sessions always took the same course, initial nervousness on entering the house, peaking when the dog came near her, then subsiding as she used the techniques until before leaving she felt more at ease. Gradually Mary got used to factoring in the sensations, reconciling herself to their presence as part of the project. Over time, since this was a dog she already knew, and a small one, she found she could relax quite easily, but doubted she could do the same with strange larger dogs.

So she stepped up the level of risk and began the same procedure with a neighbouring farmer's Labrador, and within another week of daily practice, and bargaining for even higher levels of fear, she could walk across the farmyard even if he was running around. She was also learning about doggy behaviour through talking to the owners – barking is about many things, mostly communication, but is rarely a sign of aggression towards you. There are welcome barks, territorial barks simply alerting owners to people on the property, barks to go outside to do their business, etc. Sniffing was also discussed, and she realised she'd always interpreted this behaviour as a prelude to a bite, instead of the dog's way of relating to and getting to know its world, another reason they run towards you. These conversations helped Mary to tell herself factual information whenever her mind began spiralling off into catastrophe thoughts.

Most dog phobics ask, 'but doesn't a dog sense or smell your fear, and then come after you? So won't I get bitten if he picks up mine?' Dogs don't actually smell fear, but they do notice when someone is exhibiting the behaviours which accompany fear – such as someone waving their hands around, running, screaming, or fending them off with a shopping bag – and these can be interpreted as interesting, potentially someone who wants to interact and play with them. If you stand still, and particularly if you don't eyeball them or say anything to them, they lose interest and leave you alone.

An interesting twist arose when it emerged that Mary's worst dread was puppies (because of size alone, they'd be at the lower end of most people's fear-producing scale) because they wriggled and ran about, but mostly because they did a lot of licking, which she dreaded. So the TV crew arranged a day of puppies, putting them in her bath so they were contained. By the end of the day, having stood among them wearing Wellingtons boots, then without, touching them with gloves on, then without, she could lift them up with ease.

The walk down to her sister's was next, then the park, and finally the beach. While she was doing all this I only saw Mary once more before our deadline, and was so proud to see her leading a large white Bernese mountain dog round the arena at the dog show, calm in spite of there being many hundreds of barking dogs under its roof.

Working with Mary taught me one very important thing, and I tell her story in answer to anyone who asks me 'How long will it take? Will I have to come to see you often?' Mary's story shows that it takes as long as you want to string it out, and most of the work can be done without the assistance of any therapist. But you need to be motivated and persistent, like she was, prioritising your goal by devoting the time required.

Social Phobia – No man is an Island

Evidence suggests that within the human condition we all have a biologically determined readiness to associate fear with angry, critical or rejecting faces. In other words we have become primed or conditioned to link the two without being aware of doing so. Anger or rejection which you observe being directed at others doesn't elicit the same fear, it usually has to be directed towards you to have that effect. This may be so because in primitive times shunning or imposed exile from your tribe may have had serious consequences, with such alienation almost guaranteeing your demise shortly after. In modern times perhaps our image-consciousness regarding fitting in socially is protective too.

Direct eye contact is critical to this response being stimulated, and a continuum operates along which we place individuals – at one end is the normal discomfort at being 'in the limelight', and at the other, those who are extremely fearful of public speaking or other social situations, displaying an exaggerated version of the normal sensitivity to being critiqued. The ability to memorise faces also seems to occur along a spectrum, with phobics having a more selective memory for critical than for accepting faces, and showing a bias in terms of the degree of attention they give to these, more often evaluating information as socially threatening while others ignore it.

In any fear situation, it's natural to become more self-conscious and preoccupied with our performance, but in social situations or public speaking, this inward focus is a handicap to performance, because it detracts attention necessary for carrying out the task, leading to a higher likelihood of making mistakes. More importantly, since in terms of consciousness you often find whatever you're looking for, you notice that incompetence more and then worry about it.

Considering these factors – an oversensitivity to criticism, anger or rejection, a memory bias for the negative, and an easier distractibility towards internal events – it is not hard to see how some individuals are more vulnerable than others to being shy or fearful in this area. Along the continuum we can find those who find many social situations slightly uncomfortable at first, but relax once the circumstances are right for them, such as small groups rather than large, people they know rather than strangers, etc. At the other extreme we find those who are devastated by the slightest (invariably imagined) sign of rejection or disapproval, and have adopted avoidance as a more tolerable if unfulfilling lifestyle.

This continuum seems to point to a wide variation in skills covering social situations, and it seems obvious that psychotherapy addressing the source of the fear can be very helpful. It can often be a child's own nature to be cautious and timid, but if a child was routinely criticised, or aggressive and intimidating behaviour was frequently displayed towards them either at home or at school, it would be easy to see how they might always feel on guard in the company of others. Bullying has a legacy which can reach over decades, so that even as an adult they might find themselves unable to relax, always expecting the rebuff, forever watchful that they were coming across as different or their behaviour was not reaching the group standard. Self-acceptance and independence from the opinions of others can lead to a parallel drop in fear levels and are the cornerstones on which inner confidence is built. These can be enhanced through help with adjusting any conversational and body language habits developed as a protective defence over the years but which present a less user-friendly face to others – dodging eye contact, a mumbling unclear voice, answering monosyllabically to questions, doormat behaviour – all good survival tactics to avoid the notice of a bully, but counter-productive when trying to socialise normally.

Many who panic in social situations may only have lost their confidence with the onset of the panic attacks. The sense of risk may relate not to your social skills, but solely to your ability to keep the panic hidden. Besides the unpleasantness internally, you may sweat so intensely that rivers of sweat run down your face, which blushes crimson, or your facial muscles contort into a grimace, all of which add to the excruciating experience of being judged by others. Obviously if you can be helped to gain some degree of competence in that area, your comfort in social situations will return, so those skills specific to lowering nervous system arousal are important, along with a rigorous attention to triggering thoughts, and the learning gained (through exposure to the feared situations) of being able to endure the experience.

Developing a 'so what, see if I care!' attitude to the opinions of others can substantially reduce the inner sense of threat, because anger is a stronger emotion than fear, and elicits the chemistry of 'fight' more than 'flight', through adding testosterone to the equation. I've had a few clients who found that the mental skills learnt in martial arts training – creating strong thoughts to accompany their actions – translated into not fearing people socially. So paradoxically, by becoming less attached to what people might think, you redress the power balance in your favour, your nervous arousal falls, and the symptom you're concerned about may not happen at all. It may sound paradoxical, but you get what you want by ceasing to want it.

For those suffering from phobic sensations in social situations such as a wedding or christening, practice might involve seeking out any type of opportunity which resembles these and offers you a chance to practise your anxiety-lowering techniques. Here you must become creative, and dedicated. You might attend a number of Sunday services, or even daily ones (notwithstanding any lack of religious enthusiasm, that's not the point). Although they may be only pale impressions of the big day itself, they have many elements in common – the distance from the door ruling out escape, a ceremony with a beginning, middle and end, crowds present. You can experiment with retreating rather than leaving and going home, and when the big day itself arrives it will hopefully only have a couple of added ingredients (relatives rather than strangers, etc.). Since you will know of the date well in advance there is no excuse for procrastination, so get practising the moment the invite arrives.

Any opportunity that resembles yours will do. If getting through office meetings is your difficulty, some people have found it useful to use other types of meeting as practice. Classes of any kind provide the ingredients – set time-frame, with a full room of people present, the fact that leaving would pose a slight problem – yet they don't hold any professional risk, so you lose very little if your first few attempts don't go well. The class content is irrelevant – bridge, cookery, gardening, wine-tasting, anything will do! Also parent–teacher meetings, residents' association meetings, anything where the door is closed and you begin to get the old familiar feelings.

If the social situation where you feel panicky and self-conscious is dining out, then don't wait for an invite and begin to dread the occasion from that moment on. Set up a schedule of practice rehearsals. Start easy, maybe inviting one friend who knows about your problem to meet initially for coffee, then for dinner, then with another person who doesn't know, and on up the scale to a group of strangers. Time them close together so you'll learn faster. You'll be forever learning to play the 'Moonlight Sonata' if you only sit down at the piano once a month! The procedure is the very same as for any other phobia, let the sensations build, use your strategies, watch your thoughts, retreat if you have to, then come back.

Shyness

In the case of those who are so shy that talking to anyone other than the family is a daily awesomely challenging task, individual and group psychotherapy can be very beneficial as a place in which to reality-check your negative impressions of yourself. In our relationships with others we can engage in projection, where instead of reading the situation accurately you project onto it interpretations based on your own psychological makeup. An example would be that if you were criticised a lot as a child, and as a result are highly sensitive to disapproval, you might project onto other people that they are being aggressive or intimidating when objectively they are merely giving an opinion in a neutral manner about some behaviour of yours.

Unlike in social situations, where you can get away with being silent to such a degree that you contribute very little outwards, in a therapy group you are expected to speak and encouraged to come in from the periphery and participate. It gives you a chance to practise the art of keeping your end of a conversation going in a low-risk situation, where the other participants are not your peers.

In one-to-one therapy there can be an opportunity for role-playing, where you and your therapist can decide to discuss certain topics you feel unskilled in, and try to keep the run of the conversation going despite panicky thoughts and feelings arising. As in a tennis game, the ball going over and back, each player tries to keep it moving, avoiding it going into the net. Those overtaken by shy self-consciousness can be attending so much to what they're feeling inside that they can give the impression to others that they're not interested because they contribute so little, bringing no information about themselves to the enterprise. In this way they can come across as aloof and superior, when in fact they're anything but. With a therapist, you can develop a repertoire of information-gathering questions to ask people so it diverts the attention away from you, and listening carefully to their reply. Videoing the session can give valuable feedback.

Once again, any opportunity to practise will do, so if your goal is to work up to feeling relaxed around people, start with a few comments to the man behind the counter in the local shop, engage the postman about the weather, ask directions from the person next to you on the bus, ask directions from department store staff, all the time trying to see if you can keep the sentences coming, about anything at all, it's all practice. Then work up the scale of risk, to slightly more personal conversations, about topics you actually have a view on and will reveal something about you. Attend public lectures on any subject, or visit farmers' markets resolving to strike up a conversation with someone about their product. Read the papers to have a few topics on the tip of your tongue, so silences won't freak you.

If your goal is to be less fearful socially, you can see how you have to be proactive about seeking out opportunities, can't you? No progress will be made behind the door of your house. If you want to bring your skills up to speed, it's got to be done among people, and the principle of all phobias still applies – it's only your belief which tells you that people are a risk to you, it's not the truth. So you must be rigorous at editing out threatening statements your mind is making.

Public Speaking

You don't have to be phobic to feel apprehensive about making a speech, many people are, for several reasons. First, many of the occasions on which this issue arises have a lot riding on them in a social sense – 'big days' such as graduations, christenings and weddings, professional presentations attended by peers, business meetings at which a pitch must be made to an important client, or seminars at college for which a grade will be given. So the stakes seem to be higher. Second, your awareness internally of rising unpleasant sensations is magnified by your awareness externally of being watched, scrutinised, assessed, so using the techniques which reduce adrenaline has to be done at the same time as speaking, which is anything but easy. Third, since many social events are often not spontaneous ones but scheduled for some time, it has been 'in your head', with far too much leeway to create thoughts and run catastrophe videos in advance, so that by the time the day arrives you are more likely to be awash with molecules than if it had happened without warning.

Once again, look for trial run opportunities which resemble the occasion. One very determined patient of mine, who knew that as their only child she would have to make a speech at her parents' fiftieth wedding anniversary, approached a parish priest to ask if she could read the lesson for Sunday Mass, with very successful results. She picked a church where she would know no one, figuring she would have less to lose if she stalled in the middle of it, making the prior decision that if that occurred, her plan B would be to simply say 'excuse me, I can't continue' and leave the church, without lifting her gaze from the ground. She never had to use it, and although it was awesomely fearful the first few times, she found that by reading extremely slowly, following her finger phrase by phrase along the line of writing on the page, and most importantly not looking up (and eyeballing anyone) until she had finished, that she managed her speech on the day, which she found considerably easier in comparison.

Toastmasters is an organisation which was set up for the explicit purpose of making public speaking easier, including for those who stutter or stammer. It welcomes people attending as an observer first, then if they wish, volunteering to speak on the topic of their choice. The non-judgemental atmosphere, coupled with the explicit spirit of adventure, but without any accompanying pressure to succeed, can be an ideal opportunity.

Exam Nerves

There are two aspects to this problem. One is the fear of going blank on the day, and being unable to remember anything you've studied, and the other is dreading that others in the exam hall will notice that you're having a panic attack.

The prevention of a heart attack doesn't begin in the ambulance on the way to the hospital, it starts twenty years earlier. Preventing a blank in memory is similar, with practices put in place way before the day comes. In the run-up to an exam there is the temptation to over-study, and to allow your worries about failing to push you into overdrive. This can mean you cut down on R and R activities, sleep less, take no exercise, often don't eat properly, and think about nothing else. The climate before any exam is one of degrees of fear. As you've read, fear thoughts create the corresponding molecules – adrenaline. This is where pessimists and perfectionists are particularly at risk, because their whole premise is 'expect the worst' and 'aim for the best in order to be sure'. Too many weeks or months of high levels of adrenaline will ensure that you're wound up like a coiled spring in the run-up to the day, and as the level climbs so does the prediction of catastrophe, stimulating even more production of the hormone.

We have four different brainwaves from which we operate, ranging from the fastest beta, where most of our attention is given to concentrating on outside stimuli, down through slower alpha where we focus inward with eyes closed and body still, down again into daydreamy imagery-filled theta, and finally delta, coinciding with sleep. Studying encourages mainly beta wave, and especially when time is running short, we can get stuck on a turbo setting from which it's difficult to turn the revs down, our vigilance constantly attending to (and therefore finding) gaps in our knowledge, and making good sleep less and less likely. Think of your brain as a food processor with so much material to deal with it that it jams. But simply feed it through in bite-sized pieces and it'll digest just as much in the end.

Maintaining balance is the key, and almost sounds too obvious to state. Balance in terms of hours of downtime versus hours spent studying, taking a half-hour break for every hour and a half of study, and seeing that nothing stimulates your brain for a few hours before bed, such as coffee or techno music. Regular daily exercise is a great adrenaline-buster, as is keeping a humorous sense of the absurd in the face of the insanely competitive schools points system. Some good herbal and homeopathic relaxing and sleep-enhancing remedies are available, such as valerian, avena sativa, and kava kava. Restrict the number of conversations you have with other perfectionists about what's likely to come up in order to keep paranoia to a minimum.

As I've encouraged you to examine the deeper meaning beneath your symptoms, you might ask why you are so much more fearful than your peers sitting the same exam. What is out of balance and asking to be redressed in your personality? Do you err too much on the side of negatively assessing your capabilities? The majority of those with the highest levels of anxiety are usually not those who haven't studied enough and have good reason to be nervous, but are the A students who have lost all perspective, convinced it will be the end of life as they know it if they don't achieve the results they want. If it's 'straight A's or die', this is a clear message to your fight–flight response to kick in, and your adrenaline levels will be through the roof, whereas if you could live with more moderate grades, that hormone will be lower, you'll be more relaxed and therefore less likely to blank, and will do better. So it's not a virtue to be perfectionist, but a reflection of distorted thinking which you could usefully spend time working out with a psychotherapist. One day your exams will be behind you, but if that theme remains unchecked in your personality, perhaps a reflection of doubt about your self-worth, it will rear its head again in another circumstance later in life.

The other aspect of exam nerves can be the concern over making a public spectacle of yourself in front of all the other students, and wasting valuable energy and time trying to hide it. If you've experienced a panic attack before in exam circumstances, discuss this fact confidentially with your teachers. One measure which schools are having to consider more is setting aside a special private room for someone who feels trapped and can't stay in the exam hall, but who still wants to finish the paper. On occasion I've arranged that special dispensations be given so that someone can even sit an exam at home under supervision. Set up this option with the cooperation of your doctor and the school in advance if necessary.

Gelsemium is a homeopathic remedy used for stage fright and performance anxiety, so check that option with your homeopath.

Fear of Flying

There are two versions of this fear. Those who are afraid the plane will crash and they will die, and those who fear having a panic attack on board the plane, and being unable to escape it. Taking a Fear of Flying course can help the first group tremendously because it reassures them to be presented with the statistics of how safe flying is, see the cockpit with all the controls and safeguards, to know that there are two pilots at all times, that the plane can even be run on automatic if necessary, etc. There's an opportunity to taxi round the runway without taking off, then a short flight. They are taught relaxation methods similar to the ones in this book, and instructed in how to manage their catastrophic thinking.

For the second group much of the course content is valuable also, but the core fear for them is those doors closing and cutting off their avenue of escape for some hours. For them, this equates to danger, and triggers the beginnings of an attack. Most are extremely agitated in all the stages prior to the 'door moment', often unable to sleep or keep their mind from thinking about it during the weeks since they booked, in the queue during check-in (most endeavour to avoid this by being the first there), and waiting at the gate. By the time they step onto the plane, if they haven't already decided to abort the mission, they are awash with adrenaline.

When I ask people what's the worst scenario they're imagining at that point, I hear things like 'going berserk and behaving like a lunatic, attacking the stewardess and demanding to have the plane return to the terminal, collapsing, stopping breathing' and suchlike. Most agree that in all their years of flying, although at least 5 per cent of travellers are nervous to panicky, they've never ever seen any of the above happen. In the interest of safety, if any of those were even a vague possibility, the airlines would be screening such people out, yet they don't. Why? Because these things don't happen. A panicker's reply is often 'I know that, but ...'

This inaccurate information is still the core of the problem – people who panic tell themselves lies. And the solution to the problem is the same as with all phobias – you must interrupt your old habitual patterns of thinking, breathing, and behaving, and stop dividing the world into safe and dangerous places, placing the panicky sensations which happen in enclosed spaces on a different, more serious level.

The ultimate teacher is taking flight after flight after flight, and realistically acknowledging that in spite of your predictions, you're still alive, you didn't go berserk, you did in fact survive the sensations, nothing dangerous happened in reality, only in your mind. If you've reached the point of no return, map out your campaign by scheduling a number of short flights set about two weeks apart. A good way is to start with a short one, lasting under an hour, but which is still in a regular sized plane (as the turbulence in lighter ones can give anyone an iffy tummy). If you can, have someone accompany you, and have a very loose time frame, in case you can't handle the return flight immediately. A late morning flight is ideal, in case you didn't get much sleep, and so that you're not dwelling with 'those thoughts' for the whole day.

Many people make the mistake of booking their first flight in years as the family holiday, or as a treat for the long-suffering partner, thinking that the incentive not to disappoint will spur them on. This can work sometimes, but the extra burden of pleasing others, added to an already challenging situation, can also be their undoing.

Bargain for the first time being the worst, quite possibly accompanied by really strong sensations, especially if it's been years since you last flew. What surprises most people is that these fears are short-lived, and as soon as the plane is in the air, and the option to duck out is past, they ease. They universally report a huge gap between what they predicted would happen, how severe it would be, for how long, and what actually did happen. They also find that on the second and third time the intensity of everything lessens – fewer fretful days prior, fewer sleepless nights – since you know now what to expect. Most learn that just before and at the start of the flight is the most vulnerable time, so this is the time to really concentrate on your breathing techniques, funnelling your thoughts in safe directions, focusing on the long-term gain at the cost of short-term distress.

Blood and Injection Phobias

Fainting at the sight of blood is a special case in terms of how the fight–flight response plays out, because that response rarely leads to fainting. Curiously, fear of blood needn't always be present, just the sight of blood can be enough, although if fainting recurs every time most people eventually become anxious about the possibility it will happen next time.

Although most phobias are associated with increased sympathetic nervous system arousal following exposure to a trigger, in this case a two-staged response occurs. Initially, for a few seconds or minutes sympathetic arousal increases, with heart rate and blood pressure rising, but this phase is then followed by a drop, due to the activity of the vagus nerve, part of the parasympathetic system whereupon fainting is the result. It's no more serious or complicated than that – not a sign of an imminent brain haemorrhage, stroke or anything serious.

Applied muscle tension has been found to be a successful antidote. This involves learning to tense all the muscles of the body at the same time in order to raise your own blood pressure and counteract the lowering effect of the trigger. The idea is to keep up the tension for a few minutes each time, relax briefly, then tense again until your blood pressure has been recorded as having risen. In this case the tensing practice does not necessarily have to be done during exposure to the blood or needle trigger, it can be practised beforehand with a blood pressure monitor.

17

ENERGY
BANKRUPTCY

The shift into overdraft on your bank account can be from one large withdrawal or a multitude of small ones. The result is the same – you are running on empty. The 'you' that is feeling threatened is the primitive survival part of you that literally keeps your motor running and your very cellular functions ticking over.

Like the straw that broke the camel's back, panic attacks often begin during a time when there is a greater amount of overall stress than usual. If you can't identify any one particular trigger to your panic attacks, this may be because in your case it was a series of small challenges, rather than one large one, which generated the high level of adrenaline, depleted your energy bank, and put you 'in the red'. You may need to *examine the overall background level of adrenaline that you have been running*.

For instance, you may have suffered a bereavement, or had surgery, and this may have been sufficiently distressing to generate a few panic attacks. While you may now be learning ways to control them, if you are also facing a constant level of uncertainty or conflict in a relationship, or a long and draining commute to your workplace, these factors can be undermining your efforts to lower adrenaline in one area by stimulating more of it in another. *All the combined causes of raised adrenaline are relevant* because they all contribute to it reaching that critical threshold required for an attack.

Ned had found it a testing year at work, since he'd been moved to a new division, and was increasingly taking work home, or staying late to check figures for a morning meeting. Their second child was five months old, and wasn't giving them much sleep, so Ned often ended up in the spare room trying to clock up the hours. Six months earlier his mother-in-law had developed Alzheimer's, and now he found that much of his weekend was spent minding the children while his wife helped her father adjust. She was exhausted too, and they were often irritable with each other, but there didn't seem to be anything they could do about their situation. She had given up work to stay at home, but the tighter budget meant that they couldn't afford a holiday or the use of childminders much, so they rarely got a night out. Ned often thought nostalgically of the days when he was single, when life was carefree and fun, and money and sleep were not in such short supply. Although used to feeling tired, he now began to get frequent headaches, and a series of chest infections. He knew he was stressed but didn't see any other option but to keep going and hope things would improve. The final straw came when the company moved to new premises, which involved a longer commute. The first of many panic attacks began within two weeks of battling with cross-town traffic, leaving home an hour earlier and not returning until the children were in bed. Ned had reached the limit of his reserves.

In Ned's case the threat is directly to his energy bank. It is thinly spread over too many areas, none of which are really working efficiently. Look at all the stresses – overextended at work, insufficient sleep, no time to refuel at the weekends, no fun, relationship strain, health problems, and a long commute to work. At a survival level, he is frightened that if he runs out of steam, if his tank registers empty, the present level of performance in his roles – breadwinner, husband, father – will be drastically compromised. So while he's not dealing with a life-or-death issue in the usual sense, he will have to reinvent himself if he is to find a viable new identity, one with enough 'juice' to survive his current situation.

The currency with which we 'pay' for such struggle and striving is adrenaline. Whether it is a positive challenge, like a promotion, a new baby, or a house move, or a negative one, like relationship problems or financial worries, it is all paid for out of the same purse.

BALANCING YOUR BUDGET – ENERGY BANKING

This step is an important extension of the other forms of control you learned in the chapters on breathing, muscle relaxation and safe thinking. If somebody asks you to lend them money, you would mentally check first if you have enough to give to them. If the funds aren't there you have to refuse them: you have no choice. However, with requests made for their energy, many people don't have such a realistic and pragmatic approach, and act as though there were unlimited supplies of it, since they don't regard it as a commodity in the true sense. Much of the time they don't even check to see if they have it to give, because they're used to thinking of themselves as 'givers' or 'fixers', and could never refuse someone in need.

This pattern of ignoring your own need to hold some energy in reserve can become habitual, and can lead to a deficit situation. It evolves through lack of awareness that such an 'energy account' even exists. Our culture's value system (contributed to in no small way by the various churches) has put a negative skew on saying 'no' to others, making it out to be 'selfish'. Naturally, at times when your own energy is high, it is admirable to be so giving and facilitating of others' needs. However, when it is low, continuing to give indiscriminately is not only unwise but also *unintelligent and irresponsible*. If you had a beautiful Ferrari in your garage, you'd think it wise to maintain and service it, not drive it over rough terrain as though it were an off-road vehicle. Isn't it odd that it is framed as 'bad' when you take measures to conserve your energy, and 'good' if you exhaust yourself making sure that the all the 'shoulds, musts, and have-to's' that our society dictates are taken care of?

It may be the environmental context that draws on your energy reserve more than people do. The energy to tolerate noise, crowds, traffic, hunger, cold, schedules, all comes out of the same pool of resources from which you run your thought processes, your emotional responses and your physical body. The word *tolerate* derives from toll, meaning a *tax due to be paid*, so energy is actually expended in order to 'finance' these experiences. If you're operating at a low ebb, then small things like discovering that there is no milk when you open the fridge in the morning, or no bread for breakfast, and that the natives are grumpy, can be more than you have the resources to cope with!

Even though your body may try to alert you to the fact that you're running low, through fatigue and irritability, too often these signals are ignored. Things just 'have to' be done. In this way you go on spending even though you're way over your credit limit, making 'withdrawals' without assessing whether enough is being lodged in your energy account to offset them. If you're having panic attacks, you need to become aware of all the areas in your life that are sources of adrenaline. This includes all the tasks that 'must' get done, the deadlines, the chores, and the difficult people that drain your energy reserves. Make a list of your main drains on a blank page, rating them out of 10 for cost to your account. It may help you to divide them into physical, emotional or mental sources.

Balancing the budget means not only plugging the drains, but also examining the *energy deposits – those experiences that feed and nourish you, that restore your life-force to a healthier level, acting as a counterbalance*. Control over this flow is as important and as powerful in the prevention of panic attacks as controlling your breath or your thoughts. An abundance of this vital force restores a sense of safety and confidence at a very fundamental cellular level. Now make a list of experiences that you know restore and replenish you, rating them out of 10. They can be large deposits of energy such as holidays, or small but vital, such as power naps or your favourite TV programme. Now compare your two lists, your credits and debits. Notice how drains always happen regardless, whereas deposits take more determination to put in place. And how some of your best value experiences in terms of adding energy haven't happened for years!

IS YOUR CAVE AN ADRENALINE-FREE ZONE?

Everyone dealing with stress needs to be able to rely on the safety of their cave at the end of the day. There, protected for a time from further onslaughts from the outside world, they need the opportunity to replenish their energy, and equip themselves to face another day at the coalface. But what if the home is actually a further drain rather than a sanctuary?

If you are already stressed, a sleepless baby or a teenager's noisy music can rob you of precious hours of sleep and tip you over into energy deficit if it goes on for long periods. The demands of being an active parent chauffeuring children around or participating in household chores can be more than you have the reserves for at times of extra strain. Being slightly more irritable than usual, you may not have the patience for confrontations that can seem petty compared to other burdens you're internally coping with. Add to this long hours spent commuting to work, or any other family commitments, such as caring for elderly parents, and you can find your old identity stretched beyond its limit, and having your first panic attack.

It may be possible to negotiate with others if you explain to them that *the underlying rationale is adrenaline management in the interest of health*, not to deprive them of what they want. You must learn to prioritise your need for calm and ease at home in times of extra challenge. You may feel bad about cutting down on obligatory visits to ill or ageing parents, or missing your son's soccer matches in favour of a relaxing day in the garden or an afternoon nap. Or a mother at her wits' end with exhaustion may feel guilty about asking her early-rising husband to get up to the baby at night or ordering a take-away rather than cook. People having panic attacks frequently feel negative enough already about themselves without wanting to add to it by opting out of simple demands at home. However, these are steps you may have to take for a while, in order to make your home a place of comfort and support.

An unfair and unhealthy distinction is often made between physical and psychological needs. If you break a leg or arm, it goes without saying that you will be unable to contribute in the normal way to family chores, etc., and allowances are made in all sorts of ways to facilitate your rest and immobility. You also have pain punctuating your awareness, reminding you where the limit of tolerance is. If you are burnt out psychologically, your needs are no less valid, but because you 'look normal' it is taken for granted that it is business as usual. There is also the cultural conditioning to turn a deaf ear to any psychological prompting urging you to ease up, which doesn't apply to physical illness.

You will have to change some of these attitudes if you are to free up enough energy to meet your current challenge, and avoid unnecessarily triggering panic attacks. This can set up a dilemma within you, as the symptom attempts to get your attention. It seems like a risk to stay the same, and continue triggering attacks, but also a risk to change your ways. Can you learn to accept that there is a limit to the amount of energy you are capable of putting out? Could you handle being a less than perfect parent, son or daughter, or partner for a while? How would it feel if, for the first time in your marriage, you were the vulnerable, needy one, who has to be taken care of, rather than the strong one who handles everything? Could you endure the displeasure of others if you begin saying no to their demands or setting boundaries on your energy? That part of your personality which has been denied, which you have never developed, may be at the very core of the problem, asking for integration. Through your panic attacks, attention may finally be given to your inability to feel you deserve as much ease and calm as others, or to your reluctance to be vulnerable and dependant.

WORK

To many people work can be a source of great fulfilment, to others it may merely be a generator of income, and to some it may be a daily lion's den. It is worth looking at whether it functions for you as a generator or a depletor of energy. Are deadlines contributing to your rising adrenaline? If so, are they self-imposed or part of the job? Many stressed individuals operate with a mental list that 'has to' be finished by the day's end, putting unnecessary pressure on themselves. They'll excuse themselves by claiming that 'it is just my nature', without ever considering seeking professional help to change.

There is a fine line between having enough responsibility to feel satisfaction in the job, and so much that you feel overwhelmed. The match between your level of skill and the level demanded by the job is what determines whether you'll feel out of your depth or competent. If you are getting panic attacks in certain situations at work, it may indicate that you need to increase your skills through further training, or switch to a different area, one in which you feel more in control.

Being on edge all day, vigilant in case you'll make a mistake and incur the ridicule of others, doesn't foster a feeling of safety, therefore your 'fear molecules' will be rising (like Ned's above). Clarity can often be brought to the situation through taking the decision to air your doubts about your performance with your employers. It may indeed be that you are being asked unfairly to function beyond the range of your skills or your job description, or you may find to your surprise that their feedback is that all is well, and all that's lacking is your confidence.

If there are certain personality types by whom you feel intimidated at work, this may be prompting you to examine your communication skills so that you learn ways of feeling more assertive and confident. Since there will always be difficult people in every walk of life, and since it may not be possible to avoid them, you may find they drain you less if you gain some emotional insight into why they upset you so. Psychotherapy may help you to realise that intimidating people remind you of your authoritarian father, or that highly competitive people bring to mind the brutal rivalry between you and your siblings, causing you to freeze up in fear. The most difficult people in your life can turn out to be your greatest teachers. They often embody what the philosopher Carl Jung called the 'shadow', the unintegrated and disowned parts of ourselves that we try to keep out of sight. Under the guidance of a psychotherapist you can unravel what lessons the situation is offering, what change in your identity is imminent and highlighted by your feelings of panic.

Working hours and commuting times can be hidden drains. Although the job itself can be ideal, long hours spent in traffic or shift hours that compromise sleep can mean you have fewer reserves to draw on should any extra demands come in. The absence of a lunch break undermines your reserves at a most obvious and basic level – fuel.

YOUR BODY

In order to cope with the increasing demands of today's treadmill existence, 'release' habits can creep in which help us get by. Going for a drink after work, while it can initially be a forum to vent frustrations and bond with colleagues, can mean you get home too late to bother cooking a meal, and too tired to do anything but fall into bed. With no time for exercise, an irregular diet, and the alcohol level making you sluggish the next day, if any added demand appears, you are ill-equipped to deal with it. Couple this with the extra nervous system stimulation provided by the nicotine in that first cigarette, and the caffeine 'kick' to get you going, and you're a sitting duck; you have primed your system for a panic attack.

During times of stress you may find yourself nibbling on sugary snacks rather than eating meals. To digest sugar your pancreas puts out insulin, a hormone that can overshoot after it has cleared the most recent glucose, so your sugar level tips to the low side. *The symptoms of low blood sugar are very similar to those of panic* – lightheadedness, sweating, shaking and weakness. These changes in your physiology can be misinterpreted by your 'radar' as an impending panic attack, and could easily have been avoided by regular eating.

In the case of our caveman, when his adrenaline rose, it was burnt off shortly afterwards during the fight or the chase that ensued. In modern times it climbs just as high, but often finds no release. You can feel restless and jittery, 'wired' like a coiled spring. A pressure cooker has to release steam, and it can do so through the valve on top with a loud 'hiss' as the pressure escapes, or by turning down the heat. In the case of tense muscles, regular exercise can function as a release valve, and relaxation can serve to dampen down the volume of the adrenaline response. Many a stressed executive survives the jungle of the business world only by using exercise as a counter-balance, because besides expending adrenaline, it can actually boost your energy levels.

DEADLINES – INTERNAL OR EXTERNAL?

Some deadlines are realistically imposed by the outside world and as such are non-negotiable. Your boss needs the figures for a budget meeting or your children need to be at school by a certain time. The kind of 'countdown' that accompanies Christmas, planning a wedding or preparing for a holiday imposes a schedule from which it can seem there is no escape.

Many deadlines, however, are self-imposed, but you may be relating to them as though they were non-negotiable. For example, you may have a mental list of 'must do's' which, driven by adrenaline, is making you feel tense, unsafe and panicky. *Think about what the word 'deadline' implies – instant death beyond this point, the essence of panic!* Often people lose sight of the fact that the deadline is completely internally imposed and therefore could be deferred until tomorrow or next week, and the fear defused. By stopping for long enough to ask yourself the question 'Who says I have to do this today, and who dictates to what standard?' you will often realise it is nobody but you, with your personal internal set of (usually excessively high) standards. This means you are the one to blame for raising your own adrenaline.

Finola found herself getting panicky whenever her parents visited. She cleaned the house and fussed over details about their arrival until she was exhausted. Since their youngest was a child with special needs, this kept her busy enough, so these extra chores were a real burden. Irritable and sleeping badly, she was always determined that she'd 'get everything done' before they arrived. The last thing she wanted was her mother finding anything to quibble about, since she had always been related to as the 'ditsy' one growing up, disorganised and far too laid-back in her mother's opinion. Impossible to please, her mother seemed to be not in the slightest bit surprised that Finola's child was 'imperfect', as though it was what she would have expected of her daughter.

At times her mother would be downright rude, criticising her in a way that was cruel and hurtful. Her father, a mouse of a man, would never support Finola, although she had appealed to him many times. Yet in spite of this she felt the obligation to invite them to stay periodically, and bit her lip in frustration rather than endure a confrontation. She went to a great deal of trouble to make their visit smooth, ferrying them everywhere even at great inconvenience. The strain of catering to her mother's standards was raising her adrenaline and bringing her to panic point. Following a string of severe attacks, her husband took the situation in hand, cancelled their visit, and on his insistence we began working on her relationship with her mother.

In time, she could see that many of her 'shoulds and musts' were self-made, and could be changed. She learned that she did not have to do the cooking or clean the house to her mother's standards but could dictate her own. Nor was it 'unkind' to decline to have them to stay longer than a few days, or at a time that didn't suit her. She learned to reframe saying 'no' as showing herself some respect, rather than being 'unloving' towards her mother, or a 'bad' daughter. She acknowledged that many of her beliefs had been increasing her stress, implying that something awful would happen, she knew not what, if she didn't follow them. By becoming more assertive she began to feel less drained and not as prone to panic. Insisting on her brother becoming more involved with her ageing parents and deciding that she could do without her mother's approval allowed her to feel more in control, and safer.

SCARY BELIEFS

A belief is a different thing from a truth. However, the two can sometimes become confused. For instance, you may be running a belief that says 'only disrespectful and disorganised people arrive late for appointments' or 'if things you do upset others then you're responsible'. Many would agree with this, yet is this the truth?

What if you've left your house in plenty of time to get to an important meeting, and travel the same road every day, yet today you encounter a bad accident, which creates a traffic jam that substantially delays you. Since the meeting can't begin without you, everybody will be inconvenienced. According to your belief you should by now have incurred the disapproval of all present, since by keeping them waiting you've failed to pay due respect to them, and have shown that you're negligent by not clairvoyantly choosing an alternative route! Fearful of their harsh judgement, in such an atmosphere you're likely to be frantically tense as you drum your fingers, honk at the motorist in front, and feel a lump building in your chest.

It may not have occurred to you to question your belief. Have you in fact been disrespectful or negligent in your duty to be on time? No, in good faith you left home mindful of the time, and since you didn't orchestrate the accident, you are in fact innocent of any wrongdoing. Should you be held responsible for your colleagues' impatience if a traffic jam is the real culprit? If you examined these beliefs you would see their flaws. You would also realise that if others disapproved of you in spite of your very legitimate excuse, then it reflected more negatively on them for their rigidity than it did on you. This position, one born out of active enquiry rather than habit, would allow you to feel less frantic as you waited for the traffic snarl to right itself, and safer in the knowledge that you know you have behaved impeccably. This version of yourself as 'someone who has done their best' carries less fear than 'disrespectful and negligent'. Obviously you may still feel irritation at the unpredictable nature of life, a sense of hurry to get moving, and run through several rehearsals of your apology, but at least you wouldn't feel such intense fear. This stance would keep your adrenaline at a more reasonable level.

The point here is that *there are beliefs that raise adrenaline because they scare us, and beliefs that lower it because they reassure us*. It is worth assessing yours if you are engaging in an adrenaline-lowering campaign to control panic. It is beyond the scope of this book to enumerate all the possible fearful beliefs there are, but here is a small selection to give you a flavour. It is up to you to be creative after that.

Fearful Belief:	'It is not nice to cause upset to other people.'
Reassuring Truth:	'It is a fact that, try as we might to prevent it, sometimes our actions/ words upset others.'
Fearful Belief:	'If you're careful enough, you won't make mistakes.'
Reassuring Truth:	'It is a fact that no matter how hard anybody tries, it is human to make mistakes.'
Fearful Belief:	'People who do things quickly get more done.'
Reassuring Truth:	'Often haste leads to inefficiency and incompleteness.'
Fearful Belief:	'You can judge a person's integrity by how high their standards are.'
Reassuring Truth:	'Realistic standards that are achievable are the measure of a sensible person more than unattainable ones.'

ACCEPTING LIFE AS IT IS

Safe beliefs about life in general can provide a background sense that the universe we inhabit is essentially benevolent, trying to work with us rather than obstruct us, and that the trusting philosophy 'live and let live' is a sound one. More cynical beliefs, that others are out to take advantage of us, that we need to watch our back, or that there is not enough to go around, are common in those who are stressed or panicky and in a world becoming alarmingly more driven by scarcity consciousness.

It may be worth reviewing your beliefs with the help of a therapist if they leave you ill-equipped to meet the many challenges that life presents you with. Psychologists seeking to define which ingredient all 'hardy personalities' have in common, often cite flexibility as the most advantageous in transcending major life challenges. *Beliefs which can change to incorporate new information, and which are less black-and-white, but display the shades of grey, are more productive in times of challenge.* Beliefs which contain the words 'always' or 'never' are too rigid, not allowing any adaptive movement, and imply a finality that is non-negotiable.

Suppose there were two ways of meeting life. Imagine that life was likened to a door lintel, which is described by certain attributes. Hard, made of granite, standing at five feet high. Now if human beings were six feet tall, and they attempted to walk beneath the lintel without acknowledging its characteristics, ignoring the fact that it is only five feet high, what do you expect would happen? They would traumatise their faces as skin meets granite! A painful reality check. This of course would only happen once or twice, after which time they would hopefully learn to duck whenever they saw it up ahead. No point harbouring a belief that the lintel can miraculously accommodate all six feet of them, or will bend to the impression made by their head, when the reality of the situation, and the truth of the matter, is that it is only five feet high and rock hard!

Likewise, life has certain recognisable characteristics that it pays to acknowledge early on if we want to avoid traumatising ourselves unnecessarily, or wasting vast amounts of energy on trying to alter:

- life is unpredictable by nature;

- life is often uncontrollable;

- life is at times extremely unfair (bad things do happen to good people);

- loss is built in, because things rarely stay the same;

- our illusions from childhood (the game-plan) may, to our immense surprise, fail to hold in adult life – 'if you're nice to people they'll be nice in return', 'work hard and you'll be rewarded', 'trouble won't look for you if you don't look for it', 'lightning never strikes twice', etc.

If our beliefs reflect real life, then accepting how it truly is, rather than how we'd like it to be, results in less shock-horror-surprise as we encounter its daily turbulence. The ability to adapt to change, depending on the circumstance, is a smart survival tool. Paradoxically, *by building in the notion that life by its nature is essentially ever-changing and lacking in stability, we reassure ourselves that the to-and-fro won't harm us, that we're safe, that we'll cope.* It suggests to us 'So what if you're going to be late and have to change from Plan A to Plan B – no harm done, that's life after all!' A more rigid and growth-restricting response would say 'This can't be happening, I *have* to be on time, my expected time of arrival *must* remain the same, or else something awful will happen.'

BECOMING YOUR OWN GENERATOR

Unlike cash flow, *it is always within your power to increase your vital force.* You can do this physically, emotionally, mentally or spiritually. Exercise can physically stimulate the 'chi' or life-force into action. There are other methods that can be valuable as a daily energy deposit, such as yoga, qi-gong and tai-chi. Acupuncture can identify energy blocks, and re-establish a healthy flow of chi to areas needing it. Connecting with nature energetically feeds your energy field, and particularly your first chakra, the one most concerned with survival.

Emotionally the support of others, and the intimacy of loving relationships (including pets), is a resource that can be neglected during stressful times when all you want to do is 'shut the shop down' at the end of the day. Setting up opportunities for fun, entertainment or sex can make a very healthy contribution to a depleted energy bank and pull you out of the danger zone. Mental stimulation is a buzz for some, who come alive when novel material appears, like books, courses, movies or challenging conversation.

Spiritually, if things make sense from the 'big picture' perspective, it can make the everyday struggles seem less awesome. In this way, a feeling of space is created, and a calmness develops inside, as you learn to watch the turbulence happening without as much need to haemorrhage energy into it.

Developing your own sense of a spiritual (as opposed to religious) path may require you to seek the help of a psychotherapist who works in that way. Alternatively, there is an abundance of reading material and courses available now which can be rich sources of information and guidance.

WHEN PANIC ATTACKS

18

KEYNOTE: EMERGENCY DRILL

M any of your new skills are designed to work together to cover many of the different aspects of panic. Since that information is spread out over many chapters, it may be helpful to have a summary of the core concepts to hand when you get an attack, to remind you of what most efficiently brings the sensations under control.

① *Be Still – Resist Escaping*

When you perceive the initial whispers in your body telling you that an attack is on the way, making attempts to escape or planning to run is the equivalent of telling yourself that you're going to be overwhelmed, that you are helpless in the face of what is coming, and that you'd better 'get to safety'. This misinformation generates more adrenaline and makes matters worse. By deciding to remain, you are giving yourself a powerful message that:

I will still be safe if I don't run.

This also prevents your muscles responding with a further increase in tension, which happens if you are physically running, pacing around or restlessly fidgeting.

② *Go With Your Body's Reaction – Don't Fight It*

Although you obviously didn't want to get an attack, if it has been triggered, acceptance is the stance that holds the least fear. Resisting only increases and prolongs the adrenaline surge, and makes you more tense and afraid, whereas flowing with it allows it to spend itself in the quickest time. Trying to deny that it has begun ('Oh no, not here! I don't believe it, it can't be happening again! Please, please, not now in front of all these people!') is like closing the stable door after the horse has bolted – a waste of energy.

Once panic has begun, it won't finish until the molecules of the chemical have left your bloodstream. This obviously takes time, just like an alcohol hangover takes time to clear out of your system. You cannot just 'wish' it gone, it has to run its course, so you might as well adjust to allowing that time to elapse and the concentration of molecules to eventually dissipate.

Floating with the 'wave of molecules' as it washes over you, going with whatever physical reactions your body is having, allows the adrenaline to spend itself more quickly because you're not creating any more. Make a statement of acceptance such as:

All the sensations I am feeling now will pass.
I can allow this to wash over me.

③ *Stay in the Present – Don't Futurise* Although every fibre of your being may be thinking of how to prevent the 'disaster' about to occur, try to stay with what's happening right now. By allowing your thoughts and actions to prepare you for the worst, you are again sending powerful messages of helplessness to yourself, not safety.

By keeping your attention only on what's happening now, rather than what could happen in the future, you reduce your mind's field of observation to:

- your racing heart, a highly unpleasant sensation (rather than a predicted heart attack and presumed death);
- your uncomfortable tight chest (rather than imminent suffocation);
- the confused, dizzy feelings in your head (as opposed to future admission to a mental hospital, or an operation for a brain tumour).

④ *Deflate the Danger – Tell Yourself the Facts*

This means reminding yourself of the facts regarding the sensations you are experiencing, and why you get them.

For example:

'Boy, it is hot in here, I've suddenly begun sweating – but then there are a lot of people dancing and alcohol always makes me a bit sticky so it is nothing to worry about.'

'My heart has begun to race – no wonder I suppose, since I've been fighting against the clock all day. I'll try to slow down and that'll help.'

'My fingers are tingling and that dizziness is here a bit – I've obviously let my breathing get too fast again.'

'I feel shaky and peculiar – my adrenaline is obviously higher today than I thought.'

'I feel faint and a bit nauseous – I must be more careful not to let myself get so wound up, I'd better calm down the reaction now by easing up on myself.'

Always remember:

- ★   All the sensations of panic are harmless, no matter how intense – the response is protective in nature.
- ★   You will never stop breathing because of panic.
- ★   Your heart is not at risk during a panic attack.
- ★   Nobody has ever gone mad, died or lost control as a result of a panic attack.
- ★   All panic attacks end – they are time-limited.

---

⑤ Dampen Down the Reaction

Put into action the strategies you have learned:

- Breathe slowly and abdominally, counting out your breaths.
- Let your muscles go slack and quiet.
- Ground your energy – put your right hand on your chest and your left hand on your stomach, press the tip of your tongue against the roof of your mouth as you exhale, and visualise your breath leaving through your legs into the ground.

Behaviours that would be consistent with these might include relaxing in a hot bath, placing a cold towel over your face if you're sweaty, listening to calming music, taking a walk, or in some way using your limbs as a method of 'grounding' your energy if you're feeling spaced out.

⑥ Be Consistent – Don't Resort to Bad Habits

The overall objective of this approach is to decrease the intensity of your reaction to the uncomfortable sensations, and, in time, to persuade yourself that they won't harm you. It is important to be consistent in holding that intention, so that all your strategies are pulling in the one direction. So, for example, it undermines the overall premise of the approach if you've been having success with teaching your muscles to relax and your breathing to slow down, but then try to use them while rushing round frantically looking for an exit. The overall intention isn't clear – if you are feeling safe enough to stay, then why are you planning your escape?

Most panickers have their own individual methods of calming themselves, but many of these are with the intention of staving off an attack so that 'dire consequences' won't result. It is contradictory to be too urgently forcing your body to relax, or slowing your breaths 'so you won't die of suffocation'. Both of these stances are motivated by fear, although on the surface it looks like you're trying to decrease arousal levels.

Some find that distraction or keeping busy prevents them thinking too much, and then they forget to worry. This may work in the short term, but in the long term it is perpetuating the incorrect belief that 'I had better get my mind off the subject quick, or it will escalate out of control'. The ultimate goal is that you learn to select (and have confidence in) safe truisms to replace scary lies that take over your thoughts, rather than dodge them through distraction.

WHEN PANIC ATTACKS

1. Be still – resist escaping.

2. Go with your body's reaction – don't fight it.

3. Stay in the present – don't futurise.

4. Deflate the danger – tell yourself the facts.

5. Dampen down the reaction:

   • Breathe slowly into your belly

   • Relax your muscles

   • Ground your energy

6. Be consistent – don't resort to bad habits.

19

WHAT ELSE HELPS?

KEYNOTE: COMPLEMENTARY TOOLS

The basic premise of this approach has been that panic attacks follow threats to the survival of our identity, which activates the fight or flight response, the internal sensations of which are then misread as life-threatening and dangerous. In this sense panic is seen as a reaction to something, either a thought or a sensation or both.

The emphasis has been on learning methods to dampen down that reaction, to replace misinterpretations with truths, and to encourage ways of experiencing those very thoughts and sensations in a climate of increasing safety.

The use of medication is widespread and growing, as the influence of the multi-million dollar drug industry on daily medical practice increases. Anxiety-lowering drugs, usually Valium and its other benzodiazepine cousins, act by dampening down nervous system activity, through their action on nerve endings both inside the brain and around the body. They curtail the adrenaline cascade and its effects diminish, lessening or eliminating the feared sensations. These drugs are not affecting the basic problem in any curative way, but give relief by masking its expression.

While it may seem to offer a blessed release from daily high levels of fear, medication reflects an attitude of avoidance, because the underlying fear of experiencing the sensations still persists. This book has been urging a change in how you manage your panic, from avoidance to approach, through loosening the grip these fearful sensations have over you. Through gaining the skills of controlling your thoughts and your physical reaction to them, avoidance no longer has to be your only option.

Overall the use of medication perpetuates a climate of dis-empowerment and vulnerability, by reducing adrenaline artificially. While you may feel stronger and more able to tackle threatening situations, it is not through any inherent strength of your own. So, if on occasion the medication doesn't work, or isn't available, you will still feel powerless in the situation. Since the solution is not coming from within you, this means you are still vulnerable, hoping an attack won't be triggered, always watchful in case there is one on the way. The approach offered in this book, by contrast, tries to help you to achieve the very opposite, to instil a confidence and inner strength through the acquisition of solid skills offered. It's empowering to know facts and have the ability to show yourself you can achieve mastery over the sensations. These techniques are portable, and go with you wherever you are, so that outside circumstances are not so critical.

I have tried to encourage you to take a deeper look at what possible significance panic could have in terms of expanding your consciousness and making yours a fully integrated personality. Aspects of your experience which never reach your full awareness, but rumble underneath casting a negative shadow over your life, may be resolved through the process of tackling your panic. The use of medication makes redundant the need to look for sources and meanings behind your symptoms. Its only aim is to anaesthetise, and an invaluable messenger is silenced. Any observations about fear-generating patterns of thinking or living will be kept out of conscious awareness by medication.

In this way medication offers short-term relief, and is not a long-term solution. Although your stress levels may go down, and the pills help you over a bad spot, if in the future you experience another high-adrenaline phase, all the same issues may recur. This is because your fear of the symptoms and what they signify, has not been addressed.

If depression is a feature, following months or years of feeling helpless to control attacks, anti-depressants are often prescribed. The sense of empowerment from anti-depressants is artificial and not built on any skills learned or the clear demonstration to yourself of control and mastery over your fears. These act as psychic energisers, adding a 'buzz' to your system in ways which are not clearly understood. This extra energy can instil a 'can-do' feeling into a tired system, but unfortunately, in a mind and body already speedy enough, it can lead to interrupted sleep, and restlessness, with some even finding their attacks intensified. Additionally, the withdrawal effects experienced when the time comes to discontinue them often closely mimic the symptoms of panic itself, leading to the misconception that the attacks have returned, causing a person to feel that they 'need' the medication, to resume taking them, and thereby becoming addicted to them. I discuss this in some length in my book *Depression – An Emotion not a Disease*.

If medication has a place, it should only be as an adjunct to a fuller programme of psychotherapy and adrenaline management. There are individuals who, paralysed with fear, will only move out beyond their comfort zone and begin to take risks if they have the safety net of medication to fall back on. It can guarantee them that their fear will not swamp them, and that if their initial tentative efforts at control fail to be effective rapidly enough they are not at the mercy of the dreaded sensations. The aim should be to wean them off it as their own skills bed in. I prefer that anxiety-lowering medication such as Valium or the benzodiazepine family is not taken every day without thinking, but encourage people to assess first whether they feel they need it. So, on a day when things are going smoothly, they won't use it. But if they have a challenging situation to cope with and they decide to take it, then it is being used as a safety net. It reaches the bloodstream more rapidly if dissolved under the tongue. Taken this way I have found that many people, deciding to test out their new skills before automatically taking the pills, report that they 'managed without taking them after all'.

In the case of those whose panic attacks occur irregularly, with no problems whatsoever in between, medication may also be useful. If you only ever feel panicky on planes, or when you have to visit the dentist, then you're not going to have many opportunities to practise the strategies to dampen the reaction. If you're a relaxed enough individual normally, with no high background level of adrenaline, then medication often covers that once or twice yearly occasion very efficiently.

Beta Blockers

Adrenaline stimulates heart rate through its action on a specific type of receptor in the cardiac cell wall called a beta receptor. Beta blockers are a category of drug which act selectively on the heart muscle to block the sympathetic nervous system drive to those cells. They are normally used during angina attacks or to stop irregular heartbeats, but are also prescribed in panic attacks. By reducing the sensation of a pounding heartbeat, it is hoped that those who are particularly terrified by this will be less often confronted with their fear. However, while it does reduce the overall exposure to a racing heartbeat as a trigger, it does not promote a sense of personal control or safety through mastery.

HOMEOPATHY

Homeopathy and the treatment of panic attacks fit together like a hand in a glove. The approach in this book has been to target those factors that underlie a person's state of fear, rather than eliminating the superficial symptoms of that fear. Being a holistic science, homeopathic principles hold that since the underlying causes and superficial symptoms are inseparable, there cannot be one remedy for the whole patient and a different one for each of his parts. It also acknowledges that one individual's fear may have an entirely different flavour than another's, and may need a different remedy, unlike traditional medicine which uses the same medication no matter how exquisitely unique the story.

Orthodox medicine is to homeopathy what Newtonian is to quantum physics. Homeopathic remedies work on the subtler higher vibrational levels of energy, acting on the energy field and the chakra system. These both permeate every level of our being, not only the physical but also the mind, the thoughts, and the spirit, and vibrate at a fairly consistent frequency for each individual. When our system is thrown off balance, our vibratory state changes. The word homeopathy means 'the same suffering'. The remedy given for the new state of imbalance works by cancelling out or neutralising the symptoms because of its identical match with that new vibration – the principle of 'like cures like'. From among more than 3000 remedies, only one specific plant, animal, mineral or metal substance found in nature will mirror that exact energetic signature, neutralising it. A detailed interview with a classically trained homeopath is needed to elicit the precise portrait of that illness, and find the ideal match.

Homeopathy sees disease as a disturbance of the animating life-force within us, causing a diminishing of our defence mechanism, whose aim is to maintain balance. It relates to symptoms as a reflection of the effect the battle for balance has on various parts of your body and mind. Individuals vary as to the part of their mind–body which is the 'weak link' in their defence system. Homeopathy seeks to strengthen this aspect, creating more resilience for the future.

For example, if panic attacks followed the break-up of your relationship, you could take Valium for the distress, and in time they might subside. By contrast, a homeopath would prescribe a remedy for your overall state – that feeling that your very survival is threatened by the departure of your beloved, that your prospects of happiness are compromised without them, feelings derived from a failure to develop a strong enough sense of yourself independent of that relationship. Following such a remedy, you will move to a new vibratory frequency, and being psychologically less vulnerable, will avoid feeling so bereft and disempowered if subsequent romances ends.

A homeopath will look for any signals of a weakened life-force present from early childhood, so for them a panic attack today could be a reflection of a vulnerability set up following a trauma or shock in the first years or even in the womb. They build up a portrait of your problem as it has developed over the years, as a sequence of impressions from womb to tomb, seeing your symptom today having significance along that timeline. From this viewpoint, whatever mental and emotional attributes or demeanours you have adopted, they must have been necessary in the past as a survival mechanism to counterbalance some trauma or stress. By replicating the vibrational state of that past situation through giving a remedy which exactly matches it, as like meets like, the past trauma dissolves, and leaves the energy field.

There are obvious parallels here with psychotherapy and the philosophy of this book. The homeopathic states are the equivalent of conditioned responses. Each state announces the distance the person has departed from present reality, reacting instead in a protective way to threats from a past time, but which they still see in present situations. Through the remedy, the original fearful experience is recreated and mirrored through vibrational means within them, neutralising the present state of over-reaction and bringing back perspective.

Here are examples of a few remedy portraits in which panic attacks feature, which may help you to understand why homeopathy complements psychotherapy.

Argentum Nitricum

This remedy is used for all types of fear and anxiety brought on by over-active imaginations, those who, despite reassurances, find it hard to push the impulse to catastrophise aside. If thrown off balance by an unexpected shock they can develop great anxieties about their health, and fear of death when alone at night is a big fear. Prone to panic with trembling, their fear that death is imminent often finds them in casualty departments, fearing heart attack, cancer or stroke. Claustrophobia is common, as is fear of fainting, and they will sometimes not leave the house in case something happens to them while unattended. They frighten themselves by experiencing impulses to do something like injure or kill someone, or jump from a balcony or height.

Aconite

These individuals are extremely sensitive to mental shocks of a certain kind, such as a sudden fright, or an experience in which they could have died, rather than a broken heart, financial ruin or exam failure. Car accidents, robberies, an electrical blackout in a dark tunnel, being trapped in a lift, or even sensing that death is near, as in illness or after an operation, send shocks through them like internal earthquakes. Phobias can result that last for years. These people are sure that death will come suddenly when least expected, and any kind of outside pressure makes them sure they can have a stroke or heart attack. The slightest change in heat or cold often triggers an attack. They worry excessively about others, and receive bad news badly, erupting emotionally with a disproportionate reaction. They are never stoic. They fear crowds, enclosed spaces, and suffocation, so they are frequently found sitting close to exits and will abandon cars in traffic jams. Night panics are common as the bed begins to heat up, and they can get vertigo on rising or stooping.

Gelsemium

They feel an all-pervading weakness on all levels, with no willpower to act. Emotionally this shows as severe apprehension before facing a challenge, feeling they won't be able to cope, which elicits the fight–flight or freeze response, with trembling, diarrhoea, etc. Those who suffer stage fright may need this remedy, and also those terrified by exams, or interviews. Mentally they can become confused, and even have memory blanks.

ALTERNATIVE THERAPIES

Any therapy whose aim is to dampen the fight or flight response through reducing the number of adrenaline molecules in the bloodstream will help panic.

Massage achieves this through easing the tension out of the muscles. If coupled with aromatherapy oils, it has the added advantage of their calming influence on the nervous system, since they are of sufficient molecular size to penetrate the skin and enter the bloodstream. Many memories are held in your muscular armour, and release of these into awareness can occur during massage. The experience also reminds you to nurture yourself more regularly, if neglect of your body's need for rest and timeout has been part of your adrenaline problem.

Acupuncture seeks to maintain your body's life-force energy, the chi, in a state of healthy balance. It helps to identify which lines of your energy system (called meridians) are over-loaded or blocked, reducing the supply of vital chi to those areas. By activating these channels they restore normal flow, energising some and reducing pressure on others. Depending on which channels keep blocking up, information emerges as to which areas of your life, or which aspects of your personality, are responsible.

Within the traditional Chinese medicine (TCM) framework, the emotion of fear is associated with the kidneys, one of whose functions is to support our mental abilities. When their energy is depleted, as it is in excessive fear, symptoms such as phobias, lethargy, poor concentration and memory, frequent and urgent urination, night sweating, and thirst can manifest. Whenever there is a blockage, or stagnation which manifests as paralysis or inability to breath the liver and spleen are thought of. Muscle cramping, dizziness, insomnia, blurred vision, numbness, and dry mouth can all reflect what acupuncturists refer to as liver-blood disturbance, a condition which can result from poor eating habits such as seen during periods of stress, or as a consequence of blood loss following an operation or childbirth. In TCM, excessive worry is associated with the spleen and stomach, which represent the cognitive mind, and with digestive function also, therefore a weakness here manifests as lack of mental clarity as well as poor energy, weak limbs, obsessive thinking, muzzy head, nausea and diarrhoea.

Acupuncture points will be selected to nourish the kidney energy, calm the mind, remove stagnation or blockage and open the channels. Needles are retained for up to thirty minutes as part of a calming and nourishing treatment, and seeds can be placed on points on the ear, so the patient can have a coping strategy for further attacks once the treatment is over.

Yoga means 'unity' in the Hindu culture from which it evolved. Its aim is to make your body supple and toned, with the view that this, and certain mental exercises, also keep your mind in harmony. The fostering of abdominal rather than chest breathing is fundamental to its teaching, as the very expression of the spirit through the body. This is particularly useful for those in whom hyperventilation plays a part in their panic. Additional benefits for those who panic, are its focus on body-awareness, and the fostering of a sense of commitment to change through personal effort.

Hypnotherapy helps some to access states of very deep relaxation, by allowing the mental armour to drop as they surrender control, trusting the therapist to instruct their mind to move towards health. Through working with the unconscious mind, the therapist implants empowering suggestions that reduce fear and build confidence. Neuro-linguistic programming can be seen as really another version of hypnosis, and can succeed in unseating the fear by, for example, placing humorous images side-by-side with the fearful ones, confusing the brain enough to let go the fear in such a context. Although fundamentally similar to other states of deep muscle relaxation, hypnosis may be felt by some to be more powerful if the state is created by another person, the hypnotherapist. The re-living or recalling of buried experiences and memories which may have been generating fear can have the effect of integrating these into the rest of the personality, and ending the panic attacks.

Bioenergy works directly on the energy field and chakras. Using higher sense perception, the therapist senses and removes blockages and destructive patterns of energy distribution which make you more prone to having panic attacks. By channelling healing energy directly into your chakra system, they bring integration to aspects which have become closed off or disowned, sometimes from other lifetimes, and which are still acting as a stimulus to fearful karmic patterns in the present day.

Biofeedback literally means 'feeding back to you your own biology'. Using computerised technology, a series of leads read your heart rate, sweat response, respiratory rate, hand temperature or brainwaves, making them visible to you on screen. You are then taught how to direct them to go in the direction of calm. Just by thinking of feeling safe, you can witness your muscles relax, your breathing slow down and the fight or flight response disappear in front of you on the screen. What's more, you know that you, and only you, achieved that result. It builds confidence in the use of your mind to control so-called automatic reactions, such as panic.

Eye Movement Desensitisation and Reprocessing (EMDR)

Research shows that in people who are remembering a past trauma, the amygdala, the centre for fear in the emotional brain, can be seen on scanners to have become highly activated, a not unexpected phenomenon. But less predictable is the fact that, as clients recall the past event, the visual cortex also becomes involved, as though they were looking at a photograph of the event in the present. Even more interesting is the finding that a deactivation or anaesthetising occurs in Broca's area in the left pre-frontal cortex, where language is processed, explaining why a person is often 'lost for words' to fully describe a traumatic incident.

Traumas are frequently extremely difficult to erase from emotional memory. Many a person will tell you that although they know they are safe now, they do not feel they are. Feelings often lag behind, stubbornly anchored in the past, long after our rational understanding has moved on. The woman who was sexually abused as a child may still feel tense at the moment of intimacy with her husband even though she knows she is loved and there is nothing to fear. It's as if, once a fearful memory is laid down the emotional brain isn't capable of 'listening' to the cognitive brain's advice in relation to it, more so on some occasions than others, such as when we're hungover, tired, or under the influence of mind-altering drugs.

A trauma memory is locked in place (conditioned in) within the nervous system as a complete package containing every single piece of information relating to the incident as it happened – a snapshot containing the sights, sounds, smells, touch, emotions, physical sensations, and thoughts which were impacting at the time – even the beliefs formed in that moment such as 'I'm going to die', 'there's nothing I can do', etc. This memory package can be evoked at any stage once any of its contents are called to mind – the sight of an angry face, the presence of crowds, a room that's too hot – even by something which is not identical to but closely resembles it.

EMDR works on the idea that by inducing eye movements similar to that of REM (rapid eye movement) sleep, the brain is somehow stimulated to process the dysfunctional memory by itself, although it is still not understood how. By taking one element in that snapshot image, the whole package is opened up and reviewed. The therapist sits in front of the patient and asks them to recall the incident, speaking about it if they wish, and at the same time following their finger with their eyes from left to right rapidly and repeatedly, as though following the window wipers of a car – back and forth, back and forth, for some time.

During it, patients free-associate spontaneously, seeing other scenes flow in, jumbling up the memories, finding emotions rising to the surface that have not appeared until then, forging links with the present, changing the perspective on the meaning of what happened, allowing the 'present-day eyes' to see it differently, possibly from a more empowered position. Afterwards, the old emotional 'charge' seems to be less intense, its power fading.

EMDR is being used by more and more therapists now, and does not in any way interfere with other therapies or approaches. Major progress can be made in a short time, even within one session. It seems to apply best in traumas where there is some clear image to work with, and which have their roots in a clearly remembered painful past event.

20

STIGMA AND SHAME

C ompare these two scenarios: A person is at work and suddenly experiences a piercing pain in their right knee, causing them to stumble as they're walking down a corridor. Wincing and clutching their knee, they lean up against the wall. The person nearest to them immediately offers to carry their things as they help them limp to their desk. For the remainder of the day, since they can't walk without pain, others help out with whatever tasks require movement, and they're advised to take the next day off if they need to. For the rest of the week and until the knee is healed, they receive the unquestioned support of others, and whenever they get a bout of knee pain in the future, alternative arrangements are made at work to facilitate them.

Now compare that with the following scenario: While out on a site doing technical work, someone begins to experience a panic attack. Their heart is racing, they're breathless and dizzy, and worry that they'll faint. They say nothing, hoping it will pass quickly, and pray the rest of the crew don't notice. Although they get through the task they feel exhausted, and it is a struggle to get to the end of the morning. A colleague asks if they're feeling OK, because they don't seem their usual chatty self, and they assure them they're fine, just tired from a late night. It happens a few more times during the week, and they always hide it, making excuses for any unusual behaviour. As time goes on, they begin avoiding the usual end-of-week drink, claiming they have family commitments, or some other excuse.

Why is there such a difference between those who get a physical ailment and those who have a panic attack? The vast majority of panickers automatically tend to feel ashamed of their symptoms, and create an elaborate secret life, suffering alone and afraid of the ridicule and judgement of others if they were to be 'outed'. Detesting themselves for this 'flaw', they go to great lengths to prevent their 'weakness' becoming common knowledge. They begin living a half-life, one of compromise, excuses, avoidance and playing it safe.

Why is panic such a secret agony? It is because of *stigma – the disapproval that we as a society attach to 'mental' symptoms*. There's no logical reason why, because panic is just the same as any illness. Those who get panic attacks don't choose to get them any more than those who get asthmatic attacks. Nor can they just decide to stop them by willpower alone, any more than those with angina attacks can. They also need the support of others in just the same way that any ill person does until they heal, and for the atmosphere to be created so that this can happen as smoothly as possible. As with any illness, normal function is compromised for a while. You injure your back: you can't bend or lift things. You get laryngitis: you can't sing or talk normally. You get panic attacks: you temporarily have difficulty performing certain tasks, whether that's concentrating on a conversation or giving a presentation at work.

ARE WE THINKING STRAIGHT?

These differences in attitude stem from basic *errors in cultural thinking* when it comes to mental or psychological disorders, such as:

- If an abnormality is not visible to the eye it doesn't exist. If it can't be found by your doctor either on an X-ray or medical test, it is 'all in the mind', a figment of your imagination, and as such not a bona fide illness. However, ask anyone who panics how real their pounding heart is, and mop the very real sweat from their brow, and you'll know it is certainly not imagined!

- The mind and the emotions can be controlled by willpower. Ask any bereaved or broken-hearted person to 'snap out of it' and they'll tell you it is not that simple. There is a misconception that people who panic 'just aren't trying hard enough' or are being self-indulgent. Try to imagine yourself peering over an awesome precipice and someone saying 'go on, jump, use your willpower and you'll be fine!' and you get some sense of their absolute certainty that they won't be fine if they don't run from the room right now.

- The inability to control emotions indicates an inherent 'weakness' in the person's personality, and as such is judged negatively, by the panicker and by others. The same prejudice applies to boys and men crying, supposedly a 'weak' feeling, but not to the display of 'strong' emotions such as anger (although it might be no harm if it were). Panic occurs in the most capable and competent of people; in fact, the intolerance of such feelings of fear in panickers is sometimes precisely because weakness and vulnerability is such new territory for them.

We are conditioned culturally to have a prejudice against what society has (quite arbitrarily) deemed to be an undesirable state. There are long lists of conditions that our culture has a bias against – obesity, acne, poverty, shyness, promiscuity, flatulence. Other states that were once on that list may have shifted over the years to the 'just about tolerated' position, such as being gay, jobless or having a child before you're married. This indicates that the opinion on them is changing, and as it does, thankfully there is less agony and alienation for those experiencing them.

The word 'prejudice' derives from the Latin *to judge beforehand*. This implies that even prior to interfacing with certain situations, we are literally programmed to hold a certain prescribed opinion of them. It also means that many who find themselves having certain disapproved-of experiences will *automatically, because of conditioning*, feel ashamed of doing so. Before they even examine why, they may instantly try to hide the shameful state from others, sensing what ridicule would follow if it was witnessed by others.

As you have seen in Chapter 8, when your chakra system is thrown open during a panic attack, you are in fact registering the thoughtforms of others, among them judgements and prejudices. Many who panic are only totally comfortable around those who they know would never reject them for what they're experiencing, such as family members and other panickers. In the company of these people they can be themselves, and 'let it all hang out', which is why so many find their own home to be their safest place, and feel most anxious when exposed to the public gaze.

Why panic is so explicitly disapproved of is anybody's guess. Fear is an emotion that is interesting to study cross-culturally. For example, in the Eskimo culture if a member feels intense fear they may instantly follow it with laughing, because fear is an emotion that could seriously compromise your chances of survival if you were miles out on the ice and alone. They are acknowledging that fear moves the inner state from strength to disempowerment and giving up. So denial of fear, through laughing, keeps it at bay and nudges your internal chemistry in the direction of strength and power.

Possibly our current disapproval of the open display of fear and such vulnerable or disempowered mental states used to have some survival value to our caveman ancestors. Who knows, perhaps an individual having a panic attack could have jeopardised the survival of the whole tribe by running away and in doing so attracting the attention of their enemy, or by refusing to leave their cave when it was time to move on.

We are, however, no longer at such a level of raw survival. In comparison to those times, most of our society has moved to the luxurious position of endeavouring to foster values that are more caring and compassionate to our minorities. Those who need help can now receive it with no overall repercussions or detriment to the rest of the tribe. Since the beginning of the twentieth century, the special needs of the mentally disadvantaged and the physically disabled are now being better catered for. Those who find themselves to be sexually oriented in a way different to the majority, or display some eccentric qualities, are being understood and accepted more and more.

The prejudices are breaking down gradually. One reason for this is undoubtedly the courage of those who refuse to feel ashamed of themselves for feeling vulnerable and needing help. Rightly they feel angered if acceptance is withheld. By refusing to hide themselves and by bravely announcing 'This is me, I accept myself – can you?', they have challenged us all to embrace their difference in a spirit of community.

Another reason for the shift has been education. Young children are encouraged to respond compassionately to those with an obvious physical handicap instead of pointing, staring or shrinking back in fear. Information as to the medical facts behind such disorders as leprosy, epilepsy and more recently AIDS, means there is less mystery and therefore less fear surrounding them. Panic attacks need to join their ranks.

ATTITUDES CAN SHAPE ILLNESS

I believe we could virtually eliminate panic by starving certain attitudes to it and feeding others. The advantages of a shift in our approach to it are many:

- More public naming of it would increase the communal pool of knowledge, and change our relationship to it. Panic currently isn't exactly dinner party conversation, whereas other psychological distresses, such as fear of flying, can be brought up, even if a bit sheepishly, without much sense of shame.

- If children never hear panic described, how can they know that such a phenomenon exists? Naming something brings it into existence. As adults having their first panic attack, many panickers are not relating to an experience they've ever heard about, hence their confusion, fear and sense of isolation. The majority of my clients would consider it 'unwise' to confide to their children that they're having panic attacks, and try to keep it from them. While understandably they don't want to worry them, are they in fact reinforcing the notion that it is something to be feared, instead of confidently managed?

- More public expression would occur if there were less need to hide it, and sufferers would openly show that they were having an attack. After being related to sympathetically and kindly, and space made for them to take some time out to regain their composure, all without the slightest bit of judgement, their fear levels would drop. It would become less of a big deal to have one in public, and they would have less anticipatory adrenaline in their bloodstream.

- In fairness to most people, the usual response to a person in panic is sympathy and support. Even panickers will admit they would probably react in the same way as a bystander. However, what those who panic most probably pick up is not so much the disapproval of others, but their awkwardness and confusion as to what to do. This is because most people aren't educated as to what is the best form of help to give in such a situation. For all they know it could be a heart attack you're having, and an ambulance needed, so telling you to 'relax, you'll be fine' might seem like an irresponsible act. Many might think their advice to you to tough it out, and not run, is empowering you, rather than pressure. Why don't they know what to do? Because many of them have never witnessed a panic attack before. Why haven't they? Because of the shame and secrecy.

- With more public discussion the medical profession would come up to speed on panic. As is so often the case, the public demand for knowledge could prompt a greater interest in panic among the profession. It is still far too common an occurrence for a patient to spend years on the wrong treatment – inhalers for 'asthma', antacids or anti-spasmodics for 'ulcers', anti-histamines for 'motion sickness' or 'vertigo', or anti-depressants when the reason for their 'depression' is the daily challenge of living in fear.

- Demedicalisation. Righteous anger is considered to be a reasonable response to injustice, and grief and sadness is our understandable response to the death of a loved one. These emotions aren't medicalised, so why then is the normal response to threat so often referred to in medical terms such as anxiety, panic or depression?

- By medicalising a normal response, no effort is made to reveal the source, and no other intervention is pursued but the prescribing of a drug to anaesthetise it. Once that has failed (as it so often does, because it is only obscuring the symptom, not curing it), a person feels even more desperate than before, and utterly powerless and at the mercy of the disorder. Calling it what it really is – fear – has the effect of leading on to the next obvious question – fear of what? Now a conversation can genuinely begin which actively involves the sufferer as an expert who can provide valuable input in tracking down the source of the problem, and contribute to their own healing.

DESTIGMATISING YOURSELF

If, as a sufferer of panic attacks, you recognise that fear of the disapproval of others is a contributing factor for you, consider the following:

- Your predictions of judgement by others are more than likely untrue. Do you want to live your life cowed down and constricted by something that you're not even sure exists? Why not risk testing out your suspicions by confiding to someone that you get panic attacks, and register their response?

- You could start looking for feedback from a person who is peripheral in your life, like a checkout girl in a shop, leading into it by asking her to hurry a bit, 'because I get panic attacks in queues', then ask her if she ever got one. Or ask for an aisle seat in the cinema 'because if I get panicky I may need to rush out', and see if they are supportive or dismissive. You might pretend you need assistance by requesting a glass of water in the bank and telling them why, or confide to a fellow traveller in a lift that you hate confined spaces and feel really nervous. Register their response.

- If the people you have to see regularly are more intimidating to you than strangers, then try the experiment on family friends and acquaintances. The only way to challenge the belief that 'they'd judge me, think me weird, shun me if they knew' is to test it out. If you're thinking that the risk is too great, ask yourself if it is not a greater risk to stay the way you are, living with your secret.

- Individuating beyond the need for the approval of others is a task that ought to be completed in adolescence. In the same way that a shoe you have outgrown will pinch your toes, you may need to do some adjusting to better suit your current situation. Becoming your own person, and being authentic, is movement in the direction of growth and maturity. Have you ever considered that this could be the psychological or soul message that panic is trying to have break through into your awareness, to move you towards a more mature personality?

- If you find it too daunting a task to admit to panic attacks, try a halfway measure such as this: If you need to escape, give others a half-truth, such as 'I suffer from asthma, I need to get my inhaler from the car/my desk/my coat' or 'I have low blood pressure, could you get me a chair to sit down on?' Many find they can comfortably admit to these physical (and therefore respectable) problems. So they can meet their needs to get out, or for assistance, without feeling silly or weak. In time, you may trust more in the goodwill of others and be able to be completely authentic.

Leabharlanna Poibli Chatnair Baile Átha Cliath
299
Dublin City Public Libraries

FURTHER READING

Bailey, Philip, MD, *Homeopathic Psychology*, North Atlantic Books, California, 1995.
   Portraits of the common constitutional remedies.
Barlow, David, *Anxiety and its Disorders*, 2nd edition, The Guildford Press, New York, 2004.
   A scientific look at panic and anxiety.
Benson, Herbert, *The Relaxation Response*, William Murrow, London, 2000.
   The father of the relaxation response describes its uses in stress reduction.
Bourne, Edmund J., Ph.D., *The Anxiety and Phobia Workbook*, New Harbinger Publications Inc., California, 2011.
   An excellent, practical DIY for stress and anxiety.
Bradley, Dinah, *Hyperventilation Syndrome*, Celestial Arts, California, 1991.
   A clear and simple self-help book on the dynamics behind this breathing pattern.
Capra, Fritjof, *The Turning Point*, Flamingo, 2010.
   The bridge between quantum physics and mysticism.
Chopra, Deepak, *Quantum Healing*, Bantam Books, 2015.
   The role of quantum consciousness in healing.
Chopra, Deepak, *The Seven Spiritual Laws of Success*, Bantam Press, 1996.
   A masterpiece of spiritual writing. Seven simple steps to mind-body-spirit living.
Corry, Michael and Turbidy, Áine, *Going Mad? Understanding Mental Illness*, Newleaf, Dublin, 2001 (ebook only).
   A book for those seeking to understand what madness is – or is not – and which looks at alternative ways of treating it.

Gerber, Richard, MD, *Vibrational Medicine*, Harper Collins, New Mexico, 2001.

A cutting-edge tome on the emerging role of energy in medicine.

Holford, Patrick, *Optimum Nutrition for the Mind*, Piatkus, London, 2010.

Nutrition guru's guide to getting the building blocks right for a healthy mind.

Judith, Anodea, *Eastern Body – Western Mind*, Celestial Arts, California, 2004.

The bible on the chakras and energy field and how they are expressed.

Kabat-Zinn, Jon, *Full Catastrophe Living*, Piatkus, 2013.

An accessible read on bringing meditation into everyday life.

Kornfield, Jack, *The Path With Heart*, Rider, 2002.

A heartfelt look at meditation with many beautiful exercises.

Lynch, Terry, *Beyond Prozac*, PCCS Books, 2004.

The case for psychotherapy instead of pharmaco-therapy.

Miller, Alice, *The Drama of Being a Child*, Virago, 2008.

This little gem looks at the childhood as a conditioning process.

Myss, Caroline, Ph.D., *Anatomy of the Spirit*, Bantam Books, 1997.

Examines the spiritual symbolism of the chakra system.

Pert, Candace, Ph.D., *The Molecules of Emotion*, Simon and Schuster, London 1999.

A scientific explanation of how our feelings are chemically created.

Servan-Schreiber, Dr David, *Healing Without Freud or Prozac*, Rodale, London, 2012.

Natural drug-free approaches to managing anxiety and panic.

Weiss, Brian, MD, *Many Lives, Many Masters*, North Atlantic Books, California, 1995.

A psychiatrist's introduction to past lives through one patient's experience under hypnosis.

INDEX

Page numbers bolded indicate figures, tables etc.